Policing the Monstrous

Policing the Monstrous
Essays on the Supernatural Crime Procedural

EDITED BY ASHLEY SZANTER

McFarland & Company, Inc., Publishers
Jefferson, North Carolina

Also of Interest: *Romancing the Zombie: Essays on the Undead as Significant "Other,"* edited by Ashley Szanter and Jessica K. Richards (McFarland, 2017)

This book has undergone peer review.

Library of Congress Cataloguing-in-Publication Data

Names: Szanter, Ashley, editor.
Title: Policing the monstrous : essays on the supernatural crime procedural / edited by Ashley Szanter.
Description: Jefferson : McFarland & Company, Inc., Publishers, 2020. | Includes bibliographical references and index.
Identifiers: LCCN 2020047315 |
ISBN 9781476670539 (paperback : acid free paper) ∞
ISBN 9781476641300 (ebook)
Subjects: LCSH: Supernatural on television. | Detective and mystery television programs—History and criticism.
Classification: LCC PN1992.8.S87 P65 2020 | DDC 791.45/67—dc23
LC record available at https://lccn.loc.gov/2020047315

British Library cataloguing data are available

ISBN (print) 978-1-4766-7053-9
ISBN (ebook) 978-1-4766-4130-0

© 2021 Ashley Szanter. All rights reserved

No part of this book may be reproduced or transmitted in any form or by any means, electronic or mechanical, including photocopying or recording, or by any information storage and retrieval system, without permission in writing from the publisher.

Front cover images © 2021 Shutterstock

Printed in the United States of America

McFarland & Company, Inc., Publishers
Box 611, Jefferson, North Carolina 28640
www.mcfarlandpub.com

To my wonderful husband, Michael Warren Szanter,
who supports and encourages me every day.
This is for you.

I would also like to acknowledge Jessica K. Richards for her help
shaping this volume; we worked together to handpick these
incredible essays. And, finally, a huge thank you to
Cynthia J. Miller for her expeditious editorial help
so we could get this volume out into the world.

Table of Contents

Introduction: Following the Eerie, Formulaic Steps of the Supernatural Crime Procedural
    ASHLEY SZANTER   1

Deceive, Inveigle, Obfuscate: Post-Structuralism and the Staggered Retirement of Fox Mulder
    ADAM JAMES SMITH   9

The Owls Are Not What They Seem: Uncanny Doubles in *Twin Peaks*
    MARK YATES   29

Sherlock Holmes: The Intersection of Magic and Science in Crime Detection
    MICHELLE D. MIRANDA   46

Playing Detective: Gothic Perspectives and Police Procedurals in the CW's *Supernatural*
    MARY GOING   66

Evil Is a Metaphysical Condition: Undead Melodrama, AIDS and the Crime Procedural
    TERESA CUTLER-BROYLES   80

The Hard-Boiled Detective Gone Soft: *Moonlight,* Vampire Noir and the Detective in Search of Himself
    SIMON BACON   101

True Resonance: The Intersection of the Noosphere, Spirituality and the Supernatural in *True Detective—Season One*
    PHIL FITZSIMMONS   112

Table of Contents

Pushing Daisies, Forensic Fairy Tales and Supernatural Crime Procedurals
    SCOTT ROGERS   134

"Magic's a nasty game": John Constantine as the Trickster Detective
    SHAWN EDREI   147

Runnin' with the Devil: The Procedurals from Hell
    CYNTHIA J. MILLER *and* A. BOWDOIN VAN RIPER   158

Amateur Hour: Professional Competency in Supernatural Crime Procedurals
    LYNN KOZAK   172

About the Contributors   189

Index   191

Introduction

Following the Eerie, Formulaic Steps of the Supernatural Crime Procedural

ASHLEY SZANTER

  Law & Order: 20 seasons. *Law & Order: Special Victims Unit*: 20 seasons and counting. *NCIS*: 16 and counting. *CSI*: 15 seasons. *Criminal Minds* is going into its 15th. When you look at the enduring, massive, and mainstream popularity of the scripted procedural, it is undeniable that audiences crave the formulaic, murder-of-the-week stories that have graced TV screens since 1949's first crime show, *Man Against Crime*. The very essence of the crime procedural is satisfying. Every case gets solved, every killer or criminal is brought to justice, and every victim's death is avenged in one way or another. The scripted nature of the procedural makes revelations and conclusions neat and clean, giving viewers the tidied ending that can elude law enforcement in the messy real-life business of detection and justice.

  With this popularity, it begged the question of why these massively prevalent series felt they needed a little something extra: the supernatural. We enjoy watching the inner workings of a police precinct, whether dramatic (*Rookie Blue* [2010–15]) or comical (*Brooklyn Nine-Nine* [2013–present]). We enjoy seeing our protagonist detectives experience epiphanies after catching an impossible clue at the crime scene. We have enjoyed this look behind the curtain since the dawn of television—and even longer if you count other popular culture mediums like radio and novels. Scholars (Flanders, 2014; Ascari, 2007) hypothesize a variety of potential origins for our fascination with crime and detection. Some argue that we enjoy crime stories because they appeal to the darker parts of our nature and give us a chance to see or experience those things we are cautioned to avoid in our day-to-day lives. These frightening, intoxicating parts of our minds that we do not indulge—even if we sometimes want to.

The allure of the crime narrative allows us to "try on" a variety of experiences and play out scenarios we would not dare in our real lives, at the risk of destroying our carefully cultivated and comfortable surroundings. We experience by proxy what it might be like to be a drug lord, crime initiate, or ever-elusive serial killer. Alternatively, we experience the rush we assume comes with apprehending a killer you've been tracking for decades, cracking the cold case that has haunted you your entire career, or raiding the drug den behind a string of recent busts. All of these experiences, the professional or the rogue, provide audiences with a variety of safe escapes we can use to, even momentarily, abandon our day to day lives. While I could argue that escapism is the very cornerstone of popular culture, or even entertainment as a whole, I believe there is something very specific about the dark, subversive nature of the crime procedural that feeds our desire for the unexpected, those new, sometimes terrifying elements of life far removed from the monotony of work, appointments, and child-rearing. Criminals are never boring, and, frequently, neither are the law enforcement agents hunting them.

The law enforcement officers portrayed in these kinds of series are a constant reminder of the "safety" we expect from our everyday lives, however closely it resembles "security theater" (Briganti, "Adam Ruins Security," 2015). While who gets to experience the kinds of safety promised by these series is highly dependent on identity (race, gender, education, opportunity, etc.), there is an element of escapism that comes from being able to "see" into the dark, seedy underbelly of your city, or even just a city resembling your own. These stories of criminals, detection, and justice allow us to safely experience danger while maintaining a comfortable distance. Especially with police and crime procedurals, there is an expected, almost relished repetition of tension and release. Will the criminal get away with the crime? Of course not, but there are a few adrenaline-pumping moments of "maybe they will this time." These reliable patterns give us a "hit," so to speak. They connect us to the inherent instability and unknowability of our own systems of justice and punishment. These neat, tidy representations of crime and investigative work allow us to believe, however briefly, that our own systems could one day be this perfect, cut, and dried. This, perhaps, is the real answer for why we have innumerable popular crime stories on television: they allow us a chance to see an alternate world where we could live unbound by the rules and conventions of society while quietly reinforcing the idea that law-breaking is, without a doubt, bad. Crime procedurals, especially televised procedurals, are inherently soothing because, not only can you expect a clean ending, but you can literally turn it off. It is a powerful experience that allows us the chance to peer into the deepest, darkest depths of humanity while never truly compromising our own safety.

With these little joys, why then complicate it for ourselves? Why must the detective also be a vampire? A zombie? A psychic? Satan? While the longest-running show lists are littered with criminal procedural after criminal procedural, only two "supernatural" shows even compete: The CW's cult hit *Supernatural* (15 seasons) and, of course, *The X-Files* (11 seasons, including the reboot). Perhaps the most striking similarity between these two shows is that, while prioritizing their supernatural, occasionally occult themes, both are fundamentally stories about detection, truth-seeking, and justice: justice for Mulder's sister; justice for Sam and Dean's dead mother.

But when we have perfectly crafted the most reassuring genre on television, adopting a supernatural mythos just seems plain irresponsible. By complicating these very predictable and comforting stories and conventions with the inherently unknowable, it seems we have haphazardly shot ourselves in the foot, right? Perhaps not. The cross section of the supernatural and mystical in the crime story stretches back to at least the inception of the detective fiction genre with Wilkie Collins' *The Woman in White* (1859). The presence of supernaturalism in the crime story makes several appearances in the Victorian Age, from Edgar Allan Poe's "Murders in the Rue Morgue" (1841) to even sensationalist interpretations of Jack the Ripper as an uncatchable specter. Our Victorian inheritance seems to be the foundation of our contemporary preoccupation with the supernatural crime/detective subgenre on television, at least in the last 30 or so years. But, even with the recent spate of supernatural procedurals, these come from an even more recent bread crumb trail left by the likes of *Kolchak: The Night Stalker* (1974–75) and the original *Dark Shadows* (1966–71). Though it seems that the supernatural procedural has been in the recesses of our collective imagination for some time, why has there been an increase in frequency in the last couple decades? Instead of just getting one or two narratives to quench our thirst, why are we watching them more fervently now that we have more options? Why are they lasting so long when they do pop up?

These considerations were exactly what spurred the idea for this edited collection. With so many of these shows littering television present and history, there has to be something there. Our colleagues seemed to agree, as the call for proposals received a landslide of interest from academics who finally found the appropriate home for some of their more esoteric investigations (pun intended). In the essays that follow, we encourage our readers to challenge the existence of the procedural genre and consider the even more satisfying conclusions and questions posed by the supernatural procedurals that have graced our screens for longer than we might be aware.

Supernatural. Meet Procedural.

The supernatural crime procedural has very long, often complicated roots. While *Kolchak: The Night Stalker* and *Dark Shadows* may have set an early foundation, the two most influential series to date are, arguably, *Twin Peaks* (1990–91, 2017) and *The X-Files* (1993–2002, 2016). These early, and in the case of the latter, long-running series set the tone and the stage for the long-term success of other series, like the everlasting CW series *Supernatural* (2005–present).[1] As a show with complex alien conspiracies at its core, Adam James Smith examines the challenging internal structure of *The X-Files* in "Deceive, Inveigle, Obfuscate: Post-Structuralism and the Staggered Retirement of Fox Mulder." Approaching the influential series from a post-structural theoretical lens, Smith asserts that post-structuralism places any identified coherence as a projection of the audience's need for a solid foundation. Because of the post-structural nature of *The X-Files*, Mulder finds himself as decentered as the audience in a narrative where even the conspiracies bear no identifiable center.

Similarly seminal in this subgeneric landscape is David Lynch's *Twin Peaks*. Though having a significantly shorter run than *The X-Files*, *Twin Peaks* embedded itself in the American television landscape, leaving behind incredible scars that extend into the present day with *Twin Peaks: The Return*. Embracing one of *Twin Peaks*' most identifiable characteristics, Mark Yates connects the thematic uncanniness of the series to Sigmund Freud's theory of the *heimlich* (familiar) and *unheimlich* (unfamiliar) in "The Owls Are Not What They Seem: Uncanny Doubles in *Twin Peaks*." Because the nature of the procedural is to present audiences with a familiar experience that promises closure and repetition, *Twin Peaks* lured viewers in with promises of comfort and expectation, only to subvert those expectations with supernatural mythology that unsettled audiences and placed them in unfamiliar, uncomfortable territory.

Predating *Man Against Crime* and its televised inheritors was the original, quasi-supernatural detective Sherlock Holmes. Though birthed in the detection-obsessed Victorian Age, Sherlock Holmes has gained more than cult fandom status in the 21st century. Brought to life again and again with series like *Sherlock* (2010–present) and *Elementary* (2012–present), the perceptive investigator never ceases to amaze and, occasionally, baffle audiences with his hyper-perceptive and deductive reasoning skills. In

"Sherlock Holmes: The Intersection of Magic and Science in Crime Detection," Michelle D. Miranda explores what it is about this consulting detective that has captivated audiences for over 130 years. Arguing that Sherlock Holmes narratives produce an intoxicating blend of science and illusion, reason and magic, Miranda brings Sir Arthur Conan Doyle's stories into modern context with a careful examination of Sherlock in memory and adaptation.

Though many of these series and characters share an enduring legacy long after they have "gone off the air," *Supernatural* seems to be the show that just will not die—mostly because of its incredible popularity. Starting off as a more or less traditional "monster-of-the-week" show, *Supernatural* has grown into something even more influential: the cornerstone of a new kind of detective series in and of itself, or so Mary Going argues in "Playing Detective: Gothic Perspectives and Police Procedurals in the CW's *Supernatural*." Because *Supernatural* is not really a police procedural—that is, the brothers at the heart of the show are not professionals or licensed detectives in the traditional sense—the show is really a new kind of animal. Going argues that, because the show is a procedural focused on supernatural hunts, Sam and Dean Winchester exemplify the methods of hunters, thereby creating an entirely new type of detective complete with professional, paranormal techniques of detection.

Thus far, the shows covered in this collection are chock full of normal, everyday humans tasked with uncovering the seedy, magical elements that work their way into crime and mischief. But we cannot exclude the ever-popular vampire from our analysis. While shows like *Angel* (1999–2004) and *Buffy the Vampire Slayer* (1997–2003) garner the most attention from academic circles, other vampire detectives have also had their moment in the spotlight. Teresa Cutler-Broyles places the Canadian series *Forever Knight* center-stage and argues that conflicted detective-protagonist Nicholas Knight and his vampire ilk embody a much larger, distinctly 1980s and '90s fear of AIDS and alternative sexuality. In "Evil Is a Metaphysical Condition: Undead Melodrama, AIDS and the Crime Procedural," Cutler-Broyles argues that *Forever Knight* (1992–96) uses the inherently conflicted figure of the vampire detective to tackle questions of good versus evil and while setting the stage for the vampire detective on television.

While Nicholas Knight no longer has the market cornered on the conflicted vampire detective, *Moonlight*'s (2007–08) short-lived Mick St. John expanded our understanding on what the supernatural detective drama could be if it took itself a bit more seriously than *Forever Knight*. In "The Hard-Boiled Detective Gone Soft: *Moonlight*, Vampire Noir and the Detective in Search of Himself," Simon Bacon examines how this one-season

American series mixed tropes of the "hard-boiled" detective and film noir to create an even more tortured, if problematic, vampire detective. While regularly being at odds with the characteristics of the noir detective ideal, St. John challenges the archetypes of hard-bodied masculinity by choosing love and redemption over revenge and justice.

The quest for justice is the cornerstone of any good police procedural; the promise of punishment is part of what makes the procedural so compelling and puts viewers at ease. But more modern supernatural procedurals do not just delay the comfort of promised punishment, they subvert and, occasionally, abandon it altogether. Or, as is the case in season one of *True Detective* (2014), they blend the two until they are almost uncomfortably intertwined, as Phil Fitzsimmons argues in "True Resonance: The Intersection of the Noosphere, Spirituality and the Supernatural in *True Detective—Season One*." Positing that the series brings the noosphere—a pervasive intersection of the natural and supernatural worlds—to the forefront of the show, Fitzsimmons takes a highly theoretical approach and brings *True Detective* to the forefront of a new kind of supernatural procedural where the supernatural is not an intrusion on the natural world but rather a natural psychosphere that allows humans to connect with "spirituality" as part of the detection process.

But what about a world that takes great pains to distance itself from our own? Most procedurals, even supernatural ones, try very hard to anchor themselves in the here and now—normal, everyday people in our universe who are suddenly saddled with knowledge of the supernatural. But then you have shows like *Pushing Daisies* (2007–09) that create their own set of rules and let you know that they are, without a doubt, in a different universe than we are. This is the premise that Scott Rogers takes in his essay "*Pushing Daisies*, Forensic Fairytales and Supernatural Crime Procedurals." Rogers points out that the show's home network, ABC, marketed the curious series as a "forensic fairy tale," and this description is somewhat apt as it is narratively driven by the detective-for-hire escapades of protagonists Ned and Emerson Cod. Between analyses of their "murder-of-the-week" plots and unpacking the central mystery of Chuck's death, Rogers explores how the story embraces the hallmarks of the procedural while injecting supernatural elements that really set it apart from others in the supernatural procedural genre.

Whether spirituality, intuition, or magic, supernatural procedural detectives are constantly (re)defined by their special skill sets. And, as Shawn Edrei argues in "'Magic's a nasty game': John Constantine as the Trickster Detective," so is DC comics antihero, John Constantine. Taking multiple incarnations of Constantine into consideration, Edrei argues that the procedural investigator is transformed into a trickster detective, an archetype warped by the presence of magic and inherently indefinable supernatural elements. The indefinable supernatural is often the easiest to adapt for shows and movies alike. It allows the creators unbridled imagination and creativity to construct mythologies completely unbound by established rules and generic conventions. But the construct of justice is ultimately couched in the much broader, more human need for justice. And there is no law enforcement character, detective, vigilante, or consultant more interested in punishing the wicked than the original Big Bad: the Devil himself.

As the former high-ranking angel cast out of Heaven, Satan brings an interesting set of rules to the table. When a series brings in Satan as a one-off, recurring, or even central character, there is well-developed mythos that must come with him. When you have the Devil, you also have God, Heaven, Hell, and a worldview that brings some form of Christianity into play. Cynthia J. Miller and A. Bowdoin Van Riper take a broad swing at the Devil in multiple television incarnations in "Runnin' with the Devil: The Procedurals from Hell." By closely examining *Brimstone* (1998–99), *Reaper* (2007–09), and *Lucifer* (2016–present), Miller and Van Riper discuss how the Devil, Overlord of Hell and figure of eternal damnation, is probably the ultimate figure of justice and punishment. However, when imagined as a fully fleshed out television character, certain personality traits come to the forefront and, occasionally, even serve to humanize him as he punishes the evil for interrupting the status quo.

And one of these devilish series, *Lucifer*, complicates the matter even further by stretching the limits of detection in formal institutions, asking a fundamental question: "who is allowed to police?" These questions of professionalism, teamwork, and traditional detection come to the forefront in Lynn Kozak's "Amateur Hour: Professional Competency in Supernatural Crime Procedurals." When having a protagonist who is, in essence, fully supernatural, their specific skill set can be helpful in bringing criminals to justice. But, when that character is adopted by imperfect, rule-bound officers of the law, it is challenging to reconcile those two, often competing methodologies. Whereas Lucifer Morningstar wants to circumvent any pesky rules to see that criminals answer for their crimes, the LAPD must follow rules, procedures, and protocol to make sure this is properly done. Often, this pits the two central characters at odds; they want to achieve the same goal but strongly differ on how to get that done.

Satan.
Vampires.
Tricksters.

Aliens.

Rogue Demon Hunters.

In whatever form they appear, the supernatural constantly subverts audience expectations and generic conventions. When adopted by something as formulaic as the crime or police procedural, supernatural mythologies or characters will always complicate the detection and justice promised by the procedural drama. As this particular subgenre of television grows and changes, the authors in this collection aim to be the first to tackle and unpack the intricacies offered by the supernatural procedural in its current incarnation. I believe this collection marks the beginning of a much larger, more nuanced conversation and I certainly hope that academic interest in the supernatural procedural continues past this early examination.

Notes

1. At the time of this writing, it was announced that the 15th season of *Supernatural* would be its last—the final episode airs November 2020.

Works Cited

Ascari, Maurizio. *A Counter History of Crime Fiction: Supernatural, Gothic, Sensational.* Palgrave Macmillan, 2007.

Briganti, Paul, dir. "Adam Ruins Security." Season One, Episode Two, *Adam Ruins Everything.* truTV, 2015.

Deceive, Inveigle, Obfuscate

Post-Structuralism and the Staggered Retirement of Fox Mulder

Adam James Smith

> Fox Mulder pissed away a brilliant career, lost the respect of supervisors and friends and now lives his life shaking his fist at the sky and muttering about conspiracies to anyone who will listen.
> —Morris Fletcher. "Dreamland." *The X-Files*.

> It doesn't make sense. It's incomprehensible in any real world way.
> —Fox Mulder. "Sein und Weit." *The X-Files*.

Trust No One: The X-Files *and Procedural Drama*

"Once upon a time, there was a guy with the improbable name of Fox Mulder" ("Dreamland"). With these words, Morris Fletcher opens the second installment of a two-part story told as part of the sixth season of *The X-Files* (1993–2002). This "improbably named character" is one of the show's two central protagonists: Federal Bureau of Investigation (FBI) Special Agents Fox William Mulder (David Duchovny) and Dana Scully (Gillian Anderson). Together, Mulder and Scully investigate the X-Files: unsolvable or minimal-priority status cases that exist outside the Bureau mainstream, typically associated with unexplained phenomena, fringe pseudo-scientific theories or non-verifiable evidence of paranormal investigation. Over the course of the nine years originally documented by the show Mulder drifts further away from the bureau. When the franchise is revived in the 2008 movie *X-Files: I Want to Believe*, Mulder is hiding from the FBI. Later, the 2016 "Event Series" finds him living as a hermit, fully disassociated from his former career until he is invited back to investigate the X-Files once more. Upon resuming his former occupation, Mulder catalyzes a disintegration of procedures, both within the bureau and within the genre of the show itself. This essay will chart Mulder's gradual disassociation from the FBI and, exploring this disassociation in relation to post-structuralism, argue that Mulder's career-path functions metonymically for the disintegration of the show's own genre; a procedural drama which ultimately (and recurrently) foregrounds the actual impossibility of professional procedures to secure unproblematic resolutions.

In 1996, *The X-Files* was said to be "as complex and as controversial a phenomenon as the medium of television has ever produced" (1996, 3). The first collection of scholarly essays dedicated to its analysis noted that it was incendiary:

> [N]ot least because it dared to suggest (with great seriousness) that the government of the United States is involved in a vast conspiracy with former Nazi and Japanese scientists to assist alien beings in performing experiments—including, perhaps, generic hybridization!—on American citizens, [but because] it also experimented, narratologically, semiotically—with the medium [of television] in innovative ways [Lavery, Hague and Cartwright, 1996, 3].

One such innovation was its self-conscious manipulation of the procedural drama. *The X-Files* proved so informative to procedural drama that in 2008 Chandler Harriss used it alongside only three other archetypal examples—*Law and Order* (1990–2010), *Homicide: Life on the Street* (1993–2002) and *CSI: Crime Scene Investigation* (2000–2015)—to offer what he presented as a definitive textualist account of the genre. Working with this corpus, Harriss generated the following definition:

> The procedural is a variant of the detective story, which is itself a variant of the mystery, globally speaking. Procedurals filter the ratiocinative action through characters who actively investigate the mystery for the viewer, following procedures that are prescribed by their profession (e.g., police detectives, forensic scientists, etc.) [43].

In the case of *The X-Files,* that "profession" is Mulder and Scully's work as special agents for the FBI, the ultimate signifier of institutional power in America. Michele Malach has noted that within the "pantheon of pop-culture agents," prior to *The X-Files* (and its immediate predecessor, *Twin Peaks*, 1990–91), it was typically the case that agents enforced not only the law, but also cultural standards of order and normalcy. Malach writes that "like other representations of law enforcement officials, the agent character also embodies the normal. This means that he or she represents cultural categories of correctness, acting out what it means to be normal, mainstream, not-marginalized"(64). The fundamental allure of procedural drama is the promise that order will be restored. In terms of procedural drama dealing with criminal injustice, this restoration comes when the perpetrator is caught and punished. Given that the genre deals with professional procedures, this resolution also comes with the official endorsement of the state. Here, there is also the opportunity for a second order to be restored: the restoration of state sanctioned attitudes and social behaviors. Martha Nochimson identifies the figure of the law enforcement official as the most essential ingredient in procedural drama for this reason, observing that "television government agents are the sine qua non of television's endless obsession with the restoration of limits, barriers that authorize only the most domesticated form of desire" (147).

Given that the premise of *The X-Files* sees Mulder and Scully working through a backlog of unsolved, non-normative cases, the potential for satisfactory resolution through professional procedure is high. At the same time, the show regularly foregrounds Mulder and Scully's hyper-normality. As Malach notes:

> [T]heir appearance as ordinary FBI agents in line with traditional expectations of what agents look like reminds the viewers of a time when FBI agents were trustworthy protectors of the American way of life. Because Mulder and Scully look this way, we can trust them to tell us the truth.

However, this resolution is never achieved, and rather than restoring order, *The X-Files* deconstructs the parameters by which any sense of order can be attained.

This resistance to generic expectations is deliberate, resulting from a self-conscious juxtaposition of form and content. First, the unsolved cases under investigation are unsolved because they do not obey the logic of FBI procedure. Therefore, the very procedure designed to bring order and resolution is functionally useless. Second, though Mulder and Scully may present as "normal" and thus serve as arbiters of state-sanctioned behaviors, neither is capable of acting as a dispassionate vessel for bureau attitudes and objectives. For instance, Mulder repeatedly takes psychic evidence as seriously as physical evidence, often ignoring that which is usually prized the most by law enforcement officials: proof. Even Scully, who is usually presented as the more "normal" of the two, is seen to act on visions (such as in "Beyond the Sea," an episode in the first season) or on what she perceives to be divine inspiration (such as in the ninth season episode "Improbable"). Not only are the procedures at the heart of the show utterly redundant (normal FBI procedure does not equip our agents with the skills needed to establish or evidence that a crime has been committed by an alien, a poltergeist or an entity evolved from a fluke-work, for instance), but neither can Mulder and Scully adequately police the boundaries of normalcy because neither adhere to such standards themselves. What happens instead, this essay argues, is that *The X-Files* navigates the irreconcilable contradictions built into its format by maintaining an ironic self-reflexivity from which it offers a critique of both the procedural drama and the society that lusts for its artificial conjuring of order and resolution.

Morris Fletcher, the character introduced at the outset of this chapter, offers us an intriguing perspective on Mulder's career during the sixth season episode "Dreamland." A luckless Man in Black, when we first encounter Fletcher he is counting down the days to retirement. In the previous episode, he apprehended Mulder and Scully at the gates of Area 51. As he sarcastically assures Mulder that "there's no such thing as flying saucers," a UFO rumbles overhead. The saucer's unnaturally bright lights fade to reveal that Fletcher and Mulder have swapped bodies. Told largely from Fletcher's perspective (witnessing events through Mulder's eyes), these two episodes provide a rare opportunity for the audience to encounter a new vision of Agent Mulder. Fletcher, an outsider uninitiated in the show's story and continuity, generates an alternate telling of Mulder's narrative. Famously, "Spooky Mulder" is the outsider inside the FBI, driven to find his lost sister (who he believes to have been abducted by aliens in 1973) and prove that her disappearance was part of an all-encompassing conspiracy orchestrated by a shadow organization working at the highest level of government. As our point-of-view character for much of the show, Mulder brings the audience (and our proxy, Scully) along on this quest, ever deeper into the conspiracy. However, Fletcher has not experienced our six-year initiation. From Fletcher's perspective, he has found himself in the body of a delusional man who uses his faith in an unprovable experience to justify a lack of development across both his personal and professional lives. Viewed objectively, Mulder, who left the FBI academy a rising star with an Oxford PhD, squandered his career. For his obsession, he is condemned to the basement of the bureau, while his regular insubordination gets him sacked and demoted on multiple occasions. Mulder's inability to evolve his relationship with Scully, despite their mutual insistence that they love each other, is also read by Fletcher as a sign of personal underdevelopment.

Coming six years into the show's original run, the episode mines a rich vein of comedy, bathetically juxtaposing the show's own canonical portrayal of Fox Mulder with Fletcher's far more plausible reading. At the same time, this story also allows Mulder a glimpse of the road less traveled; a life not plagued by his insatiable desire to decode, deconstruct, and decipher the narratives underpinning social reality. The appearance of this story in the show's sixth season is no mistake. Mulder's philosophy has only one logical conclusion: that there can be no totality of explanation. This revelation recalls the assertions of Post-structuralism, which emerged from the discipline of linguistics in the late 1960s. Post-structuralism promotes a linguistic skepticism of anything presented as ordered or whole. Looking at language, texts, narratives, concepts, and ideologies, Post-structuralism argues that any coherence (most often figured as "the center") is in fact projected by the observer. The post-structuralist universe is therefore commonly referred to as being "decentered." Mulder finds himself operating in such a universe, the conspiracy he perceives bearing no center.

Apology Is Policy: The Failure of The X-Files

The success of Chris Carter's *The X-Files* was stratospheric. In the U.S., *The X-Files* rapidly made the unlikely transition from small cult show to cultural phenomenon watched by billions. Observing the show's triumphant arrival on British shores, the esteemed periodical *The New Statesman* published an article titled "We all love X, but why?" (Justice). The author, Emma Justice, figured the show's popularity in terms of pandemic and addiction as it quickly became a global hit, winning awards and critical acclaim on both sides of the Atlantic and "spawning merchandising, internet sites and conventions" (Justice). It became the highest-rated program on UK television at the time (Brown). In Japan, 120,000 videos were sold before a single episode was broadcast on television (Justice). Writing six years after the show premiered, Joyce Millman observed that it was:

> [S]o much a part of the popular consciousness that the phrase "like something from *The X-Files*" regularly creeps into news stories to describe things that are scientifically ambiguous, or inexplicable, or just plain weird [Millman, "*X-Files*" 1].

Eighteen years later, this phrase persists as linguistic cultural residue of the show's phenomenal status. As early as 2002, Keith Booker was already making the claim that *The X-Files* had been the most representative show of the 1990s. More recently, Enrica Picarelli and M. Carmen Gomez-Gallisteo have asserted that *The X-Files* "occupies a special place in the SF imaginary of the late twentieth century" (71). Indeed, so common is the claim that the *X-Files* is the definitive show of the 1990s that it is now seems almost cliché to state it. A second common-place observation is that *The X-Files* crashed and burned, hemorrhaging viewers as it collapsed beneath the growing weight of its own internal continuity.

Simon Brown summarizes perceptions of the show's decline when he writes that "despite being arguably *the* defining SF series of the 1990s, by the time the last episode of *The X-Files* aired in the U.S. in 2002 (2003 in the UK), few people cared" (7). As Brown records, there are frequently two accounts given for the show's "slow death." The most obvious explanation arises from practical issues surrounding the show's production. Famously, during the final seasons, Duchovny sued Fox Television for allegedly underpaying him millions of dollars of profit (Schilling). After drastically reducing his number of appearances per season (attributed in the narrative to Mulder's convenient abduction), Duchovny left the show entirely at the end of the six season, only returning for the finale a year later after the case against Fox had been settled out of court. Naturally, viewers, critics, and commentators aware of this high-profile disagreement between Duchovny and Fox sought to find evidence from the show's production to explain developments in its ongoing narrative and characterization. In a piece published in *Salon* during the dispute, Joyce Millman wrote of "the incredible shrinking Mulder," deducing that "[Duchovny] is bored of the *X-Files* and, frankly, so are we" ("Shrinking Mulder"). Millman's coverage argues that the actor's bid for further payment was "good news for Duchovny [but] bad news for *X-Files* fans." The conclusion that the fundamental shift in the show's format that Duchovny's reduced involvement precipitated would send the show hurtling towards a creative and commercial oblivion quickly became commonly held. Brown has collated a survey of responses to these final seasons, looking at publications such as *The Hollywood Reporter* and the UK's *Guardian* as well as online commentary. He concludes that "fans argue that the machinations of Duchovny robbed the series of its principal protagonist and therefore its driving force, as well as breaking up the core relationship between the two central characters" (8).

An often cited second explanation is that the show's central conspiracy became too complex, the writers deferring resolution for too long. In 1996, Charles Taylor stated that *The X-Files* reveals a world in which "the curtain of what we except as reality seems to have torn, allowing Mulder and Scully to search for meanings usually obscured" (2). Viewed two decades on, we see that our intrepid agents were never successful in firmly establishing those meanings. It is a staggering achievement that after 201 episodes, two feature films, and a mini-series, so much remains unexplained. Just as the shadowy groups they imagined inside the corridors of institutional power, the show's writers too managed to "deny all knowledge." Like Mulder and Scully, we are left wanting to believe, no assurance that our conspiracy theories will ever be confirmed or denied. As Peter Knight eloquently observed in 2000 (while the original series was still on screens):

> [*The X-Files*] teases its audience with the promise that eventually everything will be revealed to be part of a huge, interconnecting plot. But in the same way that the

ultimate source of power is never revealed, so too is the final truth of the murky past and eerie present never fully exposed [18].

Following the broadcast of the 2016 revival, which ended on a cliff-hanger inviting further questions rather than presenting definitive answers, we see that the trend Knight identified still persists. For most commentators watching those final seasons of the original series at the time of broadcast, the perpetual deferral of resolution throughout almost a decade of continuous storytelling was seen not as an achievement but a sign of increasing weakness in the show's writing. Brown's survey of contemporary reactions leads him to observe that the most vocal critics felt that "the writers lost track of the complicated narrative arcs and started either making mistakes or cheating by reinventing history" (8). Or, as "dig-duggler" exclaimed on one online forum: "Chris Carter was just making this shit up as he went along" (8).

The Truth Is Out There: Re-Assessing The X-Files

There is, however, an alternate reading of *The X-Files* that prevailing views of later seasons refuse to entertain. The first aspect of this reading centers on the structural and thematic function of conspiracy within *The X-Files*. As Knight has noted, "the more *The X-Files* promises to reveal a traditional humanist conspiracy of top-down control, the more it seems to paint a Foucauldian portrait of decentered power which is everywhere in the system but in no particular location" (17). Rather than the writers finding themselves unable to construct a suitable explanation for how the show's various mysteries can be connected and thus resolved, this re-reading asserts that the writers deliberately resist providing such an explanation to radically foreground the extent to which narrative cohesion is always imagined, both inside and outside of the fictional text. Mulder, like the show's frustrated viewers, realizes the limitations of narrative to provide an explanation for the totality of the show's mysteries. Indeed, as seen at the outset of this chapter, "Dreamland" begins to entertain the notion that Mulder is the only one to bring narrative cohesion to the disparate events depicted on the show. Over the two seasons that follow, Mulder is, time and again, confronted with the limits of his own investigative project and prompted to reflect explicitly upon his personal raison d'être. These moments come as his core beliefs are debunked and revealed as wholly unrelated. Mulder's quest for ultimate coherent meaning becomes the ultimate challenge to the coherence of meaning, prompting generic disintegration of the procedural world he inhabits. Considering narrative events that have taken place since the original series ended in 2002, across the subsequent feature film *X-Files: I Want to Believe* (2008) and the more recent six-part "Event series" (2016), there can be seen a direct correlation between Mulder's gradual disassociation from the FBI and his character's increasing inability to function within the generic confines of the procedural drama. As he approaches enlightenment, Mulder is rendered redundant, transcending a format designed to regularly resolve with the revelation of truth. As such, in the seventh season, he vanishes. Putting aside issues of production, Mulder's disappearance is in fact consistent with the trajectory set for both his character and the show's narrative.

For all that *The X-Files* was celebrated as a ground-breaking and innovative concept during its early years, its central fusion of the procedural and the supernatural was far from new. One need only look at the works of Edgar Allan Poe, celebrated as both an early originator of crime and detective fiction and a prolific purveyor of Gothic horror, to see that the order promised by the former and the disorder threatened by the later make for a heady cocktail.[1] Indeed, in most cases, the 18th-century gothic novel features all the traits identified by Warren Chernaik, Martin Swales, and Robert Vilain as the core characteristics of the detective genre:

> The detective story is the very paradigm of the "rattling good story"; the reader cannot put the book down (as the saying goes) because of the sheer compulsion to find the explanation of "whodunit." [...] The detective story enshrines that perennial hermeneutic of the narrative mode which works with deep structures of change and stasis, of onward-moving events and retrospective reflection, of mystery and its resolution [xii].

Like detective fiction, 18th-century gothic authors such as Ann Radcliffe and Charlotte Dacre structure their novels around the deferred revelation of what has truly be terrorizing their protagonists and for what reason. Radcliffe mastered the trope of the "explained supernatural," in which the protagonist (most often a young heroine) is seemingly tortured by other worldly entities only to discover in the final pages that there was a rational explanation all along (2014). For instance, when Radcliffe's readers reach the final pages of *Mysteries of Udolpho* (1794) they discover that her heroine, Emily St. Aubert, has not in fact been terrorized by the supernatural (as implied by the preceding four-hundred or so pages) but that she has drawn misleading conclusions from coincidence, happenstance, and various unrelated conspiracies of men. The explanation comes as a relief, as Radcliffe draws the many dangling plot threads together into a satisfying and coherent whole. All the mysteries of Udolpho are resolved. This satisfaction is directly analogous to that experienced by the reader of typical detective fiction, which also culminates in the revelation of truth: "the reader-response elicited by a detective story is very specific…. A detective-story plot stimulates its audience to expect unequivocal narrative closure" (Donlan, 37).

Crucially though, 18th-century Gothic does not always necessarily resolve with a rational or earthly explanation. Like Radcliffe's *Udolpho*, Charlotte Dacre's *Zafloya* (1806) similarly defers to the closing pages the revelation of how the events that have befallen her protagonist, Victoria de Loredani, are all seemingly connected. However, Victoria has not simply stumbled upon a series of random events and misread a conspiracy into them, like Radcliffe's Emily. Instead, she finds herself confronted with the devil himself, who has carefully orchestrated her terror and has now come to claim her soul. Structurally, such novels still share a common template with crime fiction, and the euphoria of their climax is derived from the same pleasure: resolution and closure. However, the logic is not that of empirical procedure and the officious martialing of order, but instead that of the Gothic, the supernatural and the terrified imagination.

Given the close proximity of the Gothic novel and detective fiction, in terms of both their genesis and evolution, the importation of procedural crime drama into a world of supernatural terror is not a surprising development. Indeed, the use of a "professional procedure" to bring order to the dangerous and transgressive logics of the Gothic imagination is perhaps more a conservative fantasy than a radical act of generic supervision. The very premise of *The X-Files* promises that the government will bring order to Gothic chaos. However, *The X-Files* does not deliver, instead proving time and again that institutional procedures, whether endorsed by the government or not, are incapable of explaining the inexplicable.

Initially, this lurch away from closure is most obvious in the characteristic twist ending of most "monster-of-the-week" episodes. This irresolution manifests itself in two ways. Oftentimes, the agents believe that the case has been closed only for the viewer to be privileged to a final shot revealing that the phenomena they have been investigating in fact persists. More commonly, irresolution presents itself practically when Mulder and Scully are unable to file their case-report because either the evidence they have gathered does not adhere to FBI standards or the procedural infrastructure they operate within cannot accommodate the logic they have used to solve their case. For instance, at the close of the first season episode "Tooms," Scully presents FBI assistant director Walter Skinner (Mitch Pileggi) with a report accounting for the conditions under which Mulder defensively killed escaped prisoner Eugene Victor Tooms (Doug Hutchinson). The report explains that Tooms, who the agents believe to have been an adult since at least the 1930s, has an abnormal skeletal structure that allows him to elongate his limbs, and an unusual metabolism that allows him to spit acidic bile. Their investigation has apparently revealed that Tooms regularly goes into hibernation after consuming a set number of human livers. Mulder disturbed Tooms as he prepared to attack his final victim. Tooms attacked Mulder instead, who then killed him in self-defense. As will be the case many more times over subsequent years, Skinner refuses to believe this outlandish account, and Mulder and Scully have no acceptable evidence to support it. The *X-Files* peripeteia, which resists rather than delivers resolution in a last-minute sting before the credits roll, became one of the tropes for which the show was best known. Writ large, this evasion of narrative closure can be seen in Mulder's personal quest to uncover the machinations of the Syndicate (a secret shadow government with nefarious global interests) and prove his sister's abduction by aliens.

I Want to Believe: Mulder's Crumbling Faith

For much of the show's first six seasons, Mulder's core beliefs function as what Derrida terms "transcendental signifiers," fixed intellectual anchors from which all other knowledge and understanding can be mapped. Derrida figures these fixed points as the center and the knowledge, understandings, and systems that surrounding them as the whole:

> [B]y orienting and organizing the coherence of the system, the center of a structure permits the play of its elements inside the total form. And even today the notion of a structure lacking any center represent the unthinkable itself [352].

Continuing the logic of Structuralism, Derrida argues that if we can accept that language informs our understanding of the world, then that language must also be responsible for the creation of those transcendental signifiers constituting the "centers" of human society and culture. These centers, he suggested, do not originate or exist in the center at all, but are instead projected to the center by the human observer. The act of observation is what enforces linguistic coherence on that which is actually incoherent, by extension forming the illusion of a "linked chain of determinations" (352). Famously, Derrida observed that "the center is not at the center of totality" (352). Derrida talked of this revelation as a rupture within philosophy, which has subsequently been seen to seek out and deconstruct the centers around which Western intellectual thinking had previously been founded. Peter Barry highlights one such center as being the assumption that man is the measure of all things in the universe: "white Western norms of dress, behavior, architecture, intellectual outlook and so on, provided a firm center against which deviations, aberrations, variations could be detected and identified as 'Other' and marginal" (67). To an extent, this accounts for the traditional role of the pop-culture agent, as discussed by Malach. The agent provides a center, a marker of normalization, and in contrast to the agent we can see those pursued and punished as deviant and Other. Mulder, though, as already discussed, is not a typical pop-culture agent. He often implores his colleagues to have an open mind, sharing with Derrida a radical uncertainty of cultural attitudes, social mores and even, at times, reason itself. Barry's overview of Post-structuralism is surprisingly reminiscent of Mulder's worldview and, to an extent, the character and content of *The X-Files* as a whole:

> Post-structuralism inherits [from philosophy] the habit of skepticism, and intensifies it. It regards any confidence in the scientific method as naïve, and even derives a certain masochistic intellectual pleasure from knowing for certain that we can't know anything for certain, fully conscious of the irony and paradox which doing this entails [63].

Crucially, though Mulder puts little stock in the transcendental signifiers policed and installed by both the institution in which he works and his cultural episteme more broadly, he does harbor some intellectual anchors of his own. Mulder's life is structured around proving two of his personal beliefs: that his sister was abducted by aliens, and that this abduction was part of an all-encompassing global conspiracy orchestrated by a secret shadow government later identified as "the Syndicate." As the episode "Dreamland" playfully implies, much of the show's narrative cohesion comes from Mulder's own efforts to orient the cases he and Scully encounter in relation to these two beliefs. Samantha Mulder and the Syndicate become the center of Mulder's life and as a result often appear to provide the center for the show; an anchor for its dense and sprawling continuity. However, as the show enters its seventh season, each of Mulder's beliefs have been debunked.

Many of Mulder's beliefs are validated, but the grand narrative he assembles—built as it is on ideas of structure and totality—falls wide of the mark. In the sixth season episode "One Son," Mulder finally confronts The Smoking Man (William B. Davis), a dissembling agent of the Syndicate who has long since come to personify the conspiracy Mulder seeks to unravel. Held at gunpoint with nothing to lose, The Smoking Man finally tells Mulder about the Syndicate's involvement with aliens. Rather than revealing a single, coherent conspiracy that has been playing out since the 1960s, he talks of a series of largely reactionary events and decisions involving multiple players, including the U.S. government and two groups of aliens; one intent on colonizing earth, one intent on protecting it. Furthermore, though it seems that the Syndicate has been assisting in alien plans for the colonization of Earth, the Smoking Man tells the tale in such a way that this can be read as a pose, their true intention being to halt the alien invaders at the eleventh hour. Much of what Mulder has pieced together has been the result of happenstance or, in some cases, is wholly unrelated to the Syndicate's project. There is no coherent narrative, only further evidence of undersigned chaos.

Mulder is correct in his assumption that his sister was involved in the plans of the Syndicate. In the 1960s, the Syndicate had allied themselves with the colonizing aliens so that their families might be spared during the invasion. Mulder's father, Bill, was a member of the Syndicate, and he had no choice but to offer his daughter, Samantha, over to the aliens as collateral. However, in the Season Seven episode "Closure," Mulder discovers that even this may not fully account for Samantha's fate. Rather than being abducted by aliens, Mulder learns that she lived in secret with the Smoking Man, where she was regularly subjected to painful tests. He discovers that in 1979, a girl matching Samantha's description was checked into the hospital. Further investigation reveals that the girl disappeared that night. With the assistance of psychic Harold Piller, Mulder concludes that Samantha was taken by entities composed of starlight known as "walk-ins" who save children destined to suffer terrible fates. Though Mulder choses to believe that this is what happened to Samantha, similarities between her disappearance and the case that Mulder and Scully are investigating invite a far more pessimistic reading of events in which she may have fallen victim to a murderous pedophile. Though this situation remains open to interpretation, the show does at least confirm that Samantha was not abducted by aliens after all.

"Closure" also makes explicit a reading of Mulder's behavior that is usually only ever implied: that he is delusional. Concerned that Mulder's interactions with psychic Harold Piller might result in lasting psychological damage, Scully meets with a psychiatrist to discuss a videotape depicting Mulder undergoing hypnotic regression therapy a decade earlier. The tape shows Mulder vividly recounting the abduction of his sister by aliens. The psychiatrist concludes that the memory is a fantasy, conjured by Mulder's subconscious desire to never remember what really happened that night, suggesting that "his delusion is playing into his unconscious hope that his sister is still alive. And if you think about it, his delusion has the effect of giving his reason to pursue her."

Mulder's beliefs give him a reason to live. They are transcendental signifiers which allow him to orient his personal and professional lives, as well as his other beliefs, attitudes and behaviors. When he discovers that they are as artificial as any other cultural norm scrutinized by Post-structuralism, both his rationale and his role within the show begin to come unstuck. In the episode "Redux," Mulder expresses this revelation himself:

> I've held a torch in the darkness to glance upon a truth unknown. An act of faith begun with an ineloquent certainty that my journey promised the chance, not just of understanding, but of recovery. That the disappearance of my sister, twenty-three years ago, would come to be explained. And that the pursuit of these greater truths about the existence of extraterrestrial life might even reunite us. A belief which I now know to be false and uninformed in the extreme. My folly revealed by facts which illuminate both my arrogance and self-deception.

Mulder learns that there is no totality of explanation. The revelation relieves him of his goal, but as a character born of and at the heart of a procedural drama, it also relieves him of his place in the narrative. In "Requiem," Mulder's final episode as a recurring character, the case for his redundancy—both professionally and narratively—is presented to him in unambiguous terms by an FBI Auditor:

> **AUDITOR:** By FBI standards these numbers are out of control.... You're under evaluation. There has to be a point where we say no.
> **MULDER:** Well you can't really compare what we do to other departments in the bureau.
> **AUDITOR:** Right. This business with aliens?
> **MULDER:** There's more to it than that.
> **AUDITOR:** But at the end of the day you'd say that aliens are your real focus.
> **MULDER:** That's the reason I got started, yeah.
> **AUDITOR:** Investigating your sister's abduction and the government conspiracy around it Both of which have been resolved, correct?
> **MULDER:** Nothing has been resolved, exactly.
> **AUDITOR:** In this report here, it is concluded that your sister is dead, as well as the men who took her. This is your handwriting, here on the report, Agent Mulder?
> **MULDER:** Yeah.
> **AUDITOR:** So, what exactly is left to investigate?

As Mulder himself observes, "nothing has been resolved exactly," but as he has learned nothing can be resolved. In a way, Mulder has uncovered the ultimate human conspiracy: the conspiracy of meaning.

Structuralism is largely informed by Nietzschean philosophy which, in so many ways, begins by foregrounding the extent to which language informs (and distorts) human perception and understanding:

> The arrogance inherent in cognition and feeling casts a blinding fog over the eyes and sense of human beings, and because it contains within itself the most flattering evaluation of cognition it deceives them about the value of existence. Its most general effect is deception. Is there a perfect match between things and their designations? Is language the full and adequate expression of all realities? Only through forgetfulness could human beings ever entertain the illusion that they possess truth to the degree described above. If they will not content themselves with truth in the form of a tautology, i.e., with empty husks they will forever exchange illusions for truth [51].

Mulder, like Nietzsche and Derrida, discovers that there is nothing but the empty signifiers of language and the artificial projection of narrative coherence. There is no center and there is no outside. This new perspective is incompatible with the procedural drama, and as such, Mulder is not present for much of the show's eighth and ninth seasons. There is no place in the FBI for a man who has lost his faith in transcendental signifiers and by extension the promise of resolution or the discovery of truth. There is also no place for such a man in a procedural crime drama: a detective who no longer believes a case can ever be closed.

Resist or Serve: Mulder on the Outside

We encounter Mulder again in the 2008 film *I Want to Believe*. Mulder is in exile, now hiding from the FBI that he once worked for. As viewers, we are led to him by Scully (now a full-time medical doctor) and find him in his home-office, his walls plastered with newspaper clippings pertaining to strange and unusual happenings. When he is inevitably coaxed back to the FBI (who promise to drop charges against him if he assists in one final case) he is comically incompatible with the bureau, both as an institution and as an environment. Now bearded and dressed in jeans and a sweater, Mulder is a visibly irregular character as he traverses the corridors and offices, densely populated by smartly dressed men and women in suits and ties. As agents step around him, casting side-long glances, our once perceivably hyper-normal protagonist has become abnormal, transgressive and Other. The FBI is more than just a setting, it doubles as a metaphor for the show's generic confines, into which Mulder no longer fits.

Special agent Dakota Whitney (Amanda Peet) has sought Mulder out for assistance with a case that, like the X-files, does not conform to the parameters of the FBI's typical investigatory procedures. An agent has been kidnapped and a pedophilic psychic Catholic priest claims to be having visions pertaining to the case. Intriguingly, Whitney looks to Mulder for expert council, asking him to comment on existing precedents and offer alternative procedural guidance, indicating, for instance, the speed and order in which such phenomena usually progress. With access to a privileged, rarefied body of knowledge, Mulder becomes once more professionalized, but as a freelance specialist rather than an FBI agent. He can bring his own procedures to the drama, and once again inhabit the procedural genre. The film resists confirming whether Mulder's procedures work, since it is ambiguous to what extent Father Joe's vague claims actually assist in the investigation. And then, Mulder's resistance to FBI protocol during the film's finale almost results in his death. As the film closes, Mulder has been convinced that he cannot return to the FBI; neither can he continue to exist within the confines of procedural drama. As the credits roll, Mulder and Scully are seen rowing away in a small boat, out to sea and then into darkness, leaving both the franchise and the genre and finally transcending *The X-Files*.

They would of course return, nine years later, in the six-part "Event Series," which initially appears to undo the logic of *I Want to Believe* by bringing Mulder back into both the FBI and the procedural drama. Mulder suffers something of a relapse in the opening episode, "My Struggle," falling back into the convictions he held in the show's fifth and sixth seasons as he becomes once again convinced of a grand narrative that draws together all his suspicions and findings. However, "My Struggle" does not simply forget a decade of character development. Instead, it takes Mulder on a microcosmic reenactment of the character's preceding story-arc in just forty-four minutes, reminding him that there can be no such explanation. That this then results in him returning to his former office at the FBI, where he is coupled again with his former partner to work once more on the X-Files does perhaps stretch credulity to the limits. It is telling that his reinstatement happens off-screen, via voice over, in the closing seconds of the episode. However, after Mulder's return, it is far from business as usual. His worldview is now absolutely antithetical to both the profession and genre in which he is operating, triggering a volatile reaction between the show's form and content which, by the end of this short season, brings about the utter disintegration of its procedural format.

All Lies Lead to the Truth: Mulder's Rejection of Meaning

The point of no return comes in the fifth episode, "Babylon," which proves explicitly Post-structuralist in its central interest in the relationship between language and reality. The episode opens with an uncomfortably realistic sequence, depicted two men walking into an art gallery and detonating a bomb. As the dust settles, burning civilians stumble out onto the street. In total contrast to this, the title sequence is followed by a light-hearted and meta-theatrical scene in Mulder's office. There's a knock at the door, and Scully responds by directly quoting Mulder's first-ever line of dialogue on the show, before joking that she's "waited twenty-three years" to say that. Their visitors are two junior agents, Kyd Miller (Robbie Amell) and Liz Einstein (Lauren Ambrose). It clear to the viewer that the open-minded Miller and the skeptical Einstein are young doubles of Mulder and Scully, a point hammered home by the revelation that Scully wrote her dissertation on Albert Einstein's *twin* paradox. Mulder and Scully are also aware that they have come face-to-face with their own doubles, delivering a string of knowing punchlines to this effect. In contrast to the preceding scene, Mulder's office is a surreal space where anything is possible.

As in *I Want to Believe*, Mulder has been sought out for his ability to offer non-normative procedural guidance on a case that does not conform to the FBI's own procedures and regulations. Miller and Einstein hope to communicate with one of the surviving suicide bombers, who now languishes in a coma. When Einstein later reluctantly accepts Mulder's offer of assistance, he lays out his Post-structuralist philosophy, asking Einstein if she is willing to "talk about the nature of reality." He goes on:

> Do you believe that thoughts have mass? That ideas such as faith and forgiveness have weight much the same way this desk has weight? Or any material, really. I'm sure you believe that words have weight. The weight to move people to go kill other people.... Neo-Darwinists believe that every word spoken, every thought, every perception, lest I misperceive, is a step in the evolution of mankind. Agent Einstein, you have a terrorist lying in a state of existence somewhere between life and death. If he holds valuable intel on other terrorists, maybe in order to reach him, you need to expand your mind on the so-called material world.

In an exchange that emphasizes how far *The X-Files* has drifted from the typical procedural crime drama, Mulder proposes that Einstein administer him hallucinogenic drugs so that he might transcend the material word and communicate with the comatose terrorist. Citing existing precedents, Mulder explains that "test subjects report experiences that transcended space and time, confrontations with the dead, touching the very face of God.... Test subjects have also reported that once the impediment of the physical body is removed, deep and lasting truths are revealed that the conscious mind won't allow." At last, Mulder has found the means to transcend the realm of words.

Mulder's proposed procedure is remarkably simple, he will sit next to the patient and take the drug. What follows is, again, profoundly surreal, as Mulder is seen leaving the hospital to a diegetic dance beat, before participating in a montage of increasingly unlikely scenarios. He is seen jay-walking, then arriving at a line-dance, then doing a solo show-dance ending in a back-flip, before being mobbed by women and sitting down with a group of deceased characters from the show's history. Next, the bar dissolves to reveal him strapped topless to a table while being whipped by Einstein, now in the character of a dominatrix. Then he finds himself on a longboat, where, to the sound of Tom Waits "Misery Is the River of the World," he encounters the comatose terrorist who whispers to him in Arabic.

It remains unclear which aspects of the sequence actually occurred, though it is confirmed that Mulder did briefly go missing from the hospital. Einstein later reveals that the drugs she gave Mulder were a placebo, indicating the extent to which he can now self-consciously restructure his own reality. Mulder can recall the phrase that he heard during his vision, which Miller translates as the name of a hotel where more terrorists are preparing to mobilize. Mulder's procedure, such as it is, has resolved Einstein and Miller's case. Rather than there being no explanation as to why the case cannot be resolved, as was often so during earlier seasons of *The X-Files*, in "Babylon" we are instead left with no explanation for how it is solved. Mulder has become the unknowable component in the show, precipitating a radical alteration in the show's procedural format. No longer is the procedure insufficient for the task, the procedure works but it is unintelligible. Following Mulder's return, the viewer can experience the resolution of the case being closed, but is left to wonder how it is resolved.

The End: The X-Files, *Uncertainty and the Invitation to Imagine*

It is normal to seek truth from external sources and it is normal to desire closure, particularly within the procedural crime drama, which by its very nature promises resolution and the restoration and propagation of normalcy. However, *The X-Files* has always overlooked the normal in favor of the paranormal. Mr. Blockhead, a body manipulator who self-identifies as a "freak" in the episode "Humbug" hints that this is the moral behind *The X-Files* as early as the second season, telling Scully that "nature abhors normality, it can't go very long without creating a mutant. You know why? It's a mystery. Maybe some mysteries aren't supposed to be solved." In so many ways *The X-Files* is that mutant. A procedural that foregrounds the artificiality and ineffectiveness of procedure. A crime drama that knows the mystery can never be solved. Tracing Mulder's staggered retirement spotlights what it is that *The X-Files* has achieved over the past quarter of a century, and the scale of that achievement is unprecedented. It disrupts, it deconstructs, and ultimately it demonstrates time and again the creative potential of irresolution. Agent Einstein quotes her namesake to make this very observation during the closing scenes of "Babylon," responding to Miller's lamentation that some mysteries cannot be solved: "The most beautiful thing we can experience is the mysterious, the source of all true art and science."

Replacing empirical procedure with the invitation to imagine, *The X-Files* recommends an alternative way of reading the world which addresses the radical uncertainties of post-structuralism. Mulder's journey in *The X-Files* endorses the philosophical claims of post-structuralism: there is no totality of explanation and there are no transcendental signifiers, there is but the forlorn impulse of the human mind to imprint seeming order onto actual chaos. Finally acknowledging that narrative coherence, order and the "center" are all projected by the observer is a liberating revelation for Mulder. As "Babel" demonstrates, once he has learned this lesson, he is able to unlock new understanding and abilities, even briefly transcending the boundaries of human life to convene with the dead. The secret, he finds, comes in acknowledging that he was projecting the narrative all along, so transcendence comes simply with identifying and informing that narrative. Order does not come from the external, but the internal. Where, then, can we find truth? Uncharacteristically, *The X-Files* does momentarily offer an answer to this, the oldest of questions, three episodes prior to "Babel." It comes as a throwaway line during "Founder's Mutation," setting the pace for much of what follows:

> GUPTA: You guys are all alike, you know? You say you want to walk on the wild side, but when it comes down to it ... you're repressed. I finally let go of all that, that self-loathing and that judgment and I'm free. Stop tormenting yourself. The truth is in here [points to Mulder's heart].
> MULDER: Yeah, I've heard something like that.

NOTES

1. Edgar Allan Poe's character, C. August Dupin, is generally regarded as the first detective in fiction. He first appeared in *The Murders in the Rue Morgue* (1841), which is also widely considered the first example of detective fiction as we would recognize it today. Kenneth Silverman offers a comprehensive overview of Poe's role in establishing the detective fiction genre and his subsequent influence (1991).

WORKS CITED

Arp, Robert. *The X-Files and Philosophy: The Truth Is in Here*. Open Court, 2017.
Attanasio, Paul, creator. *Homicide: Life on the Street*. NBC Productions, 1993–1994.
"Babylon." *The X-Files*. Twentieth Century–Fox Television, Fox, Los Angeles, 15 Feb. 2016.
Barry, Peter. *Beginning Theory: An Introduction to Literary and Cultural Theory*. Manchester UP, 2002.
"Beyond the Sea." *The X-Files*. Twentieth Century–Fox Television, WXIA, Atlanta, 7 Jan. 1994.
Booker, M Keith. *Strange TV: Innovative Television Series from* The Twilight Zone *to* The X-Files. Greenwood, 2002.

Brown, Simon. "Memento Mori: The Slow Death of *The X-Files.*" *Science Fiction and Television*, Vol. 6. No. 1, 2013, pp. 7–23.
_____. "The X-Files." *The Cult TV Book*. Ed. Stacey Abbott. I.B. Tauris, 2010 pp. 163–6.
Carter, Chris, creator. *The X-Files*. Twentieth Century–Fox Television, 1993–2002.
_____. *X-Files: The Event Series*. Twentieth Century–Fox Television, 2016.
Chernaik, Warren, Martin Swales and Robert Vilain, eds. *The Art of Detective Fiction*. Macmillan, 2000.
"Closure." *The X-Files*. Twentieth Century–Fox Television, WXIA, Atlanta, 13 Feb. 2000.
Dacre, Charlotte. *Zofloya, or the Moor*. Ed. Kim Ian Michasiw. Oxford UP. 2008.
Derrida, Jacques. "Structure, Sign and Play in the Discourse of the Human Sciences." *Writing and Difference*. Translated by Alan Bass. Routledge, 2001. pp. 351–370.
Donlan, Marc. "The Peaks and Valleys of Serial Creativity: What Happened To/on *Twin Peaks.*" *Full of Secrets: Critical Approaches to* Twin Peaks. Ed. David Lavery. Wayne State UP, 1995. pp. 30–35.
"Dreamland." *The X-Files*. Twentieth Century–Fox Television, WXIA, Atlanta, 29 Nov. 1998.
Fiske, John. *Television Culture* Methuen, 1987.
"Founder's Mutuatuion." *The X-Files*. Twentieth Century–Fox Television, Fox, Los Angeles, 25 Jan. 2016.
Frost, Mark, and David Lynch, creators. *Twin Peaks*. Lynch/Frost Productions. 1990–1991.
"Die hand die verletzt." *The X-Files*. Twentieth Century–Fox Television, WXIA, Atlanta, 27 Jan. 1995.
Harriss, Chandler. "Policing Propp: Toward a Textualist Definition of Procedural Drama." *Journal of Film and Video*, Vol. 60. No. 1, 2008, pp. 43–59.
"Humbug." *The X-Files*. Twentieth Century–Fox Television, WXIA, Atlanta, 31 March 1995.
"Improbable." *The X-Files*. Twentieth Century–Fox Television WXIA, Atlanta, 7 April 2002.
Justice, Emma. "We All Love X. but Why?" *New Statesman*. 23 Aug. 1996. Web. 1 June 2017.
Knight, Peter. *Conspiracy Culture: From the Kennedy Assassination to* The X-Files. Routledge, 2000.
Kowalski, Dean A., ed. *The Philosophy of* The X-Files. U of Kentucky P, 2007.
Lavery, David. "Introduction: The Semiotics of Cobbler, *Twin Peaks*' Interpretive Community." *Full of Secrets: Critical Approaches to* Twin Peaks. Ed. David Lavery. Wayne State UP, 1995. pp. 1–21.
Lavery, David, Angela Hague and Marla Cartwright, eds. *Deny All Knowledge: Reading* The X-Files. Syracuse UP, 1996.
Malach, Michele. "I Want to Believe… in the FBI: The Special Agent in *The X-Files.*" *Deny All Knowledge: Reading the X-Files*. Ed. David Lavery, Angela Hague and Marla Cartwright. Syracuse UP, 1996. pp. 63–76.
Millman, Joyce. "The Incredible Shrinking Mulder." *Salon*. Salon Media Group, 22 Mar. 2000. Web. 29 May 2017.
_____. "The XEROX: *X-Files.*" *Salon*. Salon Media Group, 15 Mar. 1990. Web. 28 May 2017.
Mittell, Jason. *Genre and Television: From Cop Shows to Cartoons in American Culture*. Routledge, 2004.
"My Struggle." *The X-Files*. Twentieth Century–Fox Television, Fox, Los Angeles, 24 Jan. 2016.
Nietzche, Frederich. "On Truth and Lying in a Non-Moral Sense." *On Truth and Untruth: Selected Writings*. Harper. 2010. pp. 15–50.
Nochimson, Martha. "Desire Under the Douglas Firs: Entering the Body of Reality in *Twin Peaks.*" *Full of Secrets: Critical Approaches to* Twin Peaks. Ed. David Lavery. Wayne State UP, 1995. pp. 144–159.
"One Son." *The X-Files*. Twentieth Century–Fox Television, WXIA, Atlanta, 14 Feb. 1999.
Picarelli, Enrica, and Gomez-Galisteo, M. "Be Fearful: *The X-Files*' Post-9/11 Legacy." *Science Fiction Film and Television*, vol. 6, no. 1, 2013, pp. 71–86.
Radcliffe, Ann. *The Mysteries of Udolpho*. Ed. Bonamy Dobrée. Oxford UP. 1998.
"Redux." *The X-Files*. Twentieth Century–Fox Television, WXIA, Atlanta, 2 Nov. 1997.
"Requiem." *The X-Files*. Twentieth Century–Fox Television, WXIA, Atlanta, 21 May 2000.
Rice, Jeff, creator. *Kolchak: The Night Stalker*. Universal Television, 1974–1975.

28   Policing the Monstrous

Schilling, Dave. "David Duchovny: 'I Can't Play Mulder the Way I Did, That Would Be Obscene.'" *The Guardian*. 5 February 2016. Web. 1 June 2017.
"Sein und Zeit." *The X-Files*. Twentieth Century–Fox Television, WXIA, Atlanta, 6 Feb. 2000. Television.
Silverman, Kenneth. *Edgar A. Poem: Mournful and Never-ending Remembrance*. Harper Perennial. 1991. Print.
Taylor, Charles. "Truth Decay: Sleuths After Reagan." *Millennium Pop*, Vol 1. No. 1 (Summer 1994). Web. 2 June 2017.
"Tooms." *The X-Files*. Twentieth Century–Fox Television, WXIA, Atlanta, 22 April 1994.
Townsend, Dale. "An Introduction to Ann Radcliffe." *Discovering Literature: Romantics and Victorians*. British Library. 15 March 2014. Web. 5 July 2017.
Wolf, Dick, creator. *Law and Order*. Universal Television, 1990–2010.
Wright, Angela, and Dale Townsend, eds. *Ann Radcliffe, Romanticism and the Gothic*. Cambridge, 2014.
The X-Files. Dir. Rob Bowman. Twentieth Century–Fox Film Corporation, 1998.
The X-Files: I Want to Believe. Dir. Chris Carter. Twentieth Century–Fox Film Corporation, 2008.
Zuiker, Anthony, creator. *CSI: Crime Scene Investigation*. CBS, 2000–2015.

The Owls Are Not What They Seem

Uncanny Doubles in Twin Peaks

Mark Yates

Co-created by David Lynch and Mark Frost, *Twin Peaks* (1990–2017) adhered to and resisted the conventions of procedural dramas on television. It did so by making familiar conventions seem unfamiliar in an intertextual pastiche of soap opera, detective story, science-fiction, and horror, using but, at the same time, subverting a number of established television tropes within *Twin Peaks* (1990–91), *Twin Peaks: Fire Walk with Me* (1992), and *Twin Peaks: The Return* (2017). This experimentation with genre, which placed supernatural beings alongside the stock characters of generic television, was hinged on the utilization of a series of uncanny doubles that negotiated between public and private selves. By using Sigmund Freud's ideas about the uncanny to explore the dualities that are present throughout seasons one and two of *Twin Peaks*, this essay will demonstrate the ways in which *Twin Peaks*—much like the owls of its infamous tagline—was not as it seemed.

The experience of watching *Twin Peaks* is frequently described as uncanny.[1] However, explorations of the uncanny in *Twin Peaks* have usually been limited to the employment of this term as a convenient adjective to quickly encapsulate the unusual elements of the show. The cursory use of this term devalues the important roles that the uncanny played in the construction of the series.[2] While Lynch argues that "he knows nothing of psychoanalytic theory" (Rodley xi), his approach to filmmaking is hinged on a fundamental understanding of the uncanny: throughout his oeuvre, Lynch has explored the dualities of everyday life in America, juxtaposing the intimately familiar with the distinctly unfamiliar through the uses of quirky characters, supernatural beings, and doppelgängers. Consequently, Chris Rodley, in the introduction to *Lynch on Lynch* (1997), claimed, "if it is hard to define not only the experience of watching a Lynch film but also to pinpoint the very nature of what one has seen, it is because the uncanny—in all its nonspecificity—lies at the very core of Lynch's work" (ix). If this claim is accepted, the roles of the uncanny in *Twin Peaks* demand further exploration.

Definitions of the uncanny have proven to be problematic. According to Andrew Bennett and Nicholas Royle, "to try to define the uncanny is immediately to encounter one of its decisive paradoxes, namely that 'the uncanny' has to do with a *troubling* of definitions" (35). However, in most cases,

> the uncanny has to do with making things uncertain: it has to do with the sense that things are not as they have come to appear through habit and familiarity, that they may challenge all rationality and logic [Bennett and Royle 37].

This definition is based on Sigmund Freud's essay, "The Uncanny" (1919), in which the close but contradictory relationships between the "heimlich" and the "unheimlich" (219) are explored in terms of the former, the homely, failing to conceal the latter, the unhomely, in a process of defamiliarization which—while resulting in a distinct feeling of unfamiliarity—continued to retain some elements of familiarity as a result of its homely contexts. The uncanny, then, refers to the intellectual and emotional response to the familiar seeming unfamiliar or vice versa. Thus, in the view of Freud, the production of the uncanny within fiction necessitated the construction of a familiar setting which was compromised by the sudden disclosure of an unfamiliar component. Freud writes,

> The creative writer can ... choose a setting which ... differ[s] from the real world by admitting superior spiritual beings such as daemonic spirits or ghosts of the dead. So long as they remain within their setting of poetic reality, such figures lost any uncanniness which they might possess.... The situation is altered as soon as the writer pretends to move in the world of common reality. In this case ... everything that would have an uncanny effect in reality has it in his story.... In doing this he is in a sense betraying us to the superstitiousness which we have ostensibly surmounted; he deceives us by promising to give us the sober truth, and then after all overstepping it. We react to his inventions as we would have reacted to real experiences [249–250].

In other words, uncanniness in fiction relies on the use of a familiar setting which, for the most part, mirrors the conditions of reality. The introduction of any elements which disrupt these realistic conditions results in a feeling of the uncanny because the bounds of possibility have been confused and complicated through the juxtaposition of the familiar and the unfamiliar.[3]

With Freud's ideas about the uncanny in mind, it is clear that the consideration of *Twin Peaks* necessitates the use of a methodological framework that forms a distinction between the presentations of the familiar and the unfamiliar. Establishing this distinction makes possible the exploration of how the plot and setting of *Twin Peaks*—a police and federal investigation into a murder in a small town in Washington—achieved a familiarity that put its audiences at ease. It did so through the presentation of a homely context that was intertextually familiar to contemporaneously popular genres such as the procedural drama and the soap opera. Uncovering the intertextuality of *Twin Peaks* will lead to a consideration of how its generically familiar contexts became vulnerable to disruption through the introduction of a supernatural mythology that, with few exceptions, was unfamiliar in these formulaic genres.

The familiarity of *Twin Peaks* was not rooted in hyper-realism. Rather, this familiarity was the result of the show using a series of tropes which were connotative of contemporaneously popular television genres. These tropes served an intertextual function that grounded the contexts of *Twin Peaks* in a recognizable and familiar network of locations, characters, and storylines. John Fiske claimed that "television is essentially intertextual" (*Television Culture* 15). Therefore, when exploring the televisual coding of *Twin Peaks*, it is necessary to offer an intertextual study which investigates the familiar relationships between the signifiers and the signifieds used in the show, highlighting the ways in which the repetition of these relationships within the generic categories of television resulted in audiences being predisposed to assign conventional connotations to familiar content. This predisposition meant that the setting of *Twin Peaks*, while not absolutely true to reality, was distinctly familiar within the intertextual contexts of late 20th-century television.

Intertextuality calls attention to the ways in which texts exist in relation to other texts. This concept, introduced by Julia Kristeva, proposes that "in the space of a given text, several utterances, taken from other texts, intersect and neutralize one another" (36). The specificity of these intersections between texts can vary from explicit to ambiguous and, more often than not, it is not necessary for audiences to be intimately familiar with the exact sources of direct allusions in order to construct meanings from the text. Instead, the meanings generated from these allusions can be based on the work's intertextuality with all texts which contribute to the collective understanding of the allusion within the audience's cultural and historical contexts. This concept is demonstrated in Fiske's *Television Culture* (1987) through an intertextual analysis of Madonna's *Material Girl* (1984):

> Madonna's music video *Material Girl* ... is a parody of Marilyn Monroe's song and dance number "Diamonds Are a Girl's Best Friend" in the movie *Gentleman Prefer Blondes*: such an allusion to a specific text is not an example of intertextuality for its effectiveness depends upon specific, not generalized, textual knowledge—a knowledge that, incidentally, many of Madonna's young girl fans in 1985 were unlikely to possess. The video's intertextuality refers rather to our culture's image bank of the sexy blonde star who plays with men's desire for her and turns it to her advantage [108].

When exploring the conventional relationships between the signifiers and signifieds used in *Twin Peaks*, then, it is not necessary to isolate the exact texts that inspired its creators.[4] Instead, because signifiers function as "cues that forecast the type of genre" (Ledwon 266), it is only necessary to identify the intertextual genres to which these signifiers belonged: for instance, a lack of narrative closure would usually signal a soap opera while the appearance of a supernatural being would typically signify a work of science-fiction or horror.[5] Each of these semiotic cues, according to Robert C. Allen, "encourage the viewer to read a particular text or textual feature as belonging to a larger category of texts the viewer knows" (85). In regard to the intertextuality of soap operas, Allen claimed that "like all cultural products, soap operas exist within networks of other texts to which they inevitably in some way refer." Consequently, the audience "is constantly comparing the text being read with the encyclopedia of other texts he or she has experienced" (87). This process of intertextual comparison, if validated by consistent conformity to generic conventions, can result in a reassuring feeling of familiarity with viewers.[6]

Twin Peaks adhered to the intertextual conventions of two popular genres which were familiar to television audiences.[7] Lynch claimed that "the project was to mix a police investigation with the ordinary lives of characters" (158), offering a "strange blend" (193) of procedural dramas and soap operas. Similarly, Marc Dolan, in "The Peaks and Valleys of Serial Creativity: What Happened to/on *Twin Peaks*" (1995) argued that, at its most basic, *Twin Peaks* was a procedural drama that took place in a soap opera setting. Dolan writes:

> Instead of choosing one consistent narrative mode for all aspects of its scripting, the creators of *Twin Peaks* chose two by letting a serialized detective story (the joint local and federal investigation into the death of Laura Palmer) serve as an expositional framework for the introduction of an off-center soap opera (the ongoing plots of daily life in Twin Peaks, Washington) [35].

The intertextuality between *Twin Peaks*, procedural dramas, and soap operas was heightened as a result of the ways in which *Twin Peaks* was promoted in anticipation of its television premiere on ABC in April of 1990.

Richard B. Woodward, writing in January of the same year, described the upcoming *Twin Peaks* as a "languorous, finely textured soap opera" ("A Dark Lens" 2) which, in addition to being "laced with references to other television shows" ("A Dark Lens" 5), followed "the murder of a prom queen" by exploring "the town's involvement in her death and the F.B.I. investigation of it" ("A Dark Lens" 2). Similarly, two months later in March, Geraldine Fabrikant categorized *Twin Peaks* as a combination of "murder mystery and soap opera" (1). It was the latter of these genres, the soap opera, which spearheaded promotion in April. During a promotional interview with *The New York Times* on the day of the television premiere, Gary Levine, the vice president for dramatic series development at ABC, revealed that the network was "hoping to attract both Lynch devotees and soap-opera fans" (qtd. in Woodward, "Television" 1).[8] Promoting *Twin Peaks* as a "bizarre and quirky new nighttime soap opera" (Weinstein 1) was endorsed by its co-creators. Lynch, in the *Los Angeles Times* (1990), stated:

> I really like the idea of a continuing story and soap opera…. You can pay more attention to smaller details … to really linger over the details of a crust of cherry pie and really get into the saucer and the cup of coffee just as someone is talking about an affair, those are the things you can do in a soap opera. I think there are certain kinds of mood, especially in getting at the mood of a murder mystery, that take time to conjure up [qtd. in Weinstein 1].[9]

Likewise, Frost claimed that he and Lynch were attempting to "re-imagine the nighttime soap" by combining this genre with a "very complicated mystery story" (qtd. in Weinstein 1).

The promotion of *Twin Peaks* as a night-time soap opera that used elements from procedural dramas resulted in a series of expectations from contemporaneous audiences who were familiar with the conventions of these television genres. Indeed, according to Fiske, "the meanings of programs for viewers are influenced, even manipulated, by the genres they are fitted into" (*Television Culture* 111). More often than not, *Twin Peaks* fulfilled its generic obligations, satisfying audience expectation through the uses of intertextual signifiers which recalled the conventions that had characterized both procedural dramas and soap operas during the 1980s. The core premise of *Twin Peaks*—an investigation into the murders of Teresa Banks (Pamela Gidley) and Laura Palmer (Sheryl Lee)—was mostly faithful to the narrative structures that had underpinned contemporaneous procedural dramas, adhering to what Paul Kerr described as a "formulaic narrative structure (an equilibrium posed, fractured by villainy and recovered by heroism)" (74). The show's use of the formulaic narrative structure associated with procedural dramas was accompanied by its incorporation of a number of the conventions that had characterized soap operas during this period. Mary Ellen Brown has argued that contemporaneous soap operas were characterized by their uses of a "serial form which resists narrative closure" in addition to the inclusion of "multiple characters and plots" (4). Prior to considerable pressure from ABC, the co-creators of *Twin Peaks* had intended to resist narrative closure by postponing the reveal of Laura's killer for as long as possible—perhaps indefinitely[10]—even if that irresolution resisted the "unequivocal narrative closure" (Dolan 37) expected in procedural dramas.[11] Moreover, *Twin Peaks* included a large cast of characters whose characterization and plots adhered to the various character roles which, according to Peter Buckman had been repeated in the soap operas of the early 1980s.[12] The "romantic hero," who is "the soaps' definition a man unattached" (54), is Agent Cooper (Kyle MacLachlan). Laura Palmer, Audrey Horne (Sherilyn Fenn), and Annie Blackburne (Heather Graham) are the "heroine[s]" (58) of *Twin Peaks*. Benjamin Horne (Richard Beymer) and Catherine Martell (Piper Laurie) are the "rulers" (52) of the town, the Log Lady (Catherine E. Coulson) is the "jester, or holy fool, whose wisdom is imparted through simplicity or (more rarely) wit" (63), and Donna Hayward (Lara Flynn Boyle) is one of the "children whose rightful parentage is in doubt" (63). As a result of these similarities to procedural dramas and soap operas in terms of plot and characterization, it was likely that contemporaneous viewers would understand *Twin Peaks* through its intertextuality with night-time soap operas such as *Dallas* (1978–91) and *Dynasty* (1981–89) and procedural dramas like *Hill Street Blues* (1981–87)—the latter of which, from 1983 to 1984, was contributed to by Frost, who had worked as both a writer and an executive story editor for the serial.

The fulfillment of generic conventions in *Twin Peaks* resulted in the presentation of a familiar investigation which explored the lives of familiar characters. However, rather than allowing the intertextuality that united *Twin Peaks* with procedural dramas and soap operas to limit the creative possibilities of the show, the generic intertextuality of *Twin Peaks* was used as a framework within which further experimentation could take place. Indeed, during a promotional interview with Tracey MacLeod on *The Late Show* (1990), Frost stated:

> As *Hill Street* had, kind of, turned the idea of the cop show on its head at the beginning of the decade, we had a chance to do something like that with the night-time soap genre with *Twin Peaks*. I think the conventions of the genre had grown rather stale in the last few years and that the shows that had been the staples of that genre had grown rather tired and that there might be a way to infuse some fresh ideas and some fresh approach to the night-time soap and that's how *Twin Peaks*, kind of, came along.

The promised innovation of *Twin Peaks* materialized not only in its combination of the generic conventions of procedural dramas and soap operas—much like Frost's work in *Hill Street Blues*—but also in the show's inclusion of "some fresh ideas" which were unfamiliar to these genres. These ideas were rooted in the uses of an unfamiliar televisual style and the integration of some features from alternative genres which were rarely combined with procedural dramas and soap operas. No doubt, while *Twin Peaks* was mostly tethered to procedural dramas and soap operas in terms of its premise and characterization, the visual style and sound design of *Twin Peaks* signaled the show's refusal to be restricted by the stylistic limitations of television. Andreas Halskov, in *TV Peaks:* Twin Peaks *and Modern Television Drama* (2015), argues that "*Twin Peaks* was unconventional, as compared to traditional American television, by not employing a *three-camera set-up* and traditional lighting principles" (77). Instead, "*Twin Peaks* was more cinematic than most television series of the 1980s and 1990s" (87) because it employed "a number of overt stylistic choices, including *low-key* lighting, wide lenses, low-angle shots, long takes, *leitmotifs* and a complex *sound design*" (93), each of which "might be typical of the *noir* genre" but were "fairly unusual in television at the time" (77). These stylistic choices, within the contexts of contemporaneous television, resulted in the unfamiliar presentation of the familiar conventions of procedural dramas and soap operas.

In addition to the unfamiliar televisual style of *Twin Peaks*, the familiar generic framework of the show was gradually disrupted through the introduction of supernatural characters whose connections to horror and science-fiction imposed a feeling of the uncanny upon the audience. The uncanniness of *Twin Peaks* is usually attributed to the stylistic choices of Lynch who, while editing the alternative ending for the European version of the pilot in 1989, conceptualized what would later be described as the Red Room or, later still, the Black Lodge: an unfamiliar, interdimensional location that had a chevron floor and was enclosed by floor-length red curtains. The inhabitants of the Red Room utilized phonetic reversal in their dialogue, making the familiar—speech—seem unfamiliar. The presentation of the Red Room, which was later moved from the European pilot to the dream sequence at the conclusion of "Episode 2," made possible the integration of a supernatural mythology within the narrative of *Twin Peaks*, resulting in the surprising introductions of a dwarf, a giant, a one-armed man, and a killer named BOB. However, because supernatural subplots were uncommon but not unheard of in procedural dramas and soap operas, the supernatural content of *Twin Peaks* was still understood within the conventional contexts of its particular generic frameworks.[15] Jeremy Gerard's review of "Episode 2" of *Twin Peaks*, for instance, claimed:

> Last week's episode ended with a bizarre dream sequence that may have offended some viewers; it included a dancing midget speaking in a strangely elongated dialect as eerie music played in the background.... When F.B.I. Agent Dale Cooper blurted out, "I know who killed Laura Palmer!" in a predawn telephone call to Sheriff Harry S. Truman just before the credits rolled…, he gave the uncommon soap opera a commonplace soap-opera tease [1].

Offering an unfamiliar compound that mixed the generic conventions of procedural drama, soap opera, horror, and science-fiction encouraged critics to describe *Twin Peaks* as uncanny. Moreover, it was each of these uncanny juxtapositions that were epitomized in the character of Leland. This character, as a result of being both a loving father and a supernatural killer, embodied the intertextual compounds that underpinned the entirety of *Twin Peaks*. In order to understand the uncanniness of this antagonist, it is necessary to consider the development of Leland's character role from his first appearance in the pilot to his final appearance in "Episode 16."[14]

The Palmer family are introduced in the opening act of the pilot of *Twin Peaks*. After Laura's body is discovered on a riverbank by Pete Martell (Jack Nance), the audience meet Laura's mother, Sarah (Grace Zabriskie), in the family home. Meanwhile, Laura's father and Sarah's husband, Leland, is working at the Great Northern Hotel, acting as an attorney for the Horne Corporation. Before Sarah and Leland learn of their daughter's death, the behaviors of these characters—much like the stereotypical character roles listed above—are distinctly recognizable within the intertextual networks of soap operas: Sarah is situated within the family home, invoking what Allen describes as "the contemporary situation of the housewife/mother, whose life is given purpose and meaning by and through the family" (92), while Leland is presented as what Buckman defines as the "decent husband … whose chief ambition is honourably to fulfil his obligations" (38–39). Taken together, these characters represent "the cornerstone of hearth and home that we are all taught to revere" (Buckman 42). Frost reiterates the traditional family dynamic of the Palmers in *The Secret History of Twin Peaks* (2016), writing:

> Leland Palmer, 45. Pride and only son of a wealthy Seattle family. Private schools. Summa cum laude, University of Washington, 1966, president of the Law Review. Outstanding professional career, culminating in an eight-year run as chief counsel to the Horne Corporation, which is what brought the Palmers to town. No drugs, alcoholism, no criminal record or history of mental illness. Happily married twenty-one years to Sarah Novak Palmer, 44. Political science major. College sweethearts. One child, Laura. Homecoming queen. The golden girl next door that the whole town adored [324].

The inclusion of the seemingly conventional Palmers in the opening act of *Twin Peaks* highlighted what Allen described as "the centrality of the family" (92) within soap operas. Moreover, as a result of Laura's death, the opening act acknowledged the genre's tendency to keep "its families in a state of constant disarray" (Allen 92). The presentation of the Palmers in the pilot of *Twin Peaks*, then, was distinctly conventional and plainly familiar within the contexts of contemporaneous television.

The success of this intertextual maneuver, which grounded the Palmers within the familiar contexts of traditional soap opera families, can be measured through a consideration of the ways in which contemporaneous audiences usually failed to suspect Sarah or Leland as the antagonist of *Twin Peaks*. Indeed, during season one of the show, audiences rarely identified Sarah or Leland as Laura's killer. Following the broadcast of "Episode 1" on April 12, 1990, Greg Dawson from the *Orlando Sentinel* asked readers to submit their predictions for who killed Laura. These predictions included:

> The Log Lady.... FBI agent Cooper.... Audrey ... and an obvious choice, Dr. Jacoby, the loopy psychiatrist. Next on the viewers' hit parade was Leo, the brutish truck driver, he of the bloody shirt and homicidal aura. Leo is the most likely suspect.... Other suspects, in order of votes, were Sheriff Harry S. Truman; Laura's best friend Donna; Donna's father, the doctor who refused to perform the autopsy; the weeping deputy; the Charles Manson figure that Laura's mother hallucinated; a "mysterious stranger" not yet seen; Laura's boyfriend Bobby; Laura's other boyfriend James; Ed of Big Ed's Gas Farm; the Eyepatch Lady, Ed's drapery-obsessed wife, Nadine; Audrey's emotionally disturbed brother; the school principal; the Indian-looking deputy; unseen Diane, the one Cooper talks to on his tape recorder; the Chinese woman who owns the mill; the sister of the dead man who owned the mill; Leo's girlfriend, the waitress; Norma, Big Ed's lover; [and] the guy on the elevator [2].

The names of Sarah and Leland were notably absent. Later, following the broadcast of "Episode 6" on May 10, 1990—just two days before the finale of season one—the studio audience of *Donahue* (1967–95) made their predictions, with only three percent identifying Leland as the killer. The four-month break between seasons one and two of *Twin Peaks* resulted in further speculation. During this period, suspicions of Leland being involved in his daughter's murder increased. Tony Hellerman, in the *TV Guide* for the week of September 8, 1990, said:

> I'm inclined to pick someone as unlikely as Laura's father, Leland Palmer, as her killer. Given the kind of girl we now know Laura was, and what a neurotic guy Leland is, it's possible that he could have bumped her off in a rage after he found out she was working at One-Eyed Jacks [qtd. in Elm 4].

However, following the broadcast of "Episode 8" on September 30, 1990—the first episode of season two—Leland's murder of Jacques Renault (Walter Olkewicz) seemed to remove some of the suspicions that Laura was killed by her father. A member of the alt.tv.twinpeaks community on Usenet, Jan D. Wolter, wrote:

> Well, you folks had me half convinced with … the Leland is the killer theory.… With Leland guilty of Jacques' murder, I don't buy him as Laura's killer as well. I just can't believe that with so many fine potential villains running around, all the murders are going to be foisted off on Leland [qtd. in Bocko].[15]

In light of these contemporaneous reactions to Leland's character role within *Twin Peaks*, it is clear that Leland usually avoided suspicion from audiences as a result of his intertextuality with the husbands and fathers who, in soap operas, were primarily concerned with safeguarding their families. For that reason, it seemed "unlikely" (Hellerman qtd. in Elm 4) that Leland was involved in his daughter's death.

In the final act of "Episode 14" of *Twin Peaks*, broadcast on November 10, 1990, audiences learned that the identity of BOB's human host was Laura's father, Leland, in a scene which depicted the brutal murder of Laura's identical cousin, Madeline Ferguson (Sheryl Lee). The episode was written by Frost and directed by Lynch, signaling the last collaboration of the co-creators until the finale of season two. Ray Wise, recalling the secrecy that surrounded the reveal of Laura's killer, said: "poor Sheryl Lee had to die three times because Ben Horne killed Maddy that day, Bob killed her, then Leland Palmer killed her so even the crew wouldn't know who the real killer was" (qtd. in Dukes 203). With Ben's scenes functioning as red herrings, it was the endings that included BOB and Leland which made the final cut, with the action transitioning from Leland to BOB in a sequence which Rodley described as "very unnerving" and "uncanny" (178–179). It could be argued that the uncanniness of this dramatic conclusion, which carefully juxtaposed elements of the familiar and the unfamiliar, was the result of Lynch's signature style. Indeed, according to Philip Carr Neel, the series associate producer for *Twin Peaks*, "it was really important to him [Lynch] that it ['Episode 14'] aired properly and he told the network not to interfere with it" (qtd. in Dukes 207). Lynch's insistence that the episode "aired properly" indicates that the final act of this episode was constructed with a particular purpose in mind. For that reason, it is necessary to offer a close-reading of Leland's reveal as BOB, isolating how this scene—primarily in terms of its setting and costume—achieved the uncanny.

Prior to Madeline's murder in the final act of "Episode 14," there are a number of short scenes which take place in the Palmer house. Within the Palmer's living room, the needle of a turntable skips rhythmically on the final groove of a vinyl record. The room is presented from a series of different angles that recall previous scenes from *Twin Peaks* which were set in the Palmer house, highlighting the familiarity of this location within the show and, perhaps more importantly, the importance of "the home, or some other place which functions as a home" (Brown 4), in soap operas. Once this familiarity has been established, the act concludes with Madeline's death at the hands of Leland/BOB. Madeline's murder in the Palmer house presents a stark contrast to Ronette Pulaski's (Phoebe Augustine) visual recollection of Laura's murder by BOB in "Episode 8," the latter of which took place in an abandoned train car on the outskirts of the town. Setting Madeline's murder within the family home, according to Lenora Ledwon, captures "the domestic gone horribly wrong…. There it is, on your television screen, in your own living room—a father assaulting and killing a 'daughter' in his living room" (264). The element that distinguishes this scene from other representations of "family violence in soap operas," Ledwon argues, "is the series' insistence on the uncanny moment" (269).

The "uncanny moment" of the scene is achieved through the doubling of Leland and BOB. Before Leland/BOB encounters Madeline at the foot of the staircase, the scene centers on Leland studying his reflection in the mirror: initially, Leland's reflection is a faithful representation of his appearance; as the scene progresses, however, his reflection uncannily morphs into the supernatural visage of BOB.[16] The contrasting appearances of Leland and BOB produce an uncanny effect as a result of a series of juxtapositions which, within the domestic contexts of the Palmer house, disturb Leland's significations of familiarity with BOB's significations of unfamiliarity. Fiske argues that the appearances of actors and actresses are "encoded by our social codes," existing "for the viewer intertextually" (*Television Culture* 8). Indeed, as Fiske states, the appearance of the human body, especially "those aspects under voluntary control—hair, clothes, skin, bodily paint and adornment," sends "messages about personality, social status and, particularly, conformity" ("Communication Studies" 72–73). Exploring the contrasting appearances of Leland and BOB might help to isolate why this juxtaposition produced an uncanny effect on the audience, exposing the stereotypical ways in which heroes and villains had been presented in the television shows of the late 20th century.

Leland dresses formally throughout *Twin Peaks*. In "Episode 14," Leland wears what Yuet See Monica Owyong describes as a "power suit," a term that refers to the "ubiquitous dark-coloured matching jacket and pants ensemble that business executives, who were typically male, wore to proffer an image of power" (202). The dark coloring of the suit "functions effectively to suppress and conceal the wearer's individuality, communicating instead a distinct message about the wearer's status and designation in society"

(203).[17] Consequently, Leland's clothing connotes formality, professionalism and, within the contexts of contemporaneous television, conformity to representations of "middle-class, professional characters in ... daytime soap operas" (Fiske, *Television Culture* 175). In contrast to Leland, BOB wears a blue denim jacket and blue denim jeans. James B Salazar investigates the cultural significations of denim in terms of the "interlocking figures of the laborer, the cowboy, and the countercultural rebel" (294), writing:

> Originally identified as the useful occupational clothing of gold-rush laborers in the mountains of California, denim has come to promise the embodiment of the laborer by apportioning a body understood to be in a functional, and thereby natural, relation with the world. Such a figuration of the laborer, combined with the socially transgressive and self-reliant cowboy, underwrites the historical emergence of the countercultural rebel as a figure of liberal self-possession, critical acumen, and cultural disavowal [295].

While denim has now been appropriated into a "fashion system" that "enables it to be the uniform of everyone and anyone" (Salazar 305), denim continues to offer a performative signification which centers on what Salazar describes as the "evocation of the embodiment of the laborer" (301). Clothing Leland in a power suit and BOB in denim, then, establishes a series of immediate visual juxtapositions which—within the contexts of Leland's public persona of middle-class professionalism— were rooted in the abstract and generalized oppositions between the familiarity of white-collar conformity and the unfamiliarity of blue-collar rebellion.[18]

Capturing a series of binary oppositions—conformity and rebellion, sublunary and supernatural, good and evil, familiar and unfamiliar— within one character exposed and questioned the artificiality of the heroes and villains that had been presented in contemporaneous television shows. Indeed, Fiske claims that a number of television shows from the 1980s had promoted a myth that

> treat[ed] the belief that middle-class Anglo-Saxons are trustworthy, whereas swarthy lower-class males are not, as obvious common sense and natural.... The typical television practice of giving criminals working-class ... accents is *not* a statement about the probability that members of lower socioeconomic groups are more likely to turn to crime, because it does not require us to think through the relationships between social position and criminality. Rather it is a sign of a middle-class myth that denies the history of class relations and naturalises the explanation of class differences into the "facts" of human nature [*Television Culture* 134].

The prevalence of this "middle-class myth" in television, including procedural dramas and soap operas, is both confirmed and complicated by BOB's possession of Leland in *Twin Peaks*: on the one hand, the show perpetuates the myth of working-class criminality through the—albeit supernatural—inclusion of BOB; on the other hand, the show counters this myth with its veiled presentation of middle-class criminality in Leland. Diane Stevenson argues that

> as Lynch conceives of normality in terms of the middle class, so he tends to imagine the threat to normality as coming from the lower class.... That BOB the criminal drifter resides in Leland tells us that Leland harbors the criminal inside him, that the incestuous and murderous are to be understood as a part of his psychological make up [74–75].

Yet, confirmation as to whether Leland's crimes were earthly or supernatural is purposefully avoided. Sheriff Harry S. Truman (Michael Ontkean), following Leland's death in "Episode 16," admits that he was "having a hard time believing" in the existence of BOB. Cooper retorts, "is it easier to believe a man would rape and murder his own daughter?," to which Albert Rosenfield (Miguel Ferrer) responds: "maybe that's all BOB is: the evil that men do. Maybe it doesn't matter what we call it." The refusal to explicitly define the relationship between Leland and BOB, when coupled with the formulaic oppositions that characterized the presentations of these intertwined characters, intensified the uncanniness of the show's antagonist, doing so while remaining faithful to the contradictory narrative structures that were expected in both procedural dramas and soap operas: the narrative closure of procedural dramas was offered in the form of Cooper's heroism thwarting Leland's villainy but, at the same time, the possibility of the continuing existence of BOB worked to maintain the irresolution expected in soap operas. The non-specificity of Leland's crimes captured the essence of the uncanny, forcing audiences to choose between a contradictory pair of paradoxical interpretations that—through a process of defamiliarization—presented Leland as either a victim of a supernatural force or a villain that raped and murdered his own daughter.

Regardless of whether Leland was interpreted as a victim or a villain, the answer to the question that haunted audiences in 1990—"Who Killed Laura Palmer?"—resulted in an unprecedented demonstration of the power of the uncanny in fiction. *Twin Peaks* achieved its uncanniness by blurring the boundaries that defined contemporaneously popular genres, offering an intertextual pastiche that disturbed the familiarity of procedural dramas and soap operas with the unfamiliarity of horror and science-fiction. In doing so, *Twin Peaks* contributed to the popularization of a televisual form which was both cinematic in its style and complex in its storytelling, paving the way for the rise of the supernatural procedural drama—and *The Return* (2017) of *Twin Peaks*—in the 21st century.

Notes

1. Examples of *Twin Peaks* being described as uncanny include Christy Desmet's claim that Laura Palmer had an "uncanny refusal to be classified as either saint or as sinner" (93). Similarly, Jonathan Rosenbaum described the adults in *Twin Peaks* as "slightly uncanny art objects" (29) and Samuel Kimball stated that BOB "overwhelms everyone who comes near him by the vampiric force of his appalling, uncanny presence."

2. Ledwon's "Twin Peaks and the Television Gothic" (1993), however, is a notable exception. Ledwon argued that "*Twin Peaks* can be seen as a 20th-century reconciliation of common and uncommon, home-like and uncanny" (268), proposing that *Twin Peaks* coupled "reassuring domesticity" with the Gothic by uncovering "the specters of incest and family violence" (264) within the home.

3. Examples of situations that can produce the uncanny include "strange kinds of repetition," "anthropomorphism," "automatism," and "telepathy" (Bennett and Royle 37–40). These sources of the uncanny are utilised in *Twin Peaks*. Throughout the show, "strange kinds of repetition" take place, including the repetition of eerily similar locations in the Black Lodge in the final episode of season two. Josie Packard's conversion into a drawer-pull in "Episode 23" could be described as anthropomorphism. Automatism takes hold of both Annie Blackburn and Dale Cooper in Glastonbury Grove, signalling the hypnotic influence of the Black Lodge. Sarah Palmer demonstrates a series of telepathic traits throughout *Twin Peaks*, including her vision of Laurence Jacoby at the conclusion of "Episode 1" and her communication with Laura Palmer in "Episode 29."

4. Andreas Halskov, in *TV Peaks: Twin Peaks and Modern Television Drama* (2015), offers a useful list of films and television shows to which *Twin Peaks* refers, arguing that *Twin Peaks* introduced a large amount of intertextual references, thus demanding an *intertextual competency* on the part of the viewer.... One might argue that *Twin Peaks* requires a certain amount of *teleliteracy*, i.e., an understanding of television genres and storytelling as well as a basic knowledge of the many film and television classics to which *Twin Peaks* alludes (146).

5. It is important to note, however, that definitions of genres are problematic. Fiske states that "thinking of television generically requires us to prioritize the similarities between programs rather than their individual differences" (*Television Culture* 110). The difficulty with this approach "is that it tends to fix characteristics within genre boundaries in a way that rarely fits a specific instance.... A genre seen textually should be defined as a shifting provisional set of characteristics which is modified as each new example is produced" (Fiske, *Television Culture* 111).

6. The disruption of conventions, on the other hand, can have negative results. Allen claims that "soap opera viewers can easily sense when a new development in a soap opera does not seem to 'fit.' ... The theme might be at such odds with the soap's horizon that some viewers stop watching or switch to other soaps" (86).

7. The mixing of genres, according to Fiske, was not unusual: Any one program will bear the main characteristics of its genre, but is likely to include some from others: ascribing it to one genre or another involves deciding which set of characteristics are the most important. *Hill Street Blues* and *Cagney and Lacey* are either cop shows with characteristics of soap opera, or vice versa [*Television Culture* 111–112].

8. Tony Krantz, a former television agent at Creative Artists Agency, states that *Twin Peaks* was originally conceived of as a soap opera. Krantz recalls that, "after seeing *Blue Velvet*, I went to Nibbles with David [Lynch] and I told him, 'You should do a show about these people, the customers here in Nibbles,' and we started talking about an idea for a soap opera" (qtd. in Duke 6).

9. In 2014, when asked if *Twin Peaks* was a parody of a soap opera, Lynch responded: "No, no, no, no, no. It is a soap opera. Soap operas grow out of life and because they're continuous stories you get to go deeper into the characters' lives" (qtd. in Kay 1).

10. Frost recalls Lynch asking, "Why do we ever have to tell anybody who killed Laura?," to which Frost replied, "Because, David, they're going to hate you if you don't!" (qtd. in Thorne 133).

11. Dolan speculates: One wonders what might have happened if *Twin Peaks* had been

marketed as more soap opera than detective story. One the one hand, viewers might not have grown so impatient with the second season, but, on the other hand, they might not have watched the series in the first place, given the aesthetic snobbism that often greets the continuous-serial form. (37)

12. *Twin Peaks*'s approach to character roles is not surprising given Lynch's method of casting. Halskov writes: "Lynch's casting process has often been defined as an intertextual casting strategy, inasmuch as many actors in Twin Peaks … were cast to remind the audience of a certain character or a certain film" (66). Frost reiterates this point, stating: "We always added little asides when the opportunity arose, whether it was references to old movies or people's past work…. We knew we were making fictional narrative entertainment and we were also paying homage to things that tread similar thematic ground in the past" (qtd. in Duke 193).

13. *Kolchak: the Night Stalker* (1974–75) combined procedural drama with horror by including a series of supernatural crimes while *General Hospital* (1963-present), during the Ice Princess Saga of 1980–81, combined soap opera with science-fiction through the inclusion of a supernatural diamond that could bring about a new ice age.

14. Ray Wise does, however, return in the final episode of season two of *Twin Peaks*, performing as Leland's doppelgänger within the Black Lodge, in addition starring in *Fire Walk With Me*. Later, Wise would reprise his role as Leland in "Part 2" of *The Return*.

15. Buckman claimed that the "decent husband" stereotype might "falsify evidence or commit some (minor) crime in order to safeguard or advance the welfare of his loved one" (39). Therefore, Leland's murder of Jacques—who had been charged with the murder of Laura—might have been understood as a forgivable crime.

16. The uncanny attributes of reflections were acknowledged by Freud who, by looking at the "doubling, dividing and interchanging of the self" in fiction, explored "the connections which the 'double' has with reflections in mirrors, with shadows, with guardian spirits, with the belief in the soul and with the fear of death" (233–234). While BOB cannot be considered as a "double" in terms of appearance—that is, BOB is not a doppelgänger of Leland—he can be considered as one half of a double-consciousness which exists within Leland.

17. It is interesting to note that all three of BOB's possible hosts—Leland, Ben, and Cooper—wear dark suits throughout *Twin Peaks*, suggesting that the contrasting appearances of the host and BOB were intentional.

18. Salazar writes: "class in the United States has long been articulated in terms of a fundamental division into 'blue-collar' and 'white-collar' workers, a distinction predicated on denim's power to itself signify class difference not in terms of income but by evoking the artifactually enhanced working-class body" (302).

Works Cited

Allen, Robert C. *Speaking of Soap Operas*. U of North Carolina P, 1985.
Bennett, Andrew, and Nicholas Royle. *Introduction to Literature, Criticism, and Theory*. 3rd ed., Pearson Education, 2004.
Bocko, Joel. "*Twin Peaks* on the Internet… in 1990 (an Alt.twinpeaks Archive)." *Lost in the Movies*, 17 Nov. 2014, www.lostinthemovies.com/2014/11/twin-peaks-on-internetin-1990-alttvtwin.html. Accessed 15 May 2017.
Brown, Mary Ellen. "The Politics of Soaps: Pleasure and Feminine Empowerment." *Australian Journal of Culture Studies*, vol. 4, no. 2, 1987, pp. 1–25.
Dawson, Greg. "Readers See Suspects All Over 'Twin Peaks.'" *Orlando Sentinel*, 16 Apr. 1990, articles.orlandosentinel com/1990-04-16/lifestyle/9004165050_1_twin-peaks-nadine-killed-laura-palmer. Accessed 15 May 2017.
Desmet, Christy "The Canonization of Laura Palmer." *Full of Secrets: Critical Approaches to Twin Peaks*, edited by David Lavery, Wayne State UP, 1995, pp. 93-108.
Dolan, Marc. "The Peaks and Valleys of Serial Creativity: What Happened to/on *Twin Peaks*." *Full of Secrets. Critical Approaches to* Twin Peaks, edited by David Lavery, Wayne State UP, 1995, pp. 30–50.

Donahue, Phil, creator. *Donahue*. Multimedia Entertainment, 21 May 1990.
Dukes, Brad. *Reflections: An Oral History of* Twin Peaks. Short/Tall Press, 2014.
Elm, Joanna. "Whodunit: Four Top Authors Solve the *Twin Peaks* mystery." *TV Guide*, 8 Sept. 1990, pp. 2–6.
Fabrikant, Geraldine. "The Media Business; ABC's Top Programmer Sees His Guesses Pay Off, So Far, in Prime Time." *New York Times*, 12 Mar. 1990, www.nytimes.com/1990/03/12/business/media-business-abc-s-top-programmer-sees-his-guesses-pay-off-so-far-prime-time.html. Accessed 15 May 2017.
Fiske, John. *Introduction to Communication Studies*. Methuen, 1982.
———. *Television Culture*. Methuen, 1987.
Freud, Sigmund. "The Uncanny." 1919. *The Standard Edition of the Complete Psychological Works of Sigmund Freud*. Translated by James Strachey, vol. 17, Hogarth Press, 1971, pp. 217–256.
Frost, Mark. *The Secret History of Twin Peaks*. Macmillan, 2016.
Gerard, Jeremy. "A 'Soap Noir' Inspires a Cult and Questions." *New York Times*, 26 Apr. 1990, http://www.nytimes.com/1990/04/26/arts/a-soap-noir-inspires-a-cult-and-questions.html. Accessed 15 May 2017.
Halskov, Andreas. *TV Peaks: Twin Peaks and Modern Television Drama*. UP of Southern Denmark, 2015.
Kay, Jeremy. "David Lynch: 'I've Always Loved Laura Palmer.'" *The Guardian*, 24 July 2014, www.theguardian.com/film/2014/jul/24/-sp-david-lynch-laura-palmer-twin-peaks-unseen-fire-walk-with-me. Accessed 15 May 2017.
Kerr, Paul. "Gangsters: Conventions and Contraventions." *Popular Television and Film*, edited by Tony Bennett, Susan Boyd-Bowman, Colin Mercer, and Janet Woollacott, British Film Institute, 1981, pp. 73–78.
Kimball, Samuel. "'Into the Light, Leland, Into the Light': Emerson, Oedipus, and the Blindess of Male Desire in David Lynch's *Twin Peaks*." *Twin Peaks in the Rearview Mirror: Appraisals and Reappraisals of the Show That Was Supposed to Change TV*, edited by David Lavery, Craig Miller, and John Thorne, Kindle ed., n.p., 2012.
Kristeva, Julia. *Desire in Language: A Semiotic Approach to Literature and Art*. Translated by Thomas Gora, Alice Jardine, and Leon S. Roudiez, edited by Leon S. Roudiez, Columbia UP, 1980.
Ledwon, Lenora. "Twin Peaks and the Television Gothic." *Literature/Film Quarterly*, vol. 21, no. 4, 1993, pp. 260–270.
Lynch, David. *Lynch on Lynch*. 1997. Edited by Chris Rodley, Faber & Faber, 1999.
MacLeod, Tracey. "David Lynch & Mark Frost 1990 TWIN PEAKS BBC Interviews BBC." *YouTube*, uploaded by TaggleElgate, 26 July 2015, www.youtube.com/watch?v=4Y0C3Vy_Slg.
Owyong, Yuet See Monica. "Clothing Semiotics and the Social Construction of Power Relations." *Social Semiotics*, vol. 19, no. 2, 2009, pp. 191–211.
Rodley, Chris. Introduction. 1997. *Lynch on Lynch*, by David Lynch, Faber & Faber, 1999, pp. ix–xiii.
Rosenbaum, Jonathan. "Bad Ideas: The Art and Politics of *Twin Peaks*." *Full of Secrets: Critical Approaches to* Twin Peaks, edited by David Lavery, Wayne State UP, 1995, pp. 22–29.
Salazar, James B. "Fashioning the Historical Body: The Political Economy of Denim." *Social Semiotics*, vol. 20, no. 3, 2010, pp. 293–308.
Stevenson, Diane. "Family Romance, Family Violence, and the Fantastic in *Twin Peaks*." *Full of Secrets: Critical Approaches to* Twin Peaks, edited by David Lavery, Wayne State UP, 1995, pp. 70–81.
Thorne, John. *The Essential Wrapped in Plastic: Pathways to* Twin Peaks. John Thorne, 2016.
Twin Peaks. Created by David Lynch and Mark Frost, ABC Broadcasting, 1990–1991.
Twin Peaks: Fire Walk with Me. Directed by David Lynch, performances by Sheryl Lee and Ray Wise, New Line Cinema, 1992.
Twin Peaks: The Return. Created by David Lynch and Mark Frost, Showtime, 2017.
Weinstein, Steve. "Is TV Ready for David Lynch?: The Director of 'Blue Velvet' and 'Eraserhead' Brings His Unique Vision to the Prime-time Soap Opera 'Twin Peaks.'" *Los*

Angeles Times, 18 Feb. 1990, articles.latimes.com/1990-02-18/entertainment/ca-1500_1_twin-peaks/1. Accessed 15 May 2017.

Woodward, Richard B. "A Dark Lens on America." *The New York Times*, 14 Jan. 1990, www.nytimes.com/1990/01/14/magazine/a-dark-lens-on-america.html. Accessed 15 May 2017.

_____. "Television; When 'Blue Velvet' Meets 'Hill Street Blues.'" *The New York Times*, 8 Apr. 1990, www.nytimes.com/1990/04/08/arts/television-when-blue-velvet-meets-hill-street-blues.hml. Accessed 15 May 2017.

Sherlock Holmes

The Intersection of Magic and Science in Crime Detection

MICHELLE D. MIRANDA

The fictional character Sherlock Holmes has endured life, death, and resurrection at the hands of his creator, Sir Arthur Conan Doyle. Educated in the field of medicine, Conan Doyle introduced the consulting detective in 1887 in *A Study in Scarlet*, with Holmes' character being based on Dr. Joseph Bell, a surgeon and lecturer Conan Doyle encountered in medical school. Due to popular demand, Conan Doyle continued to write stories featuring Holmes until 1927, even after publishing "The Final Problem" in 1893, in which Conan Doyle sent Holmes to his death over Reichenbach Falls. Despite Holmes' untimely death and eventual retirement, the legacy of the famous fictional consulting detective has persisted and achieved pop culture fandom spanning generations. Credited with having substantial impact on real-world criminal investigations and forensic science, Sherlock Holmes has endured for 130 years, continually reincarnated through cinematic procedural dramas including television series and motion pictures. One recent televised crime drama based on the adventures of Holmes entitled *Sherlock* received critical acclaim and rapidly spawned a substantial fan base.[1] Inspired by Conan Doyle's fictional detective, *Sherlock* has captivated its audience through modernizing the science, reasoning, and illusion that characterizes the famous consulting detective Sherlock Holmes.

Conan Doyle's stories and novels featuring Sherlock Holmes brought forth a new approach to understanding crime and criminality by introducing science and reasoning to investigation and detection. The original adventures of Sherlock Holmes were written during the Victorian Gothic era when the public was fascinated with horror, the macabre, and the unknown, such as the causes of crime and the nature of the degenerate, "born criminal." The overlapping scientific and industrial revolutions of the 18th century brought forth advanced scientific theories and epistemological thought, while the mid–19th century saw increased interest in positivism, in which knowledge was obtained through empiricism.[2] Observation of natural phenomena, coupled with reasoning, became the fundamental basis of the scientific method, allowing for scientific endeavors to be pursued with rigor and analytical support (Miranda 3).[3] In addition to the progress being made in science and rational thought during this time, developments in criminology and the criminal justice system were taking place along with advances in forensic medicine and medicolegal investigations, forensic toxicology, criminalistics, and criminal psychology, all of which were seen as relevant to the improvement and success of criminal investigations.[4] Due to the advancement in infrastructure, organization, and the procedures of police departments and detective agencies, the public became more interested in law enforcement, the nature of the criminal, and crime solving with the aid of physical traces. Increased attention to science and criminal detection found their way into the narratives of Conan Doyle's works of detective fiction along with his personal experiences from medical school. The ability to utilize observation and medical knowledge to identify symptoms as clues to aid in diagnosing patients served as the basis for Holmes' ability to detect and observe the most seemingly trivial clues presented before him.[5] Such detection of clues and analysis of physical evidence enabled Holmes to subsequently investigate and solve the problems of those clients which came to 221B Baker Street seeking help from London's only consulting detective.

Prevailing discourse during the time of Sherlock Holmes also focused on the power of magic and the ability of magical forces to explain those occult phenomena that were otherwise unexplainable. Conan Doyle himself published a series of stories focused on the supernatural, and was a spiritualist, attending séances and believing in fairies, even disagreeing with his friend and magician Harry Houdini over the nature of supernatural phenomena.[6] Magic, including superstition and the occult, was believed to be the link between religion (faith) and science (reason). While magic and science were perceived as being at odds, magicians like Éliphas Lévi and Aleister Crowley advocated the application of scientific inquiry to magical theories and rituals in an effort to remove subjectivity and improve the rigor of magic and mysticism.[7] Crowley encouraged attention to observation, inquiry, and experimentation to advance magic to phenomena grounded in science (Crowley 15). While Crowley was advocating for the scientization of magic while still retaining the beliefs and practices of the occult, Conan Doyle was using science to explain seemingly magical phenomena through his stories, including his supernatural tales that were not part of the Sherlock Holmes series. The stories and novels featuring Holmes focused on crime solving as a scientific endeavor, and elements of the supernatural were entwined in some of Holmes' adventures, from general references to magic as a form of entertainment to references of pure "evil" such as a demon hell-hound and blood sucking vampires—phenomena which Holmes could explain using science and reason.[8]

Although viewed as a detective and scientist, Holmes' methods of detection and powers of deduction have an omniscient, superhuman quality that seem unattainable to the ordinary individual. Described throughout the *Sherlock* series as "clever" and "not ordinary," Holmes possesses powers of observation and reason, divinatory powers based on intuition and perception, and the ability to communicate with the dead to obtain the clues necessary for solving crime. These abilities, along with his extensive knowledge, memory, and imagination, place Holmes beyond the ordinary and unremarkable, and enable him to achieve superhuman status. Although Holmes himself explains his process of arriving at solutions and directs the observer to the clues that led to his conclusions, the presentation of logical solutions based on science and observation still seem out of reach to those faced with such simple explanations. Holmes often leaves his clients, police, and even his friend and biographer, John Watson in awe of his apparent supernatural abilities. Holmes' analytical abilities seem to arise from supernatural cognition, with him being likened to a magician capable of illusion, divination, conjuring, and necromancy.

Sherlock Holmes: Magician

It is easy to believe Sherlock Holmes is a magician. After all, before falling to his death in "The Reichenbach Fall," Holmes reveals that his deductions about Watson upon their first meeting were a magic trick.[9] "Clairvoyance, telepathy, and intuition … are not just uncannily reminiscent of the detective's mind-reading powers and miraculous feats of deductive reasoning, but are versions of those practices, and vice versa" (Smajić 181). Quite often in his adventures, Holmes seems to operate under unexplainable mysterious forces in which his problem-solving skills appear to demonstrate the impossible and amaze the "audience" with illusion and dramatic flair. In both Conan Doyle's works and subsequent cinematic procedural dramas like *Sherlock*, there is an overwhelming tendency to maximize the effect of Holmes' abilities and at the same time attenuate his methodology, which provides a sense of illusion and sorcery. Even when Holmes takes the time to explain his analytical methods after the fact, the rapid succession of trivial observations presented to the casual observer seem overwhelmingly obvious, yet beyond the capabilities of detection and contextual relevance. Holmes utilizes his ability to observe these clues, which are often overlooked by even the attentive observer. This enables him to make deductions appear to be derived from the possession of magical powers. As Holmes aptly states in "The Adventure of the Crooked Man" (1893), "Elementary.... It is one of those instances where the reasoner can produce an effect which seems remarkable to his neighbour, because the latter has missed the one little point which is the basis of the deduction" (Conan Doyle, II, 227). It is this sleight of hand (or mind) that mystifies the observer and makes the feat appear to be sorcery.

A magician in the period between approximately the tenth and sixth centuries BC was "no more or less than a mathematician, a man of science, who, stored with knowledge and learning, as learning went in those days, was a kind of walking dictionary to other people, and instructed the rest of mankind in any niceties and difficulties which occurred to them, and which they wanted to be informed about..." (De Foe 2).[10] De Foe continues that such magicians, serving as philosophers and scientists, studied nature and made observations in order to develop their explanations for various phenomena. As time progressed, it was asserted that the magician's abilities were divine; magicians were gifted with the spirit of the Gods. In the Middle Ages, attention was drawn to alchemy, witchcraft, and dark magic and these disciplines became part of the growing field of magic. Over time, and by the 16th century, the view of the magician as a conjurer and illusionist was widespread; their abilities exceeded knowledge and wisdom and further entered into the realm of the supernatural. During this evolution of the magician, the perception of the magician as a scientist and philosopher was replaced by the magician as an entertainer; performing prestidigitation in the form of disappearing acts, reading minds, conjuring spirits, and presenting sleight of hand tricks beyond the comprehension of spectators and audience members. Entering into the Gothic and Victorian Gothic eras, the allure of magic coupled with draw of conjured spirits became widespread among the curiosity-seeking public. Advancements in science and technology enabled the magician to practice improved acts of deception; the magician's knowledge of the natural sciences (such as physics and chemistry) could enhance the viewers experience, resulting in a performance that would defy human comprehension.

The 19th-century French magician and conjurer Robert-Houdin described several classes of conjuring: feats of dexterity, experiments in natural magic, mental conjuring, pretended mesmerism, "the medium business," and parlor magic (30).[11] Of these five, experiments in natural magic, mental conjuring, or "secret thought read by an ingenious system of diagnosis, and sometimes compelled to take a particular direction by certain subtle artifices" (Hopkins 2) and pretended mesmerism may be considered most consistent with Holmes' oft-cited powers of deduction. Robert-Houdin noted the importance of scientific knowledge in being a successful conjurer, "In order to be a first-class conjurer it is necessary, if not to have studied all [physical] sciences thoroughly, at least to have acquired a general knowledge of them and to be able to apply some few of their principles as the occasion may arise. The most indispensable requirement, however, for the successful practice of the magic art is a great neatness of manipulation combined with special mental acuteness" (29). Within this framework, Holmes' character conforms to the characteristics consistent with that of a magician.

Conan Doyle references the magical powers of Holmes throughout his adventures, likening Holmes to a wizard and a conjurer. In "A Study in Scarlet," Holmes remarks of himself, "You know a conjurer gets no credit when he has explained his trick…" (Conan Doyle, I, 174) and in "The Adventure of the Norwood Builder" (1903), when Holmes uncovers the secret hiding place of the suspect, Watson recounts, "Holmes stood before us with an air of a conjurer who is performing a magic trick" (Conan Doyle, II, 428). Referencing the historical treatment of witches in the 17th century in "A Scandal in Bohemia" (1891), Watson replies to Holmes' deductions with "You would certainly have been burned had you lived a few centuries ago" (Conan Doyle, I, 348). And, in "The Adventure of the Abbey Grange," there is reference to Holmes possessing superhuman powers. Upon announcing the location of key evidence that had been discarded, an Inspector remarks, "I believe that you are a wizard, Mr. Holmes. I really do sometimes think that you have powers that are not human" (Conan Doyle, II, 503). This reference to magic carries from Conan Doyle's works featuring the great consulting detective into depictions of Holmes in modern true crime television. In "The Abominable Bride," a disguised Dr. Molly Hooper quips, "Come to astonish us with your magic tricks, I suppose?" upon greeting Holmes at the morgue.[12]

One of Holmes' most notable traits is his ability to draw conclusions about an individual from a series of observations. Holmes' powers to read people based on their physical characteristics make him appear to possess preternatural abilities much like a mentalist or mystic. The earliest example of this in *Sherlock* is when Holmes utilizes his power of deduction on Watson upon their first encounter in the laboratory in St. Bartholomew's Hospital, when Holmes asks Watson, "Afghanistan or Iraq?" and proceeds to "read" Watson after a series of observations[13]:

> **HOLMES:** I know you're an Army doctor and you've been invalidated home from Afghanistan. I know you've got a brother who's worried about you but you won't go to him for help because you don't approve of him, possibly because he's an alcoholic; more likely because he recently walked out on his wife. And I know that your therapist thinks your limp is psychosomatic (quite correctly I'm afraid).

Such observations of trifles and consideration of their relevance escaped the ordinary observer, and the viewers are left with gaps in the sequence of events that lead to Holmes' conclusions, making him appear to possess magical powers or supernatural skills. Later in the same episode, while in a taxi to a crime scene Holmes explains his series of deductions to Watson when Watson questions how Holmes knew whether he had recently returned from service in Afghanistan or Iraq:

> I didn't know.... I saw.... Your haircut, the way you hold yourself says military. And your conversation as you entered the room.... Said trained at Bart's, so Army doctor (obvious). Your face is tanned, but no tan above the wrist.... Your limp's really bad when you walk, but you don't ask for a chair when you stand like you've forgotten about it, so it's at least partly psychosomatic That says the original circumstances of the injury were traumatic, wounded in action then. Wounded in action, sun tan: Afghanistan or Iraq...

Holmes subsequently proceeds to explain to Watson how his phone presented a series of clues by explaining:

> Your phone. It's expensive ... Scratches. Not one, many over time, it's been in the same pocket as keys and coins. The man sitting next to me wouldn't treat his one luxury item like this, so it's had a previous owner. Next bit's easy, you know it already.

And concludes by noting the significance of the engraving and the scratches on the phone:

> **HOLMES:** "Harry Watson." ... Not your father, this is a young man's gadget.... Unlikely you've got an extended family.... So, brother it is. Now Clara.... Three kisses say it's a romantic attachment. The expense of the phone says wife, not girlfriend.... This model's only six months old. Marriage in trouble then, six months on he's just given it away.... No, he wanted rid of it, he left her. He gave the phone to you.... You're looking for cheap accommodation and you're not going to your brother for help. That says you've got problems with him. Maybe you liked his wife, maybe you don't like his drinking.
> **WATSON:** How can you possibly know about the drinking?

> HOLMES: Shot in the dark. Good one, though. Power connection, tiny little scuff marks around the edge of it. Every night he goes to plug it in to charge but his hands are shaking. You never see those marks on a sober man's phone, never see a drunks' without them....

Upon arriving at the crime scene, Holmes asks Watson, "Did I get anything wrong?" to which Watson begins by remarking that Clara and Harry split up, and Harry is in fact a drinker:

> HOLMES: Spot on, then. I didn't expect to be right about everything.
> WATSON: Harry's short for Harriet.
> HOLMES: Harry's your sister.... Sister!...There's always something...

This ability to "read" a person from their physical features is referred to as cold reading when used in entertainment magic, and was referred to as characterology[14] by 19th- and early 20th-century psychologists. Characterology is the utilization and analysis of all possible combinations of features and traits of an individual in order to determine one's character, personality and disposition (McCormic 37). Character analysis, or character reading, has been described as being based on cold reading techniques.[15] Such techniques are based on the Barnum effect, a phrase coined and applied to psychoanalysis by Meehl in 1956. Based on P.T. Barnum's slogan, "Something for everyone," Meehl advocated the use of "Barnum effect" to explain the results of pseudoscientific clinical tests in which personality traits were applied to individuals based on their vagueness and general agreement with the majority of the population (266). In other words, an individual is likely to agree with a personalized character reading although it is composed of broad, sweeping statements that can be applied to most people in a given population.[16] Cold reading is the procedure by which a reader is able to persuade a client, whom he has never before met, that he knows all about the client's personality and problems (Hyman n.p.). Normally consisting of generalized statements that can fit almost any individual, cold reading is based on the reader having a good memory and acute observation skills so as to assess the client's physical features, clothing, and mannerisms (Hyman n.p.). Hyman adds that by having knowledge of actual and statistical data about various subcultures and the population, the reader is provided with the basis for making an accurate assessment of the client (n.p.). When conducted by a mentalist or mystic, such as a fortune teller, the individual will believe that the reading is based on supernatural powers or special insight possessed by the reader. Coupled with the reactions of the client to detect whether his initial assessments are correct or whether the reader is venturing down the wrong path, the reader will often benefit from the client as the client begins to let his guard down and provide details of his personal life to the reader (Hyman n.p.). The individual will often disclose personal information to the reader during the course of the reading without being aware that they are providing the information, not the reader:

> The fortune teller ... is a good reader of human nature and is helped by his client's simplicity, who, all unawares, gives him more materials than he requires to produce an impression as a great reader of the past [Gross 268].

Cold reading makes it appear that the reader possesses supernatural insight into the client's personal life. Holmes is able to ascertain information about an individual that he has never met before in what appears to be based on the techniques of cold reading. Where cold readings are based on general characteristics that could be true of any individual based on the vagueness and universal application of statements made during such readings, Holmes takes his "readings" a step further through observation, attention to detail, and reasoning based on guesses and probabilities. Allport describes characteristics of a good judge of others as including experience, similarity, intelligence, insight complexity, detachment, an esthetic attitude, and social intelligence (513). Such characteristics are found in Holmes, which enables him to "read" individuals so well. Holmes is able to observe what appear to be insignificant trifles, or details that are overlooked by many, even the subjects of Holmes' deductions. In *The Boscombe Valley Mystery* (1891), Holmes remarks to Watson, "You know my method. It's founded on the observation of trifles" (Conan Doyle, II, 148) and later in *The Reigate Squires* (1893), Holmes asserts, "It is of the highest importance in the art of detection to be able to recognize out of a number of facts which are incidental and which are vital" (Conan Doyle, I, 341). Holmes' extensive, specific knowledge (for example the nature and persistence of various types of physical traces) and experiences (based on his prior casework as well as his intimate attachment to London)[17] render his conclusions more detailed and therefore more amazing (and at the same time more likely to be correct). Holmes personifies the transition of cold reading as a pseudoscience to the analytical detection of clues based on scientific methodology.

In tracing the historical use of signs as clues in folklore, Ginzburg describes the leap from observation of apparently insignificant, silent facts, to an ordering by the observer in such a way to provide a narrative sequence of events much like reconstructing a crime (Eco and Sebeok 89). Such a "divinatory model," provides insight into the past and is based on conjecture coupled with scientific methods of observation and reasoning. The longstanding practice of observing and interpreting trace clues are characteristic of criminalistics and criminal investigation. In his memoirs, the 19th-century criminal-turned-detective Vidocq commented:

> I have been able to distinguish the character proper of each species, the physiognomy, language, habits, manners, dress, arrangement and details; I have studied all, remembered all: and if an individual pass before me, if he be a robber by profession, I will point him out, I will even tell his line of business. Frequently from inspection of a single article of clothing I would more quickly describe a thief from head to heel.... There is in the garb of a rogue hieroglyphics which can be deciphered with [more] certainty... [367].

Gross described the use of observation to determine characteristics of both witness and criminal and highlighted knowledge of man as an essential quality of an investigator in his 19th-century texts regarding criminalistics and criminal psychology (Gross 1934). Into the 20th century, medical doctors reported on the observation of markings and physical signs on an individual that were indicative of occupation or trade.[18] Ronchese makes references to works dating as far back as the 17th century:

> Many investigators have been interested particularly in rapid detection of a person's occupation or business by glance at his palms, by his general appearance, by the odor emanating from his body or his clothes, and so on [925].

The basis for such work was based on the premise that trades and professions will leave characteristic, unique marks that can be detected by the attentive observer. Forbes added, "While individual items may alone prove little, the sum total may be quite convincing and consequently each additional factor may be of importance" (266). In Conan Doyle's works featuring Holmes, references to the importance of detecting minute traces were presented. For example, in *A Case of Identity* (1891), Holmes remarks to Watson, "I can never bring you to realize the importance of sleeves, the suggestiveness of thumbnails, or the great issues that may hang from a bootlace" (I, 411) and in *The Adventure of the Creeping Man* (1923) Holmes reminds Watson, "Always look at the hands first, Watson. Then cuffs, trouser-knees and boots" (Conan Doyle, II, 762).

Another ability Sherlock Holmes has that likens him to a magician or spiritualist is necromancy. Holmes expresses the power to read the dead and elicit information necessary for leading an investigation. According to Willis, "The medium's role can be seen as being similar to that of a detective in a murder case. Both are trying to make the dead speak in order to reveal the truth" (in Chernaik et al. 60). An example of this in *Sherlock* is Holmes' evaluation of Jennifer Wilson, the lady in pink found dead in an abandoned house in "A Study in Pink." Upon examination of her body at the crime scene, Holmes is able to determine Wilson's age, handedness, residence, marital status, profession, use of a suitcase, travel plans, and even personal habits. As the investigation advances, Holmes is able to ascertain that Wilson was trying to aid in her own investigation:

She was clever.... She's cleverer than you lot and she's dead.... She didn't lose her phone.... She planted it on him. When she got out of the car she knew that she was going to her death. She left the phone in order to lead us to her killer...

Holmes continues by explaining that "Rachel" is the clue Wilson left behind, "...Rachel is not a name.... The password is [Rachel].... She's leading us directly to the man who killed her."

A major component enhancing the approach of viewing Holmes as a conjurer is the role of the observer. Clients, witnesses, law enforcement personnel, Inspectors like Lestrade, and most importantly, Dr. John Watson provide the emotions of wonder and amazement, which make Holmes' feats seem even more supernatural. The magician simulates magical powers, while the audience is unable to detect the relationship between the apparent and the concealed sequence of events that take place during the magician's trick (Nardi 29). Like a true magician entertaining with his magic tricks, the audience is amazed and perplexed by Holmes' "performances" and sleight of mind. In *A Study in Scarlet*, Watson remarks of Holmes deductions, "There still maintained some lurking suspicion in my mind that the whole thing was a prearranged episode, intended to dazzle me..." (Conan Doyle, I, 164). As the *Sherlock* series progresses, the viewer sees and hears the amazement projected by Watson, Lestrade, and clients in each instance Holmes utilizes his powers of observation and deduction. Holmes blurts out modified versions of the phrase "You see but you do not observe" throughout *Sherlock*.[19]

When compared to Holmes, what the casual observer lacks includes the ability to view and evaluate minute details with an analytical eye; the skills to detect deception and avoid being misled; the ability to reason analytically; attention to detail; and advanced scientific and technical knowledge. The audience may reason before all facts are observed, leading them to conclusions that are based on false truths. In "The Great Game," Sherlock states, "It is dangerous to jump to conclusions—I need data." Throughout his adventures, Holmes makes several important statements about his methods of deduction.[20] The dialogue between Holmes, Watson and Detective Inspector Dimmock in "The Blind Banker" illustrates this:

> **D.I. Dimmock:** We're obviously looking at a suicide.
> **Watson:** It does seem the only explanation of all the facts.
> **Holmes:** Wrong, it's one possible explanation of some of the facts. You've got a solution that you like but you are choosing to ignore anything you see that doesn't comply with it.... [Here Holmes points out several observations that are contrary to suicide, notably the handedness of the victim and the nature

of his wound].... Conclusion, someone broke in here and murdered him, only explanation for all of the facts.

Later, Holmes condescendingly responds to an inquisitive DI Dimmock, "Good, you're finally asking the right questions." And, as expected, Holmes is right—the manner of death is homicide, not suicide.[21]

In addition, the observer lacks the imagination and intuition necessary to develop expectations and alternate scenarios; the analytical ability to consider the relevance of such postulates; and the mathematical ability to consider various possibilities and determine a likelihood for each. Any combination of selective attention, such as inattentional and change blindness, coupled with myriad cognitive biases, can hinder the casual observer's ability to develop and follow a path of reasoning at a rapid pace like Holmes.[22] The only characters that exhibit skills similar to Sherlock Holmes are his brother Mycroft, his sister, Eurus, and Jim Moriarity.[23] When making decisions, there is an inherent degree of uncertainty in the reasoning process, which necessitates the ability of the observer to correctly fill in any gaps with the correct information, which may involve guessing. Methods used by magicians, such as clairvoyance and divination, can be described as alternate means of applying a measure of uncertainty to readings, much like Holmes conducts his internal process of reasoning to arrive at logical conclusions.[24]

Sherlock Holmes: Scientist and Logician

The best explanation for Sherlock Holmes' abilities rests in epistemology and the natural sciences. Holmes exhibits knowledge and intellect, including both "encyclopedic" knowledge and knowledge gained from personal experience; understanding of the scientific method, with specific focus on gaining facts through observation; proper application of methods of reasoning; the use of intuition and perception; imagination; and memory. Holmes' knowledge is obtained through learning and applying scientific methods to problem solving.[25] In addition to utilizing the scientific method as a procedural guide, the importance lies in gathering a set of observations (facts) and understanding their relevance and meaning, or knowing what to do with such information and how to apply them to the problem at hand. What Holmes does is reason backwards; beginning with the crime scene and the physical traces, Holmes discerns a series of causal links that enables him to reconstruct events and solve the crime (or identify the perpetrator who can confirm

Holmes' conclusions). "There are few people ... who, if you told them a result, would be able to evolve from their own inner consciousness what the steps were which led up to the result. This power is what I mean when I talk of reasoning backwards, or analytically" (Conan Doyle, I, 231).

In the 19th century, Mill reported the deductive method as "the mode of investigation which, from the proved inapplicability of direct methods of observation and experiment, remains to us as the main source of the knowledge we possess or can acquire respecting the conditions and laws of recurrence, of the more complex phenomena" (325). Mill further described that deduction consists of three operations: direct induction, ratiocination, and verification. "Induction to ascertain the laws of the causes; ratiocination, to compute from those laws how the causes will operate in the particular combination known to exist in the case in hand; verification, by comparing this calculated effect with the actual phenomenon. No one of these three parts of the process can be dispensed with" (350).[26] It is likely that when Conan Doyle was referring to Holmes' method of deduction, he was actually referring to a multi-step process as described by Mill. The process of reasoning was further delineated by Charles S. Peirce. Peirce distinguished three types of reasoning: deductive, inductive, and abductive. Deduction requires making an inference from a known, general principle, which provides a certainty in reaching a conclusion. With induction, there is a measure of probability assigned to a given conclusion. For example, when Sherlock and Mycroft both reference a "balance of probability" in drawing conclusions from their observations of the hat left at 221B Baker Street, they are using inductive reasoning.[27] Abductive reasoning requires creativity, intuition, and imagination to generate new ideas about observed phenomena and is the process of forming hunches about the world based on observation and perception (Eco and Sebeok 18). According to Peirce, abductive reasoning includes an element of guesswork, and provides the best explanation of observations, or facts, in reaching a conclusion since the majority of human reasoning is based on conjecture (see, Buchler, 1955; Eco and Sebeok, 1983).[28]

Abduction is the first step in reasoning in which the significance of observation is evaluated in order to develop an explanation for what one sees. According to Harrowitz, "abduction is ... the instinctive, perceptual jump which allows the subject to guess an origin which can then be tested out to prove or disprove the hypothesis" (in Eco and Sebeok 182). Upon careful reflection of the facts, the best hypothesis, or explanation of observed phenomena could be selected based on simplicity and rationality (Buchler 155). While validation through testing is necessary to establish support for conclusions resulting from abductive reasoning, the conclusions drawn by a detective from such reasoning methods during the preliminary stages of an investigation can prove useful in providing leads and guiding the investigation. Harrowitz describes a process as moving from abduction, which suggests; to induction, which shows; and finally to deduction, which proves (in Eco and Sebeok 181).ABductive reasoning involves the use of knowledge, intuition, and imagination to formulate a guess that can be subjected to the rigor of inductive reasoning. Holmes' knowledge not only rests on encyclopedic knowledge obtained from education, experimentation, and scientific inquiry, but is composed of personal experience. Sherlock also relies on imagination, which plays a critical role in the ability to reason effectively. According to Tyndall, "This idea of imagination was based on the ability to, 'magnify, diminish, qualify, and combine experiences, so as to render them fit for purposes entirely new'" (Tyndall 6).[29]

Related to knowledge is the importance of memory. In *Sherlock*, this storage of memory is referred to as Holmes' "hard drive" and "mind palace."[30] In "The Empty Hearse," Watson says, "Use your mind palace.... You've salted away every fact under the sun!" In the *Sherlock* series, the mind palace of Charles Agustus Magnussen is a focal point of "His Last Vow." Memory is the source of all knowledge, and is based on recollection, or the ability to review and pull up any stored information as needed based on contextual cues. For the magician and the consulting detective, memorization, including retention and recollection, is critical, especially when drawn up relative to scenarios that have relative associations to experience.[31] Sherlock remarks in *The Five Orange Pips*:

> To carry the art, however, to its highest pitch, it is necessary that the reasoner should be able to utilize all the facts which have come to his knowledge, and this in itself implies, as you will readily see, a possession of all knowledge, which, even in these days of free education and encyclopædias, is a somewhat rare accomplishment. It is not so impossible, however, that a man should possess all knowledge which is likely to be useful to him in his work, and this I have endeavoured in my case to do... [Conan Doyle, I, 399].[32]

Again, the dialogue between Holmes and Watson in "A Study in Pink" is instructive for demonstrating that the process of Holmes' "deductions" about Watson can be explained by reasoning coupled with knowledge [see Sherlock Holmes: Magician above for the dialogue analyzed in the following table],[33]

The Intersection of Magic and Science (Miranda) 59

Conclusion	Observations	Method of Reasoning	Type of Reasoning
Afghanistan or Iraq?	-Haircut, Manner, Verbal Statements→ Military→ Army -Tan (Nature/Location)→ Abroad -Limp→ Traumatic (Prominent, but ignored→ Psychosomatic)→ Wounded in Action	Holmes is able to narrow his options to two locations, but is not certain, thereby framing his conclusion in the form of a question that requires clarification by Watson. When Holmes states, "I know you're an army doctor and you've been invalidated home from Afghanistan" is it only because Watson confirmed Afghanistan that Holmes is able to make this statement with certainty?	-Abduction (series of guesses) -Induction (assignment of probability) -Not Deduction (the majority of Holmes' conclusions do not meet deduction due to the lack of certainty; the only conclusion that is certain upon their first encounter in the hospital is Afghanistan, which becomes a certainty only when Watson confirms this location upon being asked by Holmes)
Brother	-Phone→ Cost (the type, quality, newness and treatment of the phone are weighed against Watson's financial status)→ Previous Owner→ Young Man -Phone→ Engraving→ Family Member→ Harry=owner→ Wife (gift, cost of phone, "kisses")→ Lack of Sentiment → Failed Relationship→ Passed to Brother (John) -Phone→Drinking Problem→ Scratches by power connection	Assuming binary assignment of sex, Holmes is able to make a 50/50 guess—male or female. His conclusion is based on the name Harry. Statistically speaking, Harry is more likely to be consistent with a male (and Holmes has likely encountered more males named Harry than females), so he (incorrectly) concludes that Harry is a male based on probability and a guess; this is further extended by the conclusion that Harry is not an alternate family member (father, cousin)	-Abduction (Holmes states his conclusion about Harry's drinking problem was "a shot in the dark") -Induction (assignment of probability) -Not deduction (lack of certainty; this is clear when Watson informs Holmes that he was wrong about Harry, as Harry is short for Harriet and therefore Watson's sister)

Holmes' conclusions about Watson, based on observation and reasoning, are only made certain (or refuted) after confirmation from Watson himself. Even the matter of the limp is resolved when Watson leaves his walking stick behind at a restaurant and chases a taxi through the streets of London, leaping over rooftops in the process. By reviewing Holmes' methodology, it becomes clear that scientific reasoning and observation are the basis for Holmes' skill as a consulting detective.

Sherlock Holmes: Extraordinary

Sherlock Holmes was created in a time when science and reasoning were challenging the veracity of supernatural phenomena. As crowds were mesmerized by public performances featuring conjuring, necromancy, and phantasmagoria, philosophers and scientists were explaining the basis for such occult wonders through the natural sciences and human problem solving. Superimposed on society's attention to magic and the occult was the burgeoning focus on crime and degeneracy, and their role in the macabre, violent affairs of the ordinary citizen. Sherlock Holmes served as an answer to the mysterious—a fictional detective able to solve crimes and challenge the unknown through scientific explanations and logical reasoning. Using powers of observation and "deduction," Holmes could see what others overlooked and use those observed clues to identify criminals and the sinister motives behind their nefarious deeds. To the ordinary observer, Holmes continues to appear supernatural, with powers beyond comprehension, attributing to the enduring legacy of Sherlock Holmes. No matter how many times Holmes plummets over Reichenbach Falls, it is only a matter of time before he is reincarnated for the purpose of charming another generation of fans.

From his first case reported in 1887 to present day cinematic films and televised crime dramas like *Sherlock*, Holmes appears to be a dichotomous scientist—sorcerer. Contrary to the longstanding assertion that "[a] magician never reveals his secrets," throughout his cases Holmes explains his scientific method of detection, highlighting the observed minutia and the process of reasoning that led him to his reconstruction of the crime at hand. With methods of reasoning based on transitioning from abduction into induction and finally to deduction, Holmes uses intuition, imagination, and a vast knowledge base to contextualize his observations and develop conclusions built on the nature of physical traces and human behaviors. Those surrounding Holmes remain in amazement and utter statements of awe and incredulity, enabling Holmes to maintain his magical aura. *Sherlock* presents a modern-day account of the adventures of Sherlock Holmes, and though technology and viewer knowledge has evolved (as Holmes can now conduct an internet search to assess high tide of the Thames and text Watson their meeting location), the show still manages to captivate and amaze viewers as Holmes reasons analytically and "deduces" a series of random, but crucial facts from the observation of an otherwise overlooked clue. The character depicted in *Sherlock* maintains an intellectual arrogance that sets him apart from investigators, local law enforcement, his loyal partner Watson, and even that most attentive viewer. Such an intellectual advantage coupled with his distinct powers place him firmly in the realm of extraordinary. Holmes has unique powers that manifest themselves in his abilities to detect trifles, understand their significance, perceive patterns, and ultimately solve crimes. Because these powers remain grounded in science and reasoning that is often easily explained but lies beyond the comprehension of the ordinary individual, Sherlock Holmes continues to enchant and mystify. After all, it is Holmes who reminds us, "Omne ignotum pro magnifico" (Conan Doyle, I, 421).

Notes

1. Consisting of thirteen episodes over four series from 2010 to 2017, *Sherlock* originally aired on both BBC (UK) and PBS (USA) and was created, written and produced by Mark Gatiss and Steven Moffat, et al.

2. The Victorian Gothic era is defined as the overlap between the Gothic era (mid 1700's to 1900) and the Victorian era (1837–1901) and the period of the Enlightenment is generally described as spanning the 17th- and 18th-centuries. Epistemological thought is concerned with the study of human knowledge and understanding.

Positivism is the philosophy that knowledge is based on natural phenomena verified by the empirical sciences, and empiricism is the practice of using observation and experimentation to acquire knowledge.

3. The scientific method is characterized by the process of stating a problem, developing a hypothesis, collecting data through observation and experimentation, and either refining the hypothesis or developing a theory; it includes all principles and procedures utilized throughout the entirety of the process, including reasoning.

4. Toxicology is the detection of drugs and poisons. Criminalistics is the recognition, identification, individualization and evaluation of physical evidence using the methods of the natural sciences in matters of legal significance in an effort to aid in the reconstruction of events.

5. For more information on semiotics and the relationships between clues, signs and symptoms, see Eco and Sebeok, 1983.

6. See, for example, *Tales of Terror and Mystery by Arthur Conan Doyle*; *Uncollected Stories by Arthur Conan Doyle*; and *The Supernatural Tales of Sir Arthur Conan Doyle*.

7. Lévi (1810–1875) is best known as a magician that popularized the term occultism and Crowley (1875–1947) is best known as an occultist, magician, and founder of the magico-religious philosophy Thelema.

8. See, specifically Conan Doyle's *The Hound of Baskervilles*, *The Adventures of the Devil's Foot*, *The Adventure of the Creeping Man*, *The Adventure of the Sussex Vampire*. For a discussion of the scientific explanations of the supernatural phenomena described in these stories, see Miranda, 2017.
9. *Sherlock* Series 2 Episode 3; "Nobody could be that clever…I researched you. Before we met I discovered everything I could to impress you. It's a trick. It's just a magic trick."
10. Additional titles, which varied with historical time period and geographic location, including sage, magi, man of God, seer, prophet, illusionist, conjurer, diviner, and medium, as well as many others.
11. Including conjuring tricks; mind reading and mind control; clairvoyance and divination; and spiritualism and evoking spirits, respectively.
12. *Sherlock* Series 3, Episode 4
13. "A Study in Pink," *Sherlock* Series 1, Episode 1
14. Characterology has also been referred to as traitology; it encompasses physiognomy (the study of facial features and expressions), phrenology (the study of the shape and size of the skull; developed by Franz Joseph Gall in the late 18th-century) and pathognomy (the study of emotion and expressions). These studies have been used in various disciplines ranging from psychology, social psychology, psychiatry, forensic psychology (offender profiling and victimology), to criminology and forensic science (anthropometrics, Bertillonage), anthropology, and medicine, especially in the 19th-century. For a brief history of characterology, see Allport, 1937.
15. Character readings conducted by a medium have been reported to be based on observing and interpreting vibrations or auras given off by an individual (see, for example Crider, 1944); this differs from mediums that can reportedly communicate with dead relatives of the client based on being visited by the spirits of family members or visualizing those spirits present around the client at the time of the reading (necromancy)
16. See also, Forer, as his research resulted in the phrase "The Forer Effect."
17. Not only do we see Holmes navigate through the busy streets of London in real-time in "A Study in Pink" (drawing on his mind palace, Holmes visualizes the streets maps of road closures, detours, etc., as he is rapidly traversing the city in pursuit of a suspect), but Jeff, the cabbie-turned-killer directly states to Holmes, "You know every street in London. You know exactly where we are." This mental mapping of London is also done in "The Empty Hearse" (Series 3, Episode 1) when Holmes is racing to save Watson's life.
18. For example, see Ronchese, 1945 and 1948; Forbes, 1946
19. This statement here is repeated in "The Great Game" and "The Six Thatchers," (*Sherlock* Series 4, Episode 1) and derivatives are apparent throughout *Sherlock*. An exchange occurs between Watson and Holmes in *A Scandal in Bohemia* which clarifies the difference between two individuals that experience the same situation: WATSON: When I hear you give your reasons, the thing always appears to me to be so ridiculously simple that I could easily do it myself, though at each successive instance of your reasoning I am baffled until you explain your process. And yet I believe my eyes are as good as yours. HOLMES: You see but you do not observe. The distinction is clear (Conan Doyle, I, 349).
20. In *A Study in Scarlet* Holmes states, "It is a capital mistake to theorize before you have all the evidence. It biases the judgment (Conan Doyle, I, 166) and reiterates this in *A Scandal in Bohemia*, "It is a capital mistake to theorize before one has data. Insensibly one begins to twist facts to suit theories instead of theories to suit facts" (Conan Doyle, I, 349). In *A Study in Scarlet* Holmes declares, "All this seems strange to you…because you failed at the beginning of the inquiry to grasp the importance of the single real clue which was presented to you. I had the good fortune to seize upon that, and everything which has occurred since then has served to confirm my original suspicion, and, indeed, was the logical sequence of it. Hence things which have perplexed you and made the case more obscure have served to enlighten me and to strengthen my conclusions … " (Conan Doyle, I, 194).
21. *Sherlock* Series 1, Episode 2
22. Described as failures of visual awareness, inattentional and change blindness are concerned with failing to see something before one's eyes. Jensen et al. define change blindness as

the failure to notice an obvious change and inattentional blindness as the failure to notice the existence of an unexpected item (529).Cognitive biases that may be encountered in criminal investigation include confirmation bias, contextual bias, availability heuristic, representativeness/attribution, illusion of validity/understanding as well as premature decision making.

23. While Irene Adler proves to be a formidable opponent to Holmes he is able to gain the upper hand by the end of "A Scandal in Belgravia." Adler presents a mixture of cleverness and deception, which makes it difficult for Holmes to "read" her upon their initial encounter and also enables Adler to exploit Holmes' powers of reasoning and problem solving for her own benefit.

24. It is worth commenting at the end of this section pertaining to magic on the *Sherlock* episode "The Abominable Bride." This special episode, set in the 19th century, includes spirits of the dead conjuring, and illusion. The episode captures elements of the Gothic and Victorian Gothic eras, including the macabre, and the prevailing discourse of science and rational thought to explain the supernatural. One example is the reference to Pepper's Ghost. In 1863, Professor Pepper invented a device for projecting images of living persons in the air. The illusion, based on a simple optical effect, was based on an image reflected in glass (Hopkins 8). Pepper's Ghost was an invention that improved on the magic phantasmagoric lantern, which simply projected flat images painted on glass; it allowed for a living, moving, three-dimensional specter to appear before the viewers. Pepper's Ghost was an important part of entertainment magic, allowing for the macabre display of specters and spirits to amaze the audience Although seemingly magical and supernatural to the casual observer, the images of ghosts were based upon the natural sciences—specifically an illusion concerned with optics and the interaction of light with matter, key components of physics. For more information, see Pepper, 1869; Pepper and Walker, 1879; Hopkins, 1897.

25. See footnote 3

26. Ratiocination is characterized by the use of observation and analytical reasoning to develop a clear explanation of experiences and encounters. This method was utilized by C. Auguste Dupin, the fictional detective created by Edgar Allan Poe in a series of three tales published from 1841 to 1844. Poe's character Dupin shares many similarities to Holmes, and is believed to be an inspiration for Conan Doyle's consulting detective. For more about Poe, Dupin, and ratiocination see Miranda, 2017.

27. "The Empty Hearse." The phrase "balance of probability" is used throughout *Sherlock* and not limited to the exchange between Sherlock and Mycroft (see "A Study in Pink"; "The Final Problem," Series 4. Episode 3). Other expressions related to probability and inductive reasoning include Holmes' narrowing down possible explanations in the course of his observations—for example, in "The Great Game," when asked by Lestrade if he has any ideas, Holmes replies "7 so far" and in "A Scandal in Belgravia," Holmes narrows his ideas from eight to four to two through a series of compounding observations.

28. Intuition is knowledge without proof or evidence, often synonymous with insight, which is the understanding of someone or something. Conjecture is based on guesswork where there is an absence of proof or sufficient evidence.

29. In *The Problem of Thor Bridge* (1922), Sherlock remarks, "I have been sluggish in mind and wanting in that mixture of imagination and reality which is the basis of my art" (Conan Doyle, II, 605). When Holmes is 'accused' of guesswork in the *Hound of the Baskervilles* (1901), Holmes asserts, "[Such determinations enter] into a region where we balance probabilities and choose the more likely. It is the scientific use of the imagination, but we have always had some material basis on which to start our speculations. Now, you would call it a guess, no doubt, but I am almost certain …" (Conan Doyle, II, 24). This statement addresses imagination, guessing (abduction), probability (induction), and certainty (deduction).

30. In Conan Doyle's works featuring Sherlock Holmes, it is referred to as Holmes' brain attic. In *A Study in Scarlet*, Holmes explains, "… the skilled workman is very careful indeed as to what he takes in his brain-attic. He will have nothing but the tools which may help him in doing his work, but of these he has a large assortment, and all in the most perfect order …" (Conan Doyle, I, 154); and in *The Five Orange Pips* (1891) Holmes states, "… A man should keep his little brain attic stocked with all the furniture that he is likely to use, and the rest he

can put away in the lumber-room of his library, where he can get it if he wants is" (Conan Doyle, I, 399).

31. Rapid memorization, or mnemotechny, was an important tool of the conjurer (See Burlingame, 1891)

32. Holmes refers to his vast store of knowledge throughout Conan Doyle's works, for example, In *The Red-Headed League*, Holmes states, "…I am able to guide myself by the thousands of other similar cases which occur to my memory" (Conan Doyle, I, 419) and in *A Study in Scarlet*, he asserts, "There is a strong family resemblance about misdeeds, and if you have all the details of a thousand at your finger ends, it is odd if you can't unravel the thousand and first" (Conan Doyle, I, 160).

33. This evaluative mapping can similarly be done for of Holmes' instances of deduction throughout *Sherlock* [Jennifer Wilson ("A Study in Pink"), Alex Woodbridge (the murdered security guard in "The Great Game"), Carl Powers (the athlete in "The Great Game" whose death was unsolved until Holmes examined his training shoes), the hat of Howard Shilcott ("The Empty Hearse"), etc.]

Works Cited

Allport, Gordon. *Personality: A Psychological Interpretation*. Henry Holt & Co., 1937.
Burlingame, H. *Leaves from the Conjurers' Scrap Books Or, Modern Magicians and Their Works*. Donohue, Henneberry & Co., 1891.
Chernaik, Warren, et al., eds. *The Art of Detective Fiction*. St. Martin's, 2000.
Conan Doyle, Sir Arthur. *The Annotated Sherlock Holmes*. 2 vols., edited by William Baring-Gould, Clarkson N. Potter, 1967.
Crider, Blake. "A Study of a Character Analyst." *Journal of Social Psychology*, vol. 20, no. 2, 1944, pp. 315–318.
Crowley, Aleister. "Editorial." *The Equinox*, vol. 1, no. 1, 1909, pp. 1–3.
_____. "Liber Exercitiorum." *The Equinox*, vol. 1, no. 1, 1909, pp. 25–34.
De Foe, Daniel. *A System of Magic*. Oxford, 1840.
Eco, Umberto, and Thomas Sebeok, editors. *Dupin, Holmes Peirce: The Sign of Three*. Indiana UP, 1983.
Forbes, Gilbert. "Some Observations on Occupational Markings." *Police Journal*, vol. 19, no.4, 1946, pp. 266–274.
Forer, Bertram R. "The Fallacy of Personal Validation: A Classroom Demonstration of Gullibility." *The Journal of Abnormal and Social Psychology*, vol. 44, no. 1, 1949, pp. 118–123.
Gross, Hans, *Criminal Investigation: A Practical Textbook for Magistrates, Police Officers, and Lawyers Adapted from the System Der Kriminalistik of Dr. Hans Gross*, edited by Norman Kendal, Sweet & Maxwell, Ltd., 1924.
Hopkins, Albert. *Stage Illusions and Scientific Diversions, Including Trick Photography*. Sampson Low, Marston & Co., Ltd., 1897.
Hyman, Ray. "Cold Reading: How to Convince Strangers That You Know All About Them." *Skeptical Inquirer*, 1977. Retrieved from: http://skepdic.com/Hyman_cold_reading.htm
Jensen, Melinda, et al. "Change Blindness and Inattentional Blindness." *Cognitive Science*, vol. 2, no. 5, 2011, pp. 529–546.
McCormic, L.H. *Characterology an Exact Science Embracing Physiognomy, Phrenology, and Pathognomy, Reconstructed, Amplified and Amalgamated, and Including Views Concerning Memory and Reason and the Location of These Faculties with in the Brain Likewise Facial and Cranial Indications of Longevity*. Rand McNally & Co., 1920.
Meehl, Paul E. "Wanted—A Good Cookbook." *The American Psychologist*, vol. 11, no. 6, 1956, pp. 263–272.
Mill, John S. *A System of Logic, Ratiocinative and Inductive, Being a Connected View of the Principles of Evidence, and the Methods of Scientific Investigation*, 8th ed. Harper & Brothers, 1882.
Miranda, Michelle D. "Reasoning Through Madness: The Detective in Gothic Crime Fiction."

Palgrave Communications, vol. 3, 2017. Retrieved from: http://www.palgrave-journals.com/articles/palcomms201745
Nardi, Peter M. "Toward a Social Psychology of Entertainment Magic (Conjuring)." *Symbolic Interaction*, vol. 7, no. 1, 1984, pp. 25–42.
Peirce, Charles S. *Philosophical Writings of Peirce*, edited by John Buchler, Dover Publications, Inc., 1955.
Pepper, John. *Boy's Playbook of Science: Including the Curious Manipulations and Arrangements of Chemical and Philosophical Apparatus Required for the Successful Performance of Scientific Experiments an Illustration of the Elementary Branches of Chemistry and Natural Philosophy*. George Routledge & Sons, 1869.
Pepper, John, and J.J. Walker. Apparatus for Producing Optical Illusions. US 221,605, United States Patent and Trademark Office, 1879.
Robert-Houdin, Jean E. *Secrets of Conjuring and Magic or How to Become a Wizard*, 4th ed. George Routledge & Sons, Ltd. 1877.
Ronchese, Francesco. "Calluses, Cicatrices, and Other Stigmas as an Aid to Personal Identification." *Journal of the American Medical Association*, vol. 128, no. 13, 1945, pp. 925–932.
_____. *Occupational Marks and Other Physical Signs: A Guide to Personal Identification*. Grune & Stratton, 1948.
Smajić, Srdjan. *Ghost-Seers, Detectives, and Spiritualists: Theories of Vision in Victorian Literature and Science*. Cambridge UP, 2010.
Tyndall, John. *Scientific Use of the Imagination and Other Essays*. Longmans, Green and Col, 1872.
Vidocq, Eugene. *Memoirs of Vidocq, Principal Agent of the French Police*. Carey & Hart, 1834.

Playing Detective

Gothic Perspectives and Police Procedurals in the CW's Supernatural

Mary Going

> Dean: I hate this game. I hate that we're in a procedural cop show and you wanna know why? Because I hate procedural cop shows. There's like three hundred of them on television and they're all the freaking same.
> —"Changing Channels"

"In one sentence, this is X-FILES meets ROUTE 66": the first line of Eric Kripke's 2004 pitch for *Supernatural* epitomizes the fundamental core of his show, its relation to genre, and its generic hybridity. Originally envisaged as a horror show for the small screen, *Supernatural* (2005–present) is often categorized as a horror, fantasy, or science-fiction TV series. Acknowledging that television professionals, critics, and viewers alike typically eschew the label "Gothic" in favor of horror, the 2016 collection *The Gothic Tradition in* Supernatural also firmly identifies the show as Gothic as it locates the show's generic roots within the Gothic tradition. Although not always interchangeable, Gothic and horror are genres that remain, to a large extent, conjoined, and this is true of *Supernatural*. Heavily relying on Gothic/horror aesthetics, the show employs the monster-of-the-week format to investigate specifically American urban legends, such as the Woman in White, Bloody Mary, and Hookman, while frequently alluding to Gothic and horror texts from *Dracula*, *Frankenstein*, and the works of H.P. Lovecraft, to horror films such as *Poltergeist, An American Werewolf in London*, and *The Shining*. Yet, while horror and the Gothic appear as its predominant genres, *Supernatural*'s intrinsic generic hybridity, and its predilection to experiment with genre, has led to the inclusion of other genres throughout the series. Indeed, this generic hybridity or "conflation of genre, styles, and cultural concerns" (Hogle, 2) is, itself, a key part of the Gothic mode which manifests in *Supernatural* through the incorporation of, and gestures towards, many different genres from comedy and melodrama, metafiction and the road movie, and, perhaps most significantly, the police procedural.

Since successfully moving his initial pitch from paper to screen, Kripke's description of his show as a "modern day Western with monsters" (2.20, Audio Commentary) highlights the hybridity of *Supernatural*. Kripke further establishes horror as *Supernatural*'s key inspiration, and in so doing also locates the show's experimentation, or playfulness:

> "We set out to really make this feel like a horror movie [...] those are movies that are scary as hell, but they're funny too. And they have like a sense of playfulness to them, and that's what always attracted me and that's what we strove hard to bring to the series of *Supernatural*" [*Supernatural: Tales from the Edge of the Darkness*].

Inherent within the Gothic is a sense of play, where the boundaries of reality and fiction, authenticity, identity, and genre are explored and performed. From its creation in 1764 with Horace Walpole's *The Castle of Otranto*, the Gothic has been a space that explores the tensions surrounding claims to authenticity and, as Jerrold Hogle observes, "its insistent artificiality [...] its representation, and even its Gothicism are so pointedly fake and counterfeit from the beginning" (15). Initially claiming to be an authentic version of a 16th century Catholic manuscript, with its original title page professing itself to be a translation "From the original Italian of Onuphrio Muralto," Walpole soon revealed himself as the true author of *Otranto*. Rather than documenting a ghost story of Europe's Catholic past, this novel instead reveals Walpole's exploration of the "boundless realms of invention" (Walpole, 9) while locating the narrative and its anxieties not in the past, but in the present.[1] Moreover, the sequence of publication and subsequent revelation of its true authorship further exposes the ways that the Gothic "exaggerates its own extreme fictionality" (Hogle, 14) in order to confront, interrogate, and transgress boundaries. It is not surprising that, as other mediums have emerged—from film and TV, to online media and video-games—the transgression of boundaries, and in particular those relating to authenticity, remain integral to the Gothic together with a sense of play. Discussing survival horror gaming, Laurie N. Taylor notes that the Gothic is "best defined by its process" and its "subversion or transgression of boundaries": "Gothic texts transgress boundaries to question, define, and redefine them," often producing fear or horror (49). Within survival horror gaming, or to use Taylor's term, within ludic-gothic, this process is achieved through procedural rhetoric and subversion where gameplay norms are established and then subverted through boundary transgressions (50). This description perhaps seems antithetical to the police procedural, which "displays a pronounced preoccupation with 'authenticity' and 'realism'" (Von Mueller, 104), but it is through *Supernatural*'s relationship with this genre in particular that the Gothic aspects of play and generic hybridity are truly exposed.

Concurrent to its identification as Gothic/horror, *Supernatural* is, essentially, both a police procedural and pastiche police procedural. *Supernatural* follows brothers Sam and Dean Winchester (played by Jared Padalecki and Jensen Ackles respectively) as they travel across America in a black '67 Chevy Impala investigating "cases" or crime stories, and through their investigations the brothers perform the crux of the show: "saving people, hunting things. The family business" (1.2) Typically, such cases are self-contained within single episodes owing to the show's anthology and monster-of-the-week format, although larger, parallel narrative arcs (sometimes other cases to be solved, such as the hunt for the "Big Bad" of a season, or sometimes simply character development) are also explored. Their investigations emulate those of the police depicted in procedural shows along with many generic conventions established by police procedurals: whereas, for example, the police procedural reveals the "ordinary processes and limitations of the police force" (Davis, 11), *Supernatural* reveals the ordinary processes and limitations of their investigations and hunts. Emerging in the late 1940s as a subgenre of the detective genre, the police procedural is distinct from its parent genre through its attempts to be "an indexical replica of a 'real' world" (Von Mueller, 106), its representation of real cops, and its portrayal of "a new type of detective and a new technique of detection" (Primasita and Ahimsa-Purtra, 34). This is epitomized through the *CSI* franchise—and in particular the first three series *CSI: Crime Scene Investigation*, *CSI: Miami*, and *CSI: New York*—which functions as a distinct type of forensic procedural; here, the crime narrative is primarily investigated by scientists employing forensic methods. Other examples include: *Dragnet* (1951–9; revived 1967–70), which focuses on Los Angeles police detective Sergeant Joe Friday and his partners; *NCIS* (2003–present), a show that explores the Naval Criminal Investigative Service; and *Castle* (2009–16), which centers on a mystery novelist who works with a homicide detective to solve crimes in New York. Similarly, *Supernatural* can be viewed as a distinct type of supernatural procedural, or more specifically a procedural focused on supernatural hunts. Like the scientists within the *CSI* franchise, the Winchester brothers exemplify the methods of hunters and thus portray a new type of detective along with their paranormal techniques of detection.

Of course, the fundamental difference between traditional police procedurals and *Supernatural* is their relationship with authenticity and the real world. Although both are fiction, the former represents law enforcement teams pursuing human perpetrators and seeking legal resolutions in a way that mirrors their real life counterparts, while the latter portrays the pursuit of supernatural monsters that, as far as we know, do not have counterparts in real life. Exploring the tension that already exists within police procedurals regarding authenticity, *Supernatural* plays with the conventions and expectations of this genre. Within the show, "real" law enforcement pursue criminals to bring about their arrest and conviction, while Sam and Dean conduct their own parallel investigations in order to engender their own justice through illegal, supernatural, or violent methods. Although both methods seek to remove offenders from society, in contrast to the aim of law enforcement to put perpetrators behind bars, Sam and Dean hunt monsters with a view to kill. Moreover, to facilitate their investigations the brothers often exploit various aliases, costumes, and professional identities including those of reporters, doctors, firefighters, and even priests, but most frequently, they exploit the identities of law enforcement. In other words, the brothers are simultaneously investigators and outsiders playing detective.

Initially conceived by Kripke as a five-season show, *Supernatural*'s fifth season hinges on Sam and Dean playing their roles as the vessels of Lucifer and Michael in the final act of the apocalypse. The show establishes predetermined elements for its apocalypse storyline where the archangels, each in their Winchester "meat suit," will battle on earth to resolve their own brotherly conflict. The expected outcome: the possible destruction of earth and humans during the battle in which either heaven or hell must succeed against the other. Having established this convention, the show then plays with its predetermined storyline, and the season ends with Sam/Lucifer battling not with Dean, but their half-brother Adam; the world doesn't end, but instead the brothers reopen a cage in hell into which Sam/Lucifer and Adam/Michael are imprisoned. This playful approach to establishing and then transforming conventions, tropes, and narrative expectations can also be seen through *Supernatural*'s identification as a police procedural. Along with the genre's fixation with realism and authenticity, conventions such as the urban setting of the police precinct (Primasita and Ahimsa-Putra, 36), the investigators' distinct uniform of police blues and/or business suits (Landrum, 98), and the importance of historically bookmarking technological advances of real-world policing (Arntfield, 76) have been established. Using a textualist approach, Chandler Harriss has also identified thirteen distinct generic functions of the procedural show that occur within seven phases of the typical episode of the procedural (46). Applying Harriss' framework to *Supernatural*, we can observe how the show establishes and adheres to generic conventions of the police procedural. In particular, season one establishes these conventions from the outset and functions as a foundation or blueprint from which established conventions are first repeated, and then subsequently, and especially in later seasons, playfully adapted, modified, parodied, or even mocked. Using Harriss' textualist framework, I will focus on three episodes from season one—"Pilot" (1.1), "Hell House" (1.17), and "Something Wicked" (1.18)—to explore how these conventions are established, before turning to later seasons to examine the show's playful experimentation with the police procedural and its boundary transgressions. Although any episode from the first season could be analyzed in relation to this framework, I have chosen these episodes as being representative of the season as a whole—"Pilot" in particular sets the tone of the show itself—and also because they illustrate specific generic functions identified by Harriss.

The first phase Harriss identifies is the "Commission of Crime" where the victim is "involved in some mysterious occurrence" or crime that usually centers on their death, and which Harris classifies as the first generic function (47). In *Supernatural*, this is often blended with the second phase, the "Discovery of Crime" along with the second generic function where the victim is discovered (Harriss, 48); in most episodes, both phases are usually depicted in the teaser sequence or cold open before cutting to the show's title card.[2] Opening with a group of four teenagers playing truth or dare, the teaser for "Hell House" focuses on the group exploring a haunted house and then discovering the body of a hanged woman in the basement. Similarly, "Something Wicked" begins with a father putting his daughter to bed: we learn that her mother is at the hospital with the girl's sister, apparently suffering from pneumonia, but, once the lights are switched off, a mysterious and terrifying creature enters her room via the now open window. Like the teenagers from "Hell House," the girl screams, and the teaser cuts to the title card, having revealed both victim and mysterious occurrence. As the inaugural episode of the show, the structure of "Pilot" is slightly different, using the teaser to establish the Winchester's backstory through a prologue sequence, and then introducing its main protagonists though the opening scenes that follow the title card. However, the first two phases are not neglected, and instead scenes depicting a man picking up the ghost of a woman in white at the roadside, and then subsequently being driven to his death on a bridge, are inserted later. Revealing to the audience not simply a traditional murder or crime, but one that is immediately identified as supernatural, these teasers establish a case "worthy of the investigator's efforts" (Harriss, 48) and thus trigger the phases and investigation that follows. The third phase is categorized as "Beginning of Investigation" and consists of generic functions three and four where the investigators are made aware of the case, and then relocate to begin investigating (Harriss, 48–9). For example, in "Pilot" Dean shows his brother newspaper articles documenting several mysterious disappearances dating back twenty years, and then plays a voicemail from their also missing father which contains EVP (electronic voice phenomenon) in which a woman's voice eerily declares "I can never go home." This evidence convinces Sam to join his brother, and the pair drive off in Dean's Impala, the episode then cutting to the aforementioned scenes of the woman in white. These phases are often combined and actually take place in the Impala itself, as is the case with both "Hell House" and "Something Wicked." In "Hell House," Sam gives Dean the "lowdown" on the case, recounting first-hand accounts from the teenagers portrayed in the teaser that he discovered on the paranormal website hellhoundslair.com. In contrast, these scenes in "Something Wicked" reveal that the brothers are not pursuing a specific case, but rather coordinates sent by their father. Dean insists that "I'm sure there's something in Fitchburg worth killing," and, as a result of the episode's teaser, the audience recognizes this statement as accurate.

Scenes within the third phase function as both transitional and expository, thus laying the groundwork for the core of the procedural: the investigation itself (Harriss, 49–50). The next phase, which Harriss calls "Phases of Investigation," involves several generic functions (five to ten) including physically searching crime scenes, questioning various individuals, eye-witnesses, and experts, and identifying and apprehending perpetrators or false perpetrators (46, 49–54). For instance, the episodes "Pilot," "Hell House," and "Something Wicked" each show the brothers returning to the scenes of the crime to search for clues. At night and while examining the bridge where the disappearances occurred in "Pilot," the brothers' Impala is possessed by the woman in white and drives the brothers off the bridge. The bridge itself elucidates no clues, and Dean is also now covered in mud so the brothers relocate their investigation, but this scene nonetheless exemplifies what Harris terms a "prototypical free motif that serves to delay the resolution," where such delays are "arguably what make procedurals enjoyable" (50). Conversely, their investigations in "Hell House" and "Something Wicked" are more fruitful: examining the Mordechai house reveals several recently painted sigils from various religions, while an inspection of the house from the teaser in "Something Wicked" reveals a prominent and nonhuman handprint on the girl's bedroom windowsill. Similarly, each episode depicts the brothers questioning relevant individuals and experts, often exploiting fake aliases. Questioning the widower of Constance Welch in "Pilot" under the guise of being a reporter, Sam is able to confirm his suspicion that her husband was unfaithful and therefore the catalyst of Constance becoming a woman in white. However, in "Hell House" the brothers' interview with a teenager called Craig who works in a record shop produces snares that delay the resolution of the mystery as he provides untruthful answers to their questions. Craig is the apparent source for the original Mordechai story, and his initial false answers fit with the hypothesis that Mordechai is a ghost. Yet, when Sam and Dean discover that salt has no effect on Mordechai and therefore he cannot be a ghost, the brothers realize they must be dealing with something else, and they return to question Craig. Confronting him with a sigil from the house that is in fact simply the logo of the band the Blue Öyster Cult, Craig eventually reveals he made up the story and painted all the sigils in the house with his cousin.

Dean's passion for heavy metal and rock music leads to the identification of the Blue Öyster Cult symbol which exposes Craig's answers as snares, but in "Something Wicked" it is physical clues that function as snares or red herrings and lead the brothers to pursue a false perpetrator. Investigating the hospital where the sick children have been taken, Dean observes an old woman in a room with an inverted cross. Later, discussing the case with his brother in their motel room, Dean hypothesizes that the old woman is the monster they are hunting, in this case a shtriga which is a type of witch. Together with the fact that all of the victims live close to the hospital, and that shtrigas typically masquerade as old women when they are not feeding, Dean adds the inverted cross as evidence that she is their monster, and the brothers head to the hospital to confront their potential perpetrator. However, the old woman is in actuality not the monster they are looking for, but simply an old women unhappy that the cross in her room has been left upside down for so long. Fixing the cross, the brothers leave and return to their investigation.

The following two phases and generic functions, "Elucidation of Case and Identification of Perpetrator" and "Consequences of Identification," occur when the correct perpetrator has been discovered (Harriss, 55–6): in "Something Wicked," the monster/perpetrator is revealed to be a doctor working in the hospital, while "Pilot" uncovers the identity of the woman in white as Constance Welch. Following this correct identification of who, and also what, the monster/perpetrator is, the brothers can progress their case and work to remove them from society. In traditional police procedurals, Harris writes, these scenes are often depicted visually through the "perp walk" where the perpetrator is "handcuffed and removed from society," and where the viewer also functions as "de factor members of society" as they witness the consequences of deviating from social norms (Harriss, 56). These phases are enacted in *Supernatural*, although modified. As far as the viewer is aware, ghosts, witches, and other monsters only exist in the narrative world of *Supernatural*, and therefore they can transgress social norms in ways that real world criminals cannot; ghosts, for example, can walk through walls which creates a difficulty regarding their arrest and incarceration. Moreover, the monsters/perpetrators of *Supernatural* are not usually human, but supernatural monsters who, because they harm or kill humans, must be removed from society not through legal means but through their deaths. A ghost can be killed by burning and salting their remains, or completing their unfinished business (in "Pilot," it was simply taking the ghost home). Shtriga can be killed with consecrated iron rounds while they are feeding, as the brothers successfully perform in "Something Wicked." The resolution in "Hell House" is somewhat different as there is no monster to kill, but rather a Tupla or thought form brought to life by a Tibetan spirit sigil; with nothing to kill or take away in handcuffs, the brothers instead burn down the Mordechai house itself removing the supernatural threat from society. In these scenes, like the traditional procedural, the viewer witnesses the consequences of criminal and supernatural monstrosity, but these cases are kept hidden from society at large. Thus, playing with the relationship between reality and fiction, the viewer is here privileged with the secrets of the supernatural, while remaining removed from the dangers of these monsters through the implied knowledge that they do not exist beyond the show's narrative world.

The seventh and final phase of the police procedural identified by Harriss is the "Resolution" which encompasses the final generic function whereby investigators assess the case (56). Lacking regular sets and locations, the Impala frequently serves as the brother's home location (Beeler, 20) and it is here, as opposed to the police precinct or forensics lab, that the "Resolution" phase often takes places. Stan Beeler states that "the car and chronologically consistent music anchor the show to an anachronistic mood with the same regularity that establishing shots of identifiable location items are used in other television series" (20), and this regularity extends to the denouement of the crime story where Sam and Dean will return to the Impala and assess the case. While the location, music (both diegetic and nondiegetic), and anachronistic mood marks these scenes as, on the surface, different from the police procedural, the generic function is nonetheless the same. Assessing the case of the woman in white in "Pilot," the brothers trade remarks over the Impala; Dean congratulates his brother on finding the ghost's "weak spot" while Sam questions Dean's actions:

"What were you thinking shooting Casper in the face"? This appraisal does not occur by the Impala in "Hell House," instead taking place outside the burning Mordechai house, but the motif is repeated in "Something Wicked" as the brothers discuss that the cost of knowing about the supernatural is a loss of innocence. The frequent use of the Impala in this phase further underscores that the case or mystery has been solved, loose ends are tied up, and the brothers can physically move on to a different location and a different case.

Supernatural's first season incorporates the established conventional modes of the police procedural into its Gothic/horror narrative, stylistically changing the "formulaic narrative structure" (Harriss, 57) of the procedural through its generic hybridity and inclusion of the supernatural. In using and adapting these conventions, *Supernatural* defamiliarizes the procedural's formulaic conventions and establishes its own versions that are then repeated throughout its subsequent seasons. One convention now characteristic of *Supernatural* is the methods used by the brothers to play detectives: for instance, Sam and Dean dress up in business or "Fed" suits, flash fake FBI badges, and use aliases to gain access to crime scenes, police resources, experts and so on. Defamiliarizing law enforcement characters, behaviors, and props, fake identities have become a familiar *Supernatural* trope. Primarily derived from horror, pop culture, or heavy metal and rock music, fans enjoy identifying the references built into aliases depicted in the show such as Detectives Bachman and Turner (3.9), Agents Angus and Young (4.5) and Agents Page and Plant (5.6).[3] The show also exploits these aliases to allude to specific subjects or themes within episodes: for example, in "Heart" (2.17), an episode where the brothers investigate werewolf attacks, Dean introduces himself and Sam as "Landis, and Detective Dante," thus referencing the directors of two renowned werewolf films, *An American Werewolf in London* (1981) and *The Howling* (1981). Possibly stemming from Dean's appreciation for Horror films, or possibly a conscious nod to werewolf films inserted into the narrative by the show's writers, this name choice signals a transgression of the boundaries of fiction and reality and further demonstrates the Gothic's "extreme fictionality" (Hogle, 14).

Writer and executive producer Brad Buckner further highlights the development of this convention in the commentary of "Family Feud" from season twelve: "we've kind of dispensed with having to show their badges, or lie to everybody because everybody knows that's the convention." However, this established convention has not been dispensed with altogether, but rather it is instead occasionally parodied within the show itself. Incorporating metatextual elements and emphasizing the fictionality of the show's aliases, "The Real Ghostbusters" (5.9) places Sam and Dean in the midst of a "Supernatural" convention where fans of the book series cosplay as the brothers.[4] This episode includes a scheduled hunt or LARP, where the convention goers role-play as Sam and Dean and investigate a ghost, incorporating the brothers established use of using rock aliases (here, Agents Lennon and McCartney are used by the fans) to play the game. Unaware that the books are in fact "real" (at least within the narrative world of *Supernatural*) and also that the "real" Sam and Dean are before them, this representation playfully lampoons *Supernatural*'s own fans and conventions. Further examples of this subversion originate from the angel Castiel and moments where *Supernatural* playfully mocks his misunderstanding of the brothers preferred aliases. In "Stairway to Heaven" (9. 22) Castiel refers to Sam and Dean as his FBI partners Agents Spears and Aguilera, while in a later episode "The Foundry" (12.3) where Castiel is working a case with the King of Hell, he uses the aliases Agents Beyoncé and Z. In these scenes, dramatic irony contributes to the subversion of this trope as the viewer gets the joke while Castiel remains comically unaware.

    Other shows have differentiated themselves from earlier procedurals while still observing the genre's preoccupation with authenticity and realism (Von Mueller, 104). For example, the *CSI* franchise distinguishes itself through a focus on forensic methods and its distinct visual style while still privileging realism. However, as *Supernatural*'s subversion of the playing detective trope demonstrates, the show exploits the playfulness of the Gothic to transgress and interrogate the boundaries of reality and fiction. This is epitomized in "Changing Channels" (5.8): trapped in TV land by a supposed trickster (later revealed to be the archangel Gabriel), Sam and Dean are transported from show to show and must play the appropriate character roles to survive. This episode thus depicts and parodies distinct television genres including the medical drama (here, a show called Doctor Sexy), a Japanese game show, a sitcom, and a commercial for genital herpes medication. Demonstrating the show's generic hybridity, for example through the inclusion of Comedy throughout the episode, what makes this episode important to this discussion are the segments or "shows" that parody police procedurals, notably *CSI: Miami* and *Knight Rider*. *Supernatural*'s parody of *CSI: Miami* in particular is instantly recognizable by its heavily stylized visuals and editing, prominent crime scene markers, and the parodic performance of Lieutenant Horatio Caine. In fact, this segment includes not one but two parodic performances of Horatio. Dressed in a similar style to Horatio, Sam and Dean both take turns quipping over the victim's body ("Well I say, jackpot"; "Well I say, no guts, no glory") while comedically taking off and then putting on their sunglasses in a way that mimics and exaggerates his behavior. Yet, although this segment is clearly distinguishable from *Supernatural*, it is arguably the segment that most resembles *Supernatural*. Investigators in both shows wear business suit, physically investigate crime scenes, assess the bodies of victims, and question experts during their investigations. Furthermore, beyond this parodic segment the first three shows of the *CSI* franchise also share *Supernatural*'s anachronistic use of heavy metal and rock music: while *Supernatural* is most commonly associated with Kansas' "Carry On Wayward Son," each *CSI* show uses remixed versions of songs from The Who as their theme song. Similarly, as *Supernatural* incorporates music from Blue Öyster Cult, Black Sabbath, AC/DC, and Led Zeppelin into its soundtrack, the soundtrack of *CSI: Crime Scene Investigations* includes songs from Ozzy Osbourne, Rammstein, and Marilyn Manson. Considering the similarities between *Supernatural* and the *CSI* franchise, and *Supernatural*'s own identification as a police procedural, Dean's playful comments mocking procedurals and their formulaic conventions ("I hate procedurals") can be viewed not as criticism of the genre, but as a self conscious and playful joke at *Supernatural* itself.

While the *CSI* franchise, as with traditional procedurals, demonstrates a pursuit for realistic portrayals, these shows also reveal the tension surrounding claims to authenticity within this genre. "Living Legends" (*CSI*, 7.9) features lead singer of The Who Roger Daltrey as a guest star, and the episode is filled with references to the band; transgressing the boundaries of reality and fiction, these self-conscious references question the show's claims to authenticity through revealing its inherent fictionality. This franchise is also responsible for the "CSI effect" as it "engenders unrealistic expectations of forensic expertise" and thus affects the real world by contaminating jury pools (Arntfield, 90–1) Typically, however, where possible boundary transgression of reality/fiction and natural/supernatural are presented within the show, the narrative always conforms to the norms and conventions of realism. For example, in "Suckers" (*CSI*, 4.13) the team investigate the death of a girl involved in a vampire cult who has had all of the blood sucked from her body. Playing with vampire tropes, there is no expectation in the narrative world of *CSI* that vampires will be the perpetrators, and the episode remains firmly located in the natural world. In contrast, *Supernatural* encourages expectations that encompass the supernatural, and its season one episode "Dead Man's Blood" confirms the viewers' expectations raised by its title as it depicts vampires while also subverting established conventions of the vampire. However, whereas the resolution within traditional procedurals must adhere to the conventions of realism, the Gothic space of *Supernatural* allows the show to play with boundary transgressions and audience expectations. For example, in "The Benders" (1.15) Sam is abducted while the brothers are investigating mysterious disappearances, and Dean works with Sheriff Kathleen Hudak to find him and solve the case. Subverting viewer expectations, the monster/perpetrator is revealed to be not something supernatural, but instead simply a human cannibal family: "I'll be damned. They're just people." The horror depicted in this episode is accentuated not only because, unlike vampires, we know that cannibals exist in our world too, but also because the episode has questioned and redefined *Supernatural*'s established conventions and expectations. Introducing the possibility that the monsters/perpetrators hunted by the brothers may in fact be "just people," this therefore allows the suggestion within subsequent episodes.[5]

Within *Supernatural*, the usual suspects of the police procedural are subverted as the show plays with the conventions of the procedural and transgresses the boundaries of fiction and reality. Exposing the tension surrounding claims to authenticity with procedurals, *Supernatural* embraces its generic hybridity and exists as both a Gothic/horror show and police procedural. Creating a narrative world where the supernatural coexists alongside the natural, it is also a show where its main protagonists are characters who play detective while horror icon Linda Blair, best known for her role in *The Exorcist* (1973) guest stars on the show, emulating procedural shows by playing a detective herself. In an episode titled "The Usual Suspects" Linda Blair's character Detective Dianna Ballard is introduced to the supernatural by the Winchester brothers who help her to solve a case while being under arrest themselves. Subverting the expectations of the traditional procedural and those raised by Blair herself, the resolution of this mystery is both natural and supernatural, and involves not a demon or demonic possession but rather a ghostly death omen who tries to warns victims before they are murdered by Ballard's partner, the human Detective Sheridan. Enacting the "Consequences of Identification" phase, Ballard shoots Detective Sheridan and decides to let the brothers go free; the episode concluding with a reference to Blair's uncanny familiarity and, of course, pea soup. This episode thus typifies the ways in which *Supernatural* playfully engages with and subverts the boundaries of fiction and reality, the natural and supernatural. Merging a Gothic/horror narrative with the police procedural, *Supernatural* is a show where characters must know their roles and play their parts, while it also encourages and plays with the subversion and transgression of conventions, genres, and expectations.

Notes

1. Other notable examples that demonstrate the Gothic's relationship with play through its engagement with realism and authenticity include: James Hogg's *Confessions of a Justified Sinner* (1824) where the author inserts himself into his own narrative, and quotes from a genuine article he had published in *Blackwood's Magazine*; Paul Féval's *Vampire City* (1867), a novel that inserts the famous Gothic author Ann Radcliffe into the narrative as vampire hunter of sorts; horror films such as *The Blair Witch Project* (1999), *The Sixth Sense* 1999), and *Paranormal Activity* (2005); and, of course, countless horror games.

2. Unlike other TV shows, *Supernatural* does not use an elaborate title sequence, but instead features a title card that consists only of the show's title, 'Supernatural' with the text of the opening credits superimposed over the scenes that follow. The title card changes with each season, and several episodes have unique thematic titles cards or even title sequences such as "Changing Channels" (5.8).

3. The aliases reference the bands Bachman—Turner Overdrive, AC/DC, and Led Zeppelin.

4. The show's recurring metatextual narrative arc involves the "Supernatural" book series written by Carver Edlund where early episodes of the show have been written and published in a semi-popular series. Edlund is apparently a prophet of the Lord writing the Winchester Gospels, although he is later reveal to be God himself.

5. *Supernatural* returns to this trope in "Family Remains" (4.11) where the brothers assume they are hunting a ghost, but it eventually turns out to be a girl and her brother living in the walls of a house.

Works Cited

Arntfield, Michael. "TVPD: The Generational Diegetics of the Police Procedural on American Television." *Canadian Review of American Studies*, vol.41, no. 1, 2011, pp. 75–95.
Beeler, Stan. "Two Greasers and a Muscle Car: Music and Character Development in *Supernatural*." *TV Goes to Hell: An Unofficial Road Map of Supernatural*, edited by Abbott, Stacey and Lavery, David, ECW Press, 2011, pp. 18–30.
"The Benders." *Supernatural: The Complete First Season*, created by Eric Kripke, season one, episode one, Warner Bros., 2017.
Bucker, Brad. Audio Commentary. "Family Feud." *Supernatural: The Complete Thirteenth Season* created by Eric Kripke, Season twelve, episode thirteen, DVD extra, Warner Bros., 2017.
"Changing Channels." *Supernatural: The Complete Fifth Season*, created by Eric Kripke, season five, episode eight, Warner Bros., 2017
Davis, J. Madison. "He Do the Police in Different Voice: The Rise of the Police Procedural." *International Crime and Mystery*, vol. 9, 2012, pp. 9–11.
Edmundson, Melissa, ed. *The Gothic Tradition in* Supernatural. McFarland, 2016.
"The Foundry" *Supernatural: The Complete Twelfth Season*, created by Eric Kripke, season twelve, episode three, Warner Bros., 2017.
Harriss, Chandler. "Policing Propp: Toward a Textualist Definition of the Procedural Drama." *Journal of Film and Video*, vol. 60, no. 1, 2008, pp. 43–59.
"Heart." *Supernatural: The Complete Second Season*, created by Eric Kripke, season two, episode seventeen, Warner Bros., 2017.
"Hell House." *Supernatural: The Complete First Season*, created by Eric Kripke, season one, episode seventeen, Warner Bros., 2017.
Hogle, Jerrold E. "Introduction." *The Cambridge Companion to Gothic Fiction*, edited by Jerrold E. Hogle, Cambridge UP, 2006, pp. 1–20.
Landrum, Larry. "Instrumental Texts and Stereotyping in *Hill Street Blues*: The Police Procedural on Television." *MELUS*, vol. 11, no. 3, 1984, pp. 93–100.
"Pilot." *Supernatural: The Complete First Season*, created by Eric Kripke, season one, episode one, Warner Bros., 2017.
Primasita, Fitria Akhmerti, and Ahimsa-Putra, Heddy Shri. "An Introduction to the Police Procedural: A Subgenre of the Detective Genre." *Humaniora*, vol. 31, no. 1, 2019, pp. 33–40.

"The Real Ghostbusters." *Supernatural: The Complete Fifth Season*, created by Eric Kripke, season five, episode nine, Warner Bros., 2017.

"Something Wicked." *Supernatural: The Complete First Season*, created by Eric Kripke, season one, episode eighteen, Warner Bros., 2017.

"Stairway to Heaven." *Supernatural: The Complete Ninth Season*, created by Eric Kripke, season nine, episode twenty two, Warner Bros., 2017.

"Supernatural: Tales from the Edge of the Darkness." *Supernatural: The Complete First Season*, created by Eric Kripke. DVD extra. Warner Bros., 2017.

Taylor, Laurie N. "Gothic Bloodlines in Survival Horror Gaming." *Horror and Video Games: Essays on the Fusion of Fear and Play*, edited by Bernard Perron, McFarland, 2009, pp. 46–61.

@therealKripke. "In honor of #SPN300, here's my original #SPN pitch from 2004. The pilot story is very different, but the tone always rang clear to me. could never have imagined what this show became and the good it's done. Humbled and grateful beyond words to you all. #SPNFamily @CW_SPN." *Twitter*, 7 February 2019, 6:08 p.m., https://twitter.com/therealKripke/status/1093557218346061824.

"The Usual Suspects" *Supernatural: The Complete Second Season*, created by Eric Kripke, season two, episode seven, Warner Bros., 2017.

Von Mueller, Eddy. "The Police Procedural in Literature and on Television." *The Cambridge Companion to American Crime Fiction*, edited by Nickerson, Catherine Ross, Cambridge UP, 2010, pp. 96–109.

Walpole, Horace. "Preface to the Second Edition" *The Castle of Otranto*, edited by E.J. Clery, Oxford UP, 2008, pp. 9–14.

Evil Is a Metaphysical Condition
Undead Melodrama, AIDS and the Crime Procedural

Teresa Cutler-Broyles

The supernatural crime series *Forever Knight* ran on CBS and the USA Network in the United States[1] for 70 episodes over three seasons from 1992 to 1996, showcasing Nicolas de Brabant (Geraint Wyn Davies), a nearly 800-year-old vampire trying to find his way back to humanity. Guilt-ridden after centuries of killing innocent mortals, de Brabant roams the night-time streets of Toronto, Canada, as Nicolas Knight, an undercover police detective who uses his supernatural abilities to hunt down murderers, the embodiment of a purely human form of evil, in pursuit of his own redemption. Knight's inhuman desires for blood and his lust for the sensual in all things are represented as effectively identical, and are almost insatiable. He fights these as he would any dangerous foe. Played out in unerring, perhaps unintentional camp against a backdrop of unabashed melodrama, his righteous crime-fighting endeavors force him to face the darkness he knows still exists within him when he uses his supernatural abilities and his friendship with other vampires to find the criminals he seeks. Shown through flashbacks in every episode, his troubled past becomes entwined with his present to offer him insights into the minds of his foes while bringing to the fore for viewers his deep self-inflicted torment, and torturous inner turmoil.

This show's entry into the vampire TV canon came relatively early in what has become a vast cornucopia of undead on screen in various pursuits over the years and across the globe. From Germany and Denmark to Japan and the Philippines, from Israel and India to Italy and the UK, and from Brazil to Canada and many places in between, television vampires have been stalking their victims and insinuating themselves into our homes and hearts since the early 1960s. Much work[2] has been done on the particular allure vampires have, and their sensuality and appeal despite the inherent danger of falling for their dark designs, and many of the more than forty TV shows[3] with vampires as main or supporting characters have capitalized on that appeal, using it to draw viewers and drive plots. Perhaps the epitome of the tall, dark and handsome figure, to say nothing of being the ultimate bad boy, vampires have in some ways become de rigueur in the 21st century.

But, in 1992 when *Forever Knight* hit the airwaves, vampire TV was still a relatively new field, with many of its vampires' characteristics still to be formalized. While virtually all the time-tested vampire tropes are adhered to meticulously, this was the first show to meld the detective and vampire genres and introduce to the viewing world a literal vampire detective. As horror it misses the mark, too self-consciously invested in questions of morality and a search for atonement, as well as being too campy[4] to be frightening.

The television crime procedural had been around for nearly 40 years by this time. On the surface, adding a vampire wouldn't necessarily require adjustments to the way crime procedurals worked, and the show indeed adheres to the tropes that had been established for decades. In one area, though, it took full advantage of an important limit imposed on it by the inclusion of these supernatural creatures—their inability to tolerate sunlight. Because its main character can only be at large between sunset and sunrise, it was perhaps inevitable that *Forever Knight* was steeped in both the mise-en-scene and thematic elements of film noir.

Film noir, literally "dark film" was an American film style of the 1940s and '50s[5] whose movies were heavy on symbolism and shared a common set of themes, stock characters, a specific setting, and a particular look and acting style. And never, ever a happy ending. They typically starred a hardened detective[6] with a dark and mysterious past, often wearing a trench coat and a hat as a kind of uniform. Two other stock characters were the mysterious, morally questionable dark-haired woman or *femme fatale* who threatened to lead him astray, and the pure-of-heart lighter-haired good girl. The detective's loyalties were torn between the two, making them emblematic of the two sides of himself that were always in tension. This tension, and the typically dark themes of murder, betrayal and corruption were mirrored in the mise-en-scene. Its low-key lighting created deep shadows that often half-covered the detective's face—signifying his dual nature—and provided hiding places for unsavory criminals and their dark deeds. Grimy city streets are always the backdrop and sometimes squarely centered in the films' stories, functioning as setting and metaphor, and most often the acting is melodramatic with fast-paced dialogue and witty repartee.

Forever Knight took these elements to their logical conclusion when it made its main character a detective who is literally a creature of the night. He lives in the shadows because he has no choice, and the murderers he pursues are firmly rooted there as well. The city is both setting and character; it's impossible to imagine the stories taking place anywhere else. The two women who feature in his day-to-day—or really night-to-night—existence are the epitome of the femme fatale and the good girl. Janette DuCharme (Deborah Duchêne) is a dark-haired vampire, overtly sensual, a former and sometime lover (and sister, but we'll come back to that) who openly and often tries to tempt him back to the dark side, to abandoning his quest for his lost humanity. Natalie Lambert (Catherine Disher) is blonde, wholesome, a scientist, and urges him in every episode to continue his search for his own humanity and his quest for mortality The dialogue between Knight and his male partner, Don Schanke (John Kapelos) echoes back to that between any detective and his sidekick in classic film noir films. And finally, dressing Knight in a trench coat as they did for much of the show was not simply a nod to the film noir style but a full-on catapulting into it. Basically, with its thematic angst, a conflicted hero with a criminal past and a drinking problem, heavily shadowed urban, nighttime settings, a heavy music soundtrack, the pure good girl/friend and the bad ex-girlfriend, and an overkill of dark sexuality suffused with elements of mystery, danger, and BDSM, *Forever Knight* is the perfect vehicle for addressing important social and cultural issues of the late 20th century.

In addition to vampires allowing for, or really demanding, the interplay with film noir elements, they also almost necessitated adding two other characteristics often seen in film, melodrama, and camp. When utilized properly as they were for many of the *Forever Knight*'s episodes, the interplay of these two elements enabled the show to take the subject matter from potentially banal or ridiculous to important and sometimes sublime.

In its purest form melodrama is a highly exaggerated form of acting that accompanies heart-wrenching plots meant to highlight often devastating events, and is meant to appeal to emotion; it was also an important element of Film Noir, unlike camp. Camp, as defined by Susan Sontag in "Notes on 'Camp'" is many things. As the first theorist to try to explain this phenomenon, Sontag spends 17 pages circling the concept, ultimately arriving at this: at its core camp is artifice and exaggeration, a certain aesthetic of what could be considered bad taste, and it is melodramatic and absurd. It is an intentional exaggeration of thematic elements, visual components, or acting, often taking the form of affected, theatrical, overly effeminate or hypermasculine behavior. Some of the relevant references Sontag makes are to Gothic literature, dandyism, drag queens, and film noir. As she notes, it "converts the serious into the frivolous," and, in so doing, allows for quite serious subjects to be brought to the fore.

This quality ultimately offers us a way into considering how this particular detective crime procedural is far more than it first appears. It is in fact a work that delves deeply into issues of identity and loss of self, good and evil, free will and fate, the existence of God, faith as a state of being, the moral dimensions of illness, questions of choice about how and who we love, and the dire consequences of loving the wrong person. And it does all this while balancing, generally successfully, overblown hyperbolic characters and stories, and campy melodrama that hides a far more serious issue.

From the first episode, it is made clear to viewers that Knight believes he is the embodiment of pure evil. That he is damned in a very real sense. And while the presence, confrontation, even questioning of evil are de rigueur in any story that includes vampires, creatures as they are who must kill in order to survive, *Forever Knight* takes this to the next level. Evil becomes not just a factor in the *creation* of vampires or the method of their finding sustenance, but an underpinning of their identity, an unquestioned reality of their existence. Its opposite, goodness or ultimately God, is unquestioningly present as well, all integral elements of each episode. Ultimately the show does not shy away from asking, and attempting to answer, just what the nature of true evil is; this question defines the series from the beginning, thematically wrapped into each episode via Knight's unending angst. As we learn from the flashbacks that are part of each show, he is the perfect person to both embody and ask these questions about God, about the condition of mortality and the existence of a soul, about the nature of identity and desires of the flesh: In 1228 at the time of his being brought across,[7] or turned into a vampire, he was a knight in service to his Lord, on a crusade to the Holy Land. A number of episodes in Season One deal directly with questions of faith and allow viewers to ask their own questions about the nature of evil and the possibility of redemption. This sets the stage for the possibility of his failure to achieve it.

All of this is compounded by the inclusion in the show of an unapologetic, powerful sexuality. While virtually all vampires from the 18th century onward exhibit sexuality as *part* of their nature, *Forever Knight* revels in representing its vampires as wholly sensual, sexual creatures. This conflation of vampires and sexuality is of course not new, but *Forever Knight* makes another important, explicit connection. From the first episode vampirism is intimately entwined with an overt, *dark* sexuality that contains deviant[8] sexual themes including not a few BDSM elements in the vampires' clothing, behavior, and language. In addition, and to ensure that the viewer does not miss the point that vampires and evil, and that sexuality and deviance and darkness go together, there is an intense sensual relationship between the three main vampires, Nicholas, Janette, and Lucien LaCroix (Nigel Bennett) that adds another element to the mix. LaCroix, an ancient vampire, is the one who turned each of them, making him their Master and making them his "children" in the parlance of the show, thereby turning Knight and Janette's relationship as lovers into a form of incest.[9] While the theme of incest does not factor overtly into the show until the penultimate episode of the series, it exists strongly as an unspoken underpinning throughout, one of the ways the show's sensuality is made to be both alluring and terrifying, compelling and off-putting. Even uncanny.

In their interactions with humans, their sensual selves come most strongly to the fore in their feeding. As they take a human for his or her blood, they experience what for all intents and purposes is an orgasm. Janette and LaCroix, in effect daughter and father, hunted humans together for centuries before she seduced Knight with the intention of bringing him back for LaCroix to feed on, to turn into a vampire or "bring across," making Knight his symbolic son. This element of sexual predation continues after he is brought across. Knight and Janette continue to be lovers, hunting and feeding together as a couple, finding beautiful, mortal women they both want; Knight feeds on their warm blood, killing them while indulging in the pleasures he desires. The sexual aspect of the hunt and the killing are emphasized when Janette urges him to "take them." LaCroix and Knight often travel together and find delectable, always young and desirable young men or women whom LaCroix urges Knight to take while he watches avidly.

LaCroix and Knight speak often in sensually loaded language to each other about the pleasures of the flesh, particularly the pleasures of *feeding* on the flesh. About the tastes and the smells and the physical sensations it evokes. Their wordplay is a kind of dark seduction, an entendre-laden banter just this side of actual coupling.

All this is possible because, unlike many vampires before and since, Knight and his ilk are able to consummate their desires[10] and have sex with humans as long as they're careful not to become too aroused. This is difficult for them; they tend to "take too much,"[11] and need to learn how not to kill their lovers, to be intimate, in other words, without causing death.

The connections between sex and death extend farther, both implicitly and explicitly. In *Forever Knight*'s Toronto, most of the murders that

Knight and his partner(s) investigate are related to sex as well. As any crime procedural should, each show begins with a death and the arrival of detectives Knight and his partner. Each of these deaths is connected in one way or another to sex workers, sexual escapades, and/or sexualized women, or they happen in sexualized locations. This is not new; sex and violence have been connected and conflated in film and TV for decades.[12] But here it is blatant as the show goes overboard to make sex and deviance and darkness and unnatural desires co-complicit. The connotations are clear: wanton sexuality and a penchant for murder are intimately entwined. Death a consequence of sex.

What makes it important in this case is that here it is represented in ways that would have spoken to a late 20th-century audience in poignant and pointed ways. In utilizing vampires and their inherent darkness and moral depravity, and adding or exaggerating the connection between their feeding *on blood* and the sexual act—and simultaneously inserting elements of forbidden desires and sexualities—the show offers up particularly dark kind of sex, one that is uncontrolled, deviant, depraved. And so it is that these disparate elements—the crime procedural, vampires and blood, sexuality, melodrama, camp, darkness in theme and subject matter, the unquestioned existence of true good and evil, and God—that gave this show its power made it a perfectly suited venue through which to discuss one of the most culturally important issues of the 1990s—the AIDS crisis.

It is important to note here that the show's creators may or may not have had AIDS and its devastating presence in mind at the outset or even as they produced the 70 episodes that made up the series (though I would argue that they must have). In film studies parlance, their intent is unimportant. Film scholars have debated a text's (film or TV show's) meaning and authorial (filmmaker's) intent for as long as celluloid has been used to tell stories, vacillating between early on locating meaning in the creator of the text, to eventually locating it in the audience's perceptions. In much film scholarship,[13] meaning has recently been located in the audience with, the argument goes, their perceptions mattering more than the intent of the author. According to Stuart Hall[14] and others, audiences interpret media texts in particular ways that are in large part context- and culturally dependent and grounded in subject-position, often regardless of what an author meant when they wrote or created the text itself. In essence, this idea goes, there are three ways to read a text: the preferred, the negotiated, and the oppositional.[15] The preferred reading is defined as the one most likely to coincide with what an author intended, and is based in understanding cues and representations that reside within the normative culture surrounding the time period of the text's creation. The negotiated and the oppositional interpretations depend as much on an understanding of those cultural norms, but bring the audience's subject positions more into play; a negotiated reading might accept some of those norms but is filtered more through the audience members unique way of interpreting the world, and an oppositional reading understands the preferred reading but rejects it outright.

All of these, as noted, depend on an awareness of, a lived-in-ness, of the culture surrounding the text's creation. For a late 20th-century audience living in a world in which AIDS was the number one cause of death for males aged 25–44, where Freddie Mercury had recently, publicly died from the disease and Magic Johnson had announced his positive status, where the stigma attached to it was still huge, and no one in power was talking about it, a show about vampires—virtually synonymous with blood and death—and deviant sexuality would certainly draw parallels.[16]

And it wasn't just vampires who signaled the underlying meaning. Nearly every episode includes either a discussion or a visual representation of same-sex desire, the overwhelming power of lust and desire, and/or the exchange of bodily fluids. And while AIDS itself is never mentioned by name in the show, references are made as early as the second episode[17] to a disease that is spread by biting, and by an exchange of blood. Vampires and AIDS wrapped into one neat package.

Gay Vampires

Forever Knight was not the first time vampires had been connected to either same-sex desire or the AIDS crisis, of course. Richard Dyer, noted film theorist, explores this connection in some detail and finds indications of the vampire being a recurring metaphor for same-sex desire for more than a century.[18] Bram Stoker himself, the father of today's modern vampire in his novel *Dracula*[19] was, according to a number of scholars, a closeted gay man; his vampire's subtext indicates that Dracula may have been as well. Dracula's dark, hidden, and forbidden desire for blood and his claiming of Jonathan Harker—"This man belongs to me!" he tells the female vampires—were nothing less than coded language and action, effectively an exploration of homoeroticism in a society in which being gay was often punished by prison or hard labor.

This tradition runs through depictions of vampires to the 20th- and 21st centuries, until recently[20] most famously in Anne Rice's *Vampire*

Chronicles series. As George Haggerty notes, Rice's vampires are easily read through the lens of same-sex desire. While he references earlier vampires and posits that "vampires [perhaps] have almost naturalized homoerotic origins," his point that Rice's vampires are homoerotic "for reasons that tell us more about their moment of creation than they tell us about any historical precedents"[21] is an important one. Vampires, and indeed all cultural artifacts, are the products of the times in which they are created, and they change accordingly as needed by the society in which they (re)appear. Their utility and their continued relevance is due not to their unchanging nature but to the uses to which that nature can be put at the moment of their reappearance. *Interview with the Vampire*, Rice's first foray into the vampiric supernatural, was published in 1977, twenty years before *Forever Knight* appeared, and long before AIDS became a societal and political issue (quagmire). As such its vampires speak to slightly different concerns; Haggerty suggests that they in fact "express our culture's secret desire for and secret fear of the gay man; the need to fly with him beyond the confines of heterosexual convention and bourgeois family life to an exploration of unauthorized desires, and at the same time to taste his body and his blood; to see him bleed and watch him succumb to death-in-life" (6). And in a nod to both Sigmund Freud and Rene Girard's monstrous double, Haggerty later suggests that "[t]he vampire represents the return of the repressed in a culturally significant way" and "the vampire represents everything that the culture desires and everything that it fears" (9).

While this essay will not unpack all the meanings free-floating in those statements, what is easily discerned is that vampires and homoerotic desires are comfortable bedfellows, and that vampires have significance and import that is far-reaching and powerful. They signify in important ways, and their messages must be deciphered if their presence is to matter.

Nicolas Knight is a paragon of both good and evil. He struggles with his innate nature, wanting desperately to overcome his dark, compelling, uncontrollable desires—offered to viewers in the visual and verbal languages of sexual passion, addiction and alcoholism. As a vampire he is multivalent, able to represent not just desire and sexuality but *same-sex* desire. Each episode is heavy-handed in moral messages, and ethical questions abound. As an alcoholic might, as a gay man who is trying to deny his nature, Knight fights against all things that might lead him down the damned path. His fear that he cannot overcome his inner nature, and the struggle he is always engaged in against it, echo prevailing cultural fears.

I Am What I Am: Episode One

The first episode of the series, "Dark Knight," is a compendium of everything we need to know about Nicolas Knight and the struggles he will face throughout three seasons of being Toronto's nighttime vampire detective. Living in the shadows and hunting in darkness are characteristic of both the murderers he pursues and vampires, setting up from the very beginning the entwinement of the two.

Adhering closely to both vampire and detective show tropes, augmented by the deployment of elements of film noir, camp and melodrama, the episode highlights Knight's dark side by default as it reveals the bases upon which the entire series will be built. We learn of Knight's vampiric birth via being brought over by LeCroix in 1228, and his current desire to be human and make amends for centuries of death and destruction he has wrought; we witness his existential angst at his undead state and hear about his sensitivity to light; we witness what will soon become familiar melancholic stares into space as he sits at home at his piano, alone in his loft apartment contemplating the wine bottle full of blood he dare not drink; we are introduced to The Raven, the nightclub run by his ex, Janette, and witness their openly sensual, familiar relationship; we learn that The Raven is a haven for lost souls, among them vampires who drink blood from wine glasses and other creatures of the night, namely and importantly prostitutes, again reinforcing the show's thematic interconnectivity. We meet Janette's antithesis, Knight's platonic friend Natalie Lambert, Toronto's finest coroner and the only human who knows who and what he really is; and we watch as Knight uses his supernatural powers to solve crimes.

Simultaneously, he is in constant metaphysical pain as he battles his inner demons. He seems to move no closer to being human as the season progresses—he still drinks blood (albeit not human) and Janette continually derides him for his attempts at moral and ethical goodness—and nothing is resolved by the end of the first season. In the last episode we watch a flashback in which Knight and LaCroix discuss a young woman Knight has become obsessed with. LaCroix tells him "Consummate your intense love for her in the most intense way. Take her. Kill her." Knight does, only to realize he has destroyed the purity he so desired in her. Metaphor at its most obvious: giving in to desire is akin to murder. Unnatural desire equals death. Not a large leap to what "the culture desires and everything that it fears."[22]

Season Two opens with LaCroix's return from the dead[23] as a radio host, adding perhaps the last element to the film noir characteristics: the voiceover or narrator. Because he and Knight ended on bad terms, they don't speak to each other anymore so LaCroix uses his radio show for the duration of the series to speak to Knight at night as he drives around the city contemplating his undead existence. LaCroix's voice functions as a mirror into which Knight must look if he hopes to find himself, and offers life lessons in the form of almost koanlike questions to ponder about the nature of life, the close proximity of death, and the moral dimensions of good and evil.

Again the season flirts with answering Knight's desire to be human, but balances it always with his struggle to hold on to himself; when one's life is defined by the concept of evil, moving in any other direction means a negation of one's self. This makes for a relatively difficult choice: choosing the light means losing who he is—perhaps losing his life. This theme is picked up in Season Three.

The Coming of the End

The third season continues apace. It loses its way somewhere in the middle, but returns with a vengeance to the themes that made it so much more than the cheesy melodrama it could have been. The third to last and the penultimate episode are rife with the themes of dark, forbidden desires of various sorts, characters carefully coded as gay, open homosexual desire expressed by a possessed cross-dresser, Knight capitulating to desires he cannot any longer deny, and an attempt by a young girl to seduce her father.

But first we must deal with Janette. Through the first two seasons Janette is the anti–Natalie, a woman unashamed of her dark desires with a propensity to scoff at Knight's attempts to become human. Throughout she has pressured him to give in to his inner nature, his darkness, and become once again the creature of the night she is. However, despite her constant derision of Knight's search for humanity she falls in love with a mortal and chooses to become human herself in "The Human Factor," about two-thirds of the way through the last season. She accomplishes this feat through the true, pure love of a man; during multiple sex acts she took (from) him a tiny taste of blood, letting it infuse her with tiny doses of his goodness, theoretically inoculating her against all dark desires and redeeming all her past actions. All should have been well, but instead she dies. This deserves a bit of unpacking.

The message throughout the show to this point has been: unnatural desires are morally deplorable, a death sentence. Janette's sins should have been forgiven and she should have lived a long and healthy life once she chose to leave her morally corrupt world and become human. But instead of being satisfied with her mortality and her vanilla world which included dressing in bland, nondescript clothing (a far cry from her vampire attire of black lace and leather), she decides she must avenge her lover's killer. Without her inner core and the strength that came with being true to her darker self, she is easily overpowered and killed.

Ultimately Janette was "cured" of her deviance by straight, heterosexual sex. In the process, though, she became something that was not in accordance with her innate self. And she died as a result. The message seems clear. As representative of a particular subculture, vampires offer this warning: to let society's values and judgments about love and the right way to do it change your behavior is just as sure a way to death as any other.[24]

After Janette's death the show lost its way for a while and, for a few episodes, was merely a detective show, and a bad one at that. Without emphasis on the vampiric elements and the deeper themes of dark sexuality and desire, the camp and melodrama overrode the stories and foregrounded the artifice that was otherwise in service to the deeper messages. Then, as if suddenly realizing the end was nigh, the last three episodes of the series came into their own. Each of them coalesced and concentrated the overarching themes of good and evil, sexuality and identity, the nature of faith and of God, and the connection between death and desire that the show had begun with and so intricately wove together throughout.

The last three sections will examine those last episodes for the purposes of driving home the connection between sex, unnatural desire, vampires, AIDS and death. I will discuss them in the order in which they appeared, in which incest and filicide are given a higher billing than homosexual desire in a ranking of deviance. Yet, as a buildup to the end these three episodes each draw power from the themes that have swirled within them, building on the depravity of the episode before to drive home the point that if it isn't normative, desire is equally morally reprehensible. Conflating homosexual desire with cross dressing killers, and allowing daughters to desire fathers in incestuous relationships puts them all on a par. Evil is evil. And death the only way out.

"Francesca"

The episode that deals most fully and dramatically with the concept of homosexual desire and its connection to vampires and death is "Francesca," third from the last. This show features a cross-dressing man and his explicit recounting of having a male lover, and a female therapist coded as gay. It is the only episode in which the word gay (or homosexual) is used and that only to immediately refute the idea that the character is indeed that.

Francesca (Catherine Winters) is a vampire from Knight's past who possesses a man, Frank (Maurice Dean Wint), in the present. The show opens with two parallel vignettes playing out, past and present. A scene featuring a woman we later learn is Francesca is intercut with another, exceptionally strong woman we learn is a man in drag. In both timelines, the woman kills a man by stabbing him in his heart. In the past, Francesca drinks his blood from a chalice; in the present, the other woman holds a knife to her victim's throat, and then they both lean over and leave a lipsticked kiss on their respective dead man's forehead.

After the credits, we fade in to a slow-motion scene of Francesca making love to Knight in the past, with another man's voice overlying it. Until now, the narrator of each episode has been LaCroix; this one is different. This scene is intercut with a therapist's office in which a man in the present is recounting the scenario from the past. It is his dream, and Francesca and Knight's lived experience, both violent and passionate, and quite sexually explicit. The terminology Frank uses is graphically sexual as well. This is a marked divergence from most of the series. While the drinking of blood—the taking of humans—has always been presented as explicitly sexual through the entire show, not just drunk for food but for pleasure and for the thrill, and while the homoerotic undertones of vampires have been utilized as well, when Frank describes the act of sex in his dream it includes the drinking of blood as part and parcel, and makes the connection explicit. Frank's dream of being Francesca is vivid, the memory of sex and blood is relentless, and Frank's voice relating the whole thing weaves the disparate threads together and leaves no room for doubt about what the entire series has told us: Deviance is intricately wound up in the kind of sex in which blood and death are interchangeable; and death is inevitable.

> **FRANK, AS FRANCESCA:** The first sip is like explosion. We taste everything. I know his dreams, his fears, his loves. I can feel myself against him. Taste my own blood returning through his. He's younger than me. A crusader turned away from the light. I can taste the sands of Jerusalem in his veins. Sweet with his hunger for me. I die a hundred times in his arms. He dies in mine. He dies in mine....[25]

Frank has no idea of the content of his therapy sessions nor a memory of saying this. He knows only that he is theoretically reliving past life memories. While Knight and his partner Tracey (a woman who replaced his first partner who was killed in a plane crash at the end of Season One)

(Lisa Ryder) investigate the mysterious murder of the man we saw at the beginning and the draining of his blood, flashbacks to Knight's past fill in the blanks.

Sometime in the late 17th century, LaCroix and Knight arrive at the home of the lovely Countess Francesca du Montaigne, where LaCroix introduces them to each other as brother and sister; he is the connection, having brought them both over to the vampire realm. Incest of the vampire kind is hereby invoked, and adds to the discomfort viewers feel throughout the episode. Immediately attracted to each other, the two of them verbally spar for the evening and soon eagerly engage in the edgy, nearly violent sexual episode described above. As a kind of nightcap, Francesca hands Knight a chalice that he drinks from. Immediately he realizes it is the blood of the young violinist who had played for them at dinner and whose proficiency and future he had lauded. He is horrified, disgusted with the way Francesca wantonly kills. That is the last of their liaison.

In the present, Knight explains to Natalie just what the drinking of blood entails:

> **KNIGHT:** You have to understand that every drop of blood has your wholeife in it. It's not just our food. It's the way we feel life. Imagine if you could know someone's soul just by sharing their blood. Everything you know, everything you are, transformed into touch and taste. Imagine the temptation to take just one sip. One sip, and then another, and another. To take them inside you and know every secret. To let them know yours. To be them. That's why it's such a tough habit to break.[26]

Couched as an addiction that has at its base the essence of evil that Knight has been fighting since the series began, this describes penetrative sex. A habit he is trying to break; a desire he wishes he did not have. Echoes of repressed sexuality are not just hinted at, they are spelled out by the therapist, Lisa Kadlec (Brooke Johnson) later in the episode as she explains Frank's cross dressing and his murdering of women in a pseudo-scientific psychological psychobabble. Explaining Frank's impulses in sexually deviant—i.e., homosexual urges—terms, she says:

> **LISA KADLEC:** He ... sublimated his hunger for sexual attention into this vampire fantasy, complete with mysterious lover, the dark and dangerous Nicholas Chevalier. Francesca du Montaigne is a manifestation of his desire projected onto another facet of his personality that he could feel separate from. She was a way of controlling his own impulses.
>
> The vampire fantasy is a ... is an archetype that's deeply embedded in our collective unconscious. It stems from ... *the sublimation of sexual desire.* The deeper the frustration, the greater the desire. And in creating Francesca, Frank created a persona who had the freedom that he's never had, a sexual freedom[27] [Emphasis mine].

Moments later, she tells Knight and Tracey, "I've been treating Frank for gender confusion, for issues of sexuality and identity, not for violent tendencies." It's too late, though; for viewers, the connection is not just already made but indelible. Gender confusion and violence go hand in hand and there is no way out. And just like that, the episode fully embraces the deeply troubling, damaging stereotype of the confused gay man who sublimates his desire and represses it to the point of violent, deadly explosions of violence. Even Natalie, earlier in the episode, speculates that the killer is sexually repressed. Ultimately the message to viewers is that sublimated, non-normative desires are dangerous. Accept them or you'll die; accept them *and* you'll die. Either way, the world will be well rid of what infects it: a blood-borne disease spread by unnatural desire.

Or will it? That has been Knight's belief for all sixty eight episodes so far, and the 1990s audience nods in agreement; vampires are manifestations of repressed sexuality, vampires are evil, and that which they represent— deviant sexuality, i.e., homosexuality—continually rises.

The episode concludes as Knight kills Frank who, dressed as Francesca, has kidnapped his therapist, but not before Frank asks her, in a strange tossed-off comment, "What do you taste like, Doctor." It is as if the writers had to make a quick stab at reasserting some facsimile of socially constructed normalcy into what until this point has been an unrelenting foray into decidedly non-normative events. Too little too late. Vampires again have served their purpose for us as a way to discuss otherwise unacceptable subjects, and come to truly horrific conclusions. When Knight swoops in and effectively eviscerates Frank, and Francesca, with iron spikes we learn the lesson: Death is the only way to escape unnatural desire. The world is right(ed) again.

But not for long. Vampires, as it turns out, are vehicles for not only repressed same-sex desire but even more sinister yearnings. Deviance in the form of homosexuality having been dispensed with for the moment, the series leaps with abandon into something far darker, incest, in the penultimate episode, "Ashes to Ashes."

"Ashes to Ashes"

This episode starts with a grave robber breaking into a sarcophagus in search of treasure. When he breaks the seal, he is immediately decapitated by the as-yet unseen spirit of the 2000-year-old girl who had been imprisoned within it. Days later in Toronto, LaCroix enters The Raven[28] and in the process of organizing it for another evening of patrons he finds a headless corpse in his beer fridge. Knight and other detectives arrive, having been tipped to the corpse's presence by an anonymous call. The corpse is identified as that of the grave robber and a nearby box contains his head. A necklace in the box identifies the killer for LaCroix but he does not yet reveal that she is his long-dead daughter, Divia (Kathryn Long).

Over the course of the episode in a series of flashbacks as LaCroix tells Knight his deepest, darkest secret, we learn that 2000 years ago in Pompeii, when LaCroix himself was still mortal, Divia had been turned by an ancient vampire who she subsequently killed. Later, as Mount Vesuvius erupts, Divia turns LaCroix into a vampire to save his life, effectively becoming both his daughter and (vampire) mother. Once LaCroix is undead, he laments the murder of Divia's master—who would, he believes, have been able to impart to them a wealth of knowledge of their kind—and she defends her actions. "[He] thought he controlled me. He said he brought me across because I was young and my evil was as pure as he had ever seen. But then he tried to harness it, to make me in his image.[29] That could not be. I would choose my own way. I did what I had to do to ensure that."

This sets the stage for what LaCroix does next in that it sets up this young girl—likely fourteen or so years old—as truly evil. Not only a vampire, not only one who kills wantonly, but worse than others, more evil than anyone. Divia continues, in more explicit dialogue than any of the earlier episodes, barring "Francesca." She tells her father:

> **DIVIA:** I want us both to experience everything that our nature offers without restriction. To kill as often as we desire. Bathe in mortal flesh and blood. To do everything that is forbidden.... Everything we lust after can be ours. Including love. Let us do what must not be done. Make love to me, Father.[30]

Their inherent nature as vampires is equated with killing, bathing in blood, lusting after the forbidden, and love—of a forbidden, taboo kind. LaCroix's refuses, perhaps redeeming him a bit in viewers' eyes—he's been a huge source of angst for Knight, and us, since the beginning of the series in his refusal to believe that Knight's search for mortality and humanity is either possible or right. "You are my daughter," he says, horrified. "Daughter, mother, lover," she answers. "Why can't I be all three? Come. Touch me." No same-sex desire here, she slips right past that and tries to seduce her own father. This in turn makes explicit an intriguing hierarchy within the parlance of the show itself and allows for a simultaneous exposure and erasure of the incestuous undertone that has underlain the entire series: Same-sex desire may be bad, but incest is worse. And really, it doesn't matter in the end because they are both deviant and need to be expunged.

LaCroix kills her by beheading her with a scythe—filicide the only possible solution—and puts her headless body in a handy sarcophagus. Two thousand years later in the episode's present, she has managed to regenerate and is on the hunt for all those whom her father loves. She goes after a number of the vampires that effectively make up his contingent, and finally attacks Knight and leaves him for dead. Satisfied that she has eradicated all those who had taken her place in his affections she goes after LaCroix himself at The Raven. She is preternaturally strong and tortures him physically as she tells him that she has killed Knight, his "son," He is incensed but unable to overpower her. Just before she is about to strike off his head, she is impaled on a wooden spear. Knight, not dead after all, has killed her and saved their father in the process.

While this episode is unique in that it ventures away from the underlying homosexual undertones of the series for the most part,[31] it comes to the same conclusion. Vampires are evil. Filicide. Fratricide. Sororicide. Incest. Same-sex desire. Vampires embody them all. But can they be saved? When LaCroix burns Divia's body in the end, he says he will stay with her until she has returned to ashes and that he may even say a prayer. This from him is certainly a commentary on the show's other underlying concept—that of goodness, faith, humanity, and the presence of God. The hope is still that those things can overpower the evil that makes up a vampire's very nature.

This is, after all, the overarching conceit of the series and Knight's driving force. Forgiveness and redemption are what he seeks, what he has worked toward, killed for—ironically enough—and why he has resisted the nearly constant temptation to give in to his desires. It is what LaCroix has mocked him for, what Janette attempted to seduce him from,[32] and what Natalie has continually helped support him in. His entire vampire existence has been, in other words, a struggle between good and evil, and from the first he has believed he is beyond the very redemption he seeks. And yet, he never quite gets there.

For its late 20th-century audience the entire *Forever Knight* series[33] has only confirmed the idea that there is no turning back once a person has been taken across. With AIDS as an underlying fact of life and the death associated with it an existential cultural fear, a sexually active male vampire who "takes" both women and men through the exchange of blood in a deviant, violent, unnatural act is not far off from the idea of a gay man exposing his lovers to the possibility of infection; the line is crossed, blood—or body fluid—is exchanged, and death will likely follow. The final episode drives this point home.

"Last Night"

The episode begins with LaCroix discussing suicide, arguing against it with Christianity-laden verbiage.

> **LACROIX:** Life is a gift as sweet as a ripe peach, as precious as a gilded jewel. I have never been able to understand the logic of willfully surrendering such a treasure. And what is there to gain? How dark can your existence be when compared to an eternal void? Unless, of course, you have faith that there is something beyond. What do you see from where you stand? A bright light at the end of the tunnel? Is it a ray of hope? A glimmer of something better? Or will it burn you like the rising sun? Is that sound you're hearing the trumpeting of St. Peter's angels or the screams of Memnoch's tortured souls? You can't answer that, can you? Because you will never know the answer until after the deed is done. And is your faith really that strong?

The questions overlay a scene in which a woman slits her wrists in a bathtub. We learn that she was Natalie's friend, and her diary soon provides Natalie with both insight and desperation. She realizes that she is living a lonely sad existence. She confesses her love for Knight and asks that he bring her across so that they can be together. Effectively she puts herself in a position of sacrifice, willing to take the chance of death in order to have the love she craves. "I have faith in you and whatever follows" she tells him. Knight refuses Natalie's request, telling her he refuses to damn her into becoming what he is.

Though couched in heteronormative terms, her desire for Knight and her willingness to risk death to be with him can be read as analogous to the prevailing belief that gay men who willingly engaged in sex were rolling the dice each time. Sex came with inherent danger; infection was likely, blood the intermediary and the means, and death waited on the other side.

Through the course of the episode Knight loses his partner to the bullets of an escaped convict. In the throes of his grief and existential despair he goes to LaCroix—father figure, friend, sometime adversary—for advice. LaCroix is packing. It is time to move on, he says, and he implores Knight to go with him, to leave Natalie if he loves her, because loving her, bringing her across, will damn her. Of course, it's not that easy. She might be his salvation. The woman who might be able to change his very nature. Vampire to mortal; same-sex desire to heterosexual.

> **NATALIE:** "Make love to me, Nick," she says in the final scene. "Don't be afraid. I'm not afraid of death. Or of an eternity of darkness as long as I can spend it with you. All I have is faith and love ... all I'm asking is for you to make love to me. I trust you."

He gives in, seduced by her pleas, his love for her, and his belief, finally, that there is no other way for him but through the darkness. And if it doesn't work, if he can't become mortal and redeem himself, the only other option is death. Hers and his own. "I won't leave you," he says. "Whatever happens, we'll be together." He kisses her, his vampire identity emerges, and he drinks her blood. Flashbacks to many similar moments in his past, all violent, equate his lovemaking with the inevitable. When LaCroix arrives after it's all over and asks if Knight will be adding Natalie to their entourage, he puts it in stark terms: "There she lies at the brink. Her fate is in your hands. Bring her across or let her die.... You cannot deny what you are." You cannot deny what you are; you cannot be otherwise, no matter how hard you try.

"I can't condemn her to this darkness," Knight says, effectively affirming that premise. He kisses Natalie and in the last moments just when LaCroix thinks all is well and they can bury Nat and be on their way, Knight reveals that he desires to follow her into whatever is beyond. He professes his faith in her belief that this would be a beginning, not an end. In essence, he chooses his own death.

LaCroix speaks here—the episode's opening monologue, as it turns out, now put into context. "Is your faith really that strong?" he asks at the end. Instead of answering, Knight calls LaCroix his closest friend and hands him a wooden stake, then kneels by Natalie's side. As LaCroix raises the stake above his head and slashes downward, the camera moves upward, preventing us from watching as (we assume) he kills Knight in one last act of unnatural fatherly love. This death is Knight's only way out of his darkness, the only way he will be released from the evil he embodies. And LaCroix's last words echo as the screen fades to a full moon rising into the night sky. "Damn you, Nicolas." Indeed. For they are all damned.

The series doesn't answer many of the questions it poses. Most of them are tangential to the main issue: an exploration of the concept of evil as a metaphysical condition, as Knight says of his own existence early on.[34] However, one answer is clear: the condition of being a vampire is unchangeable, their unnatural desires part and parcel of their existence, and they must pay for their sins. As must we all in the end. Redemption is but a dream for those who live so far outside the norm.

Perhaps "the slaying of the vampire represents the triumph of 'dominant' culture, sustaining heteronormative practices and beliefs."[35] Knight's death may signal a possible recapitulation of heteronormativity, an outcome that would resonate with a society in which AIDS was feared but ignored, and in which deviant sexualities and death were seen as equivalent.

Forever Knight gave the late 20th century a vampire detective dedicated to fighting the evils of society, and the evil that resided at the core of his being. He strove to be free of his dark desires, to no longer crave blood or engage in sensual, often sexual acts, and to no longer kill because of his deviance. As has been the case throughout this essay, this term is used advisedly, without judgment, to refer to the heteronormative point of view that was struggling to retain its stranglehold on society in the face of both the AIDS crisis and a growing acceptance of people who were beginning to openly reject that same standard. Perhaps *Forever Knight*'s vampires, long signifiers of fears and carriers of meaning, had fulfilled their purpose, dying to redeem our sins. And yet, the show seems to say in the end, if death is the only answer perhaps it is time to rethink the cultural belief systems that created them.

Notes

1. *Forever Knight* originated in the U.S. as a CBS television movie in 1989. By 1992 the series had moved to Canada and was produced by Glen Warren Productions (part of the CTV Television Network in Canada) and the now defunct Paragon Entertainment Corporation. It was broadcast on CBS and USA Network in the United States between 1992 and 191996. It was then syndicated and ran through the late 1990s.

2. See for example Auerback, Craft, Frayling, Roth, Showalter, and Senf.

3. This does not include the more than twenty-five animated vampire shows, the more than 30 shows not dedicated to vampires but in which they appear for an episode or two—or in the case of Supernatural, a multitude of times—or the nearly 10 web shows in which they feature.

4. Camp is an important element of this show, and will be addressed later in the chapter.

5. Some film scholars date this era from the mid-1920s through 1959.

6. See Simon Bacon's excellent chapter in this volume, "The Hard-boiled Detective Gone Soft: Moonlight, Vampire Noir and the Detective in Search of Himself."

7. Bringing a person across is always figured as sexual in *Forever Knight*.

8. This term is used in two ways: to define how the show itself represents various behaviors, activities, and themes; and to designate how those same behaviors, activities and themes would have been understood by viewers. There is no inherent judgement about those behaviors, or in the use of the term.

9. This is not unlike the relationship between vampire and victim in many vampire tales, wherein the vampire becomes master, mother or father, mentor and sometimes lover, and almost always teacher of his (or her) victim, seducing the newly born vampire into killing again and again in order to continue to exist; essentially, the new vampire is "born again" as hunter.

10. This does seem to be changing in the last few iterations of this creature. See *Twilight*, among others.

11. This is a direct quote from many episodes of *Forever Knight*. It becomes a plot point early on, and is essential to understand about these vampires by the end of the series, the last episode of which hinges on it.

12. In horror films this connection has become a parody of itself, so much so that avid horror filmgoers know that generally the girl who has the sex will be the first to die.

13. See Graham Turner, *Film as Social Practice IV*, for more details on reception theory.

14. In his encoding/decoding theory.
15. A fourth way, the perverse, has been suggested and developed by Janet Staiger in her book *Perverse Spectators: The Practices of Film Reception*. While this is as valid a mode of reading a film as the others, it will not be developed here in the context of this particular show.
16. In fairness to the text and to the modes of interpretation, other means may be read into this particular show, among them Proof for the Existence of God, The Power of Faith, The Nature of Evil, The Nature of Identity, The Performativity of Evil, or even The Nature of Camp or Melodrama. Choosing to interpret a text in a particular way means, as Edward Said once said (paraphrased) picking a point from which to begin speaking and ignoring all the rest.
17. Entitled "Dark Knight: The Second Chapter" and it first aired in 1992.
18. Dyer, Richard (1988). "Children of the Night: Vampirism as Homosexuality, Homosexuality as Vampirism."
19. *Dracula*, 1897.
20. Netflix's *Dracula* (2020) makes this explicit.
21. Haggerty, George E. "Anne Rice and the Queering of Culture."
22. Haggerty, George E. "Anne Rice and the Queering of Culture."
23. In "Dark Knight: The Second Chapter," Episode 2 of Season 1, Knight kills LaCroix, adding a particular kind of patricide to his sins.
24. This episode, seemingly a tossed-off wrap-up of one of the more interesting characters in *Forever Knight*, did not do justice to some of the important themes of the series and could merit its own analysis.
25. Frank in "Francesca," Episode 20 of Season 3, during a therapy session. He is remembering and reliving Francesca's interlude with Knight as they made love and drank of each other's blood.
26. "Francesca," Episode 20, Season 3.
27. *Ibid*.
28. He had taken over the running of it when Janette left earlier in the show.
29. Echoes of Christianity are no mere accident. The entire series was built on Christian beliefs, questions of evil and goodness, right and wrong, temptation and fate, destiny and the punishment of sin. That is the subject for a later examination of this same show.
30. Divia to LaCroix in "Ashes to Ashes."
31. Though there are the usual sexual inuendoes and passion-laced wordplay between Knight and LaCroix.
32. Until she found her own redemption through true love.
33. And even its title.
34. In Episode 16 of Season 1, "Only the Lonely."
35. Marty Fink, "Reimagining Illness in Butler's *Fledgling*."

Works Cited

Aurback, Nina. *Our Vampires, Ourselves*, U of Chicago P, 1997.
Craft, Christopher. "'Kiss me with those red lips': Gender and Inversion in Bram Stoker's Dracula," *Representations*, No. 8, Autumn, 1984, pp. 107–133
Dracula. Netflix, Hartswood Films, 2020.
Dyer, Richard. "Children of the Night: Vampirism as Homosexuality, Homosexuality as Vampirism." *Sweet Dreams: Sexuality, Gender, and Popular Fiction*, edited by Susannah Radstone, Lawrence & Wishart, 1988, p. 64.
Fink, Marty. "AIDS Vampires: Reimagining Illness in Octavia Butler's *Fledgeling*," *Science Fiction Studies*, Volume 37, No 3, November 2010, pp. 416–432.
Forever Knight, Glen Warren Productions and Paragon Entertainment Corporation. CTV Television Network, Toronto, 1992–1996.
Frayling, Christopher. *Vampyres: Lord Byron to Count Dracula*, Faber & Faber, 1992.

Haggerty, George E. "Anne Rice and the Queering of Culture," *Novel: A Forum on Fiction*, Vol 32, No. 1, Autumn, 1998, pp 5–18.
Roth, Phyllis. "Suddenly Sexual Women in Bram Stoker's Dracula," *Dracula: The Vampire and the Critics*, edited by Margaret L. Carter, UMI Research Press, 1988.
Senf, Carol A. *Dracula: Between Tradition and Modernism*. Twayne Publishers, 1998.
Showalter, Elaine. *Sexual Anarchy: Gender and Culture at the Fin de Siecle*. Virago, 1992.
Sontag, Susan. "Notes on Camp," *Against Interpretation and Other Essays*. Picador, 1966.
Staiger, Janet. *Perverse Spectators: The Practices of Film Reception*. NYU P, 2000.
Stoker, Bram. *Dracula*. Archibald and Company, 1897.
Turner, Graham. *Film as Social Practice IV (Studies in Culture and Communication)*, 4th ed. Routledge, 2006.

The Hard-Boiled Detective Gone Soft

Moonlight, *Vampire Noir* and the Detective in Search of Himself

SIMON BACON

This essay will look at the ways in which the American series *Moonlight* uses the tropes of the hard-boiled detective and film noir to construct its idea of a vampire detective. However, many of the characteristics of the main protagonist of the show, Mick St. John (Alex O'Loughlin), set up multiple points of dissonance with the noir detective ideal. Consequently, as argued by this study, rather than conforming to the hard-bodied masculinity of his hard-boiled predecessors, Mick, the vampire detective, is consistently made soft by his quest for redemption and his love for a human.

There seems to be almost an obvious connection between the idea of vampires and detectives. Maybe because Bram Stoker's Count Dracula and Conan Doyle's Sherlock Holmes are contemporaries and vie for the title of the fictional character most portrayed on film, or that now in the early 21st-century vampire detectives are not uncommon—heightened senses and physical abilities being particularly useful—it seems a natural fit. Indeed, both characters share a predisposition for the shadows and dark, hidden recesses of society where the American Dream has become the American Nightmare (Hibbs 52). One could also argue that the connection between the two became cemented in the popular consciousness in the early 2000s with films and series such as the *Buffy the Vampire Slayer* spin-off, *Angel* (Greenwalt: 1999–2004) quickly followed by *Blood Ties* (Huff: 2007),[1] and *Moonlight* (Koslow: 2007–8), though this is not to downplay the importance of the slightly earlier show *Forever Knight* (Cohen:

1992–6).² *Moonlight* will be looked at here as it is primarily based on the idea of the vampire detective, knowingly references its film noir precursors, and neatly shows the intersections and conflicts between the detectives' "code" and the vampires' quest for redemption, which form the core of this study.

The Vampire Detective

The creation of the vampire detective obviously produces something of a contrast to seminal vampire texts such as *Dracula* (1897) where the undead are the ones being investigated and tracked down. That said, vampires are not totally unfamiliar with investigations of their own and an early example is *Mark of the Vampire* (Browning: 1935)—the remake of the now lost *London After Midnight* (Browning: 1927)—though, at the film's end, it is revealed the vampire is not real. More useful precursors are films like *Dracula's Daughter* (Hillyer: 1936) and *House of Dracula* (Kenton: 1945) where the vampire, while not trying to solve a murder or a crime, is searching for a cure to their vampirism. *Dracula's Daughter* is of particular interest as the vampire, Countess Zeleska (Gloria Holden), is on something of a quest to find herself as a person free from her vampiric past.³ It should be noted that the much earlier story, and precursor of *Dracula*, *Varney the Vampire* (Rymer and Prest 1845–7), itself something of a long running series that appeared as Penny Dreadfuls in 19th-century Britain, saw the vampire ultimately searching for redemption, but which only ended in his self destruction in the heart of Mount Vesuvius. In fact, this points to the almost inevitable conclusion of the vampiric search for redemption and identity beyond vampirism, and that is death, or at least the realization that they were better off being a vampire.⁴ However, what the spate of vampire detectives in the early 21st century specifically seems to involve is an increased sense of morality, which is inevitably problematic for a creature driven to drink human blood. Mainly this is solved through a kind of vampiric vegetarianism which sees them feeding from (often killing) certain members of society deemed deserving of such an end, generally murderers, rapists, and the like. This then involves the creation of a "code" of sorts as one will never be seen to be worthy of regaining one's humanity if one is not seen, by whatever powers might decide such things, to be humane. The idea of a code links directly into the construction of the hard-boiled detective that features in film noir, which the series *Moonlight* specifically cites throughout its duration.

The fictional hard-boiled detective arose in Prohibition America in the

1920s. A lone figure fighting organized crime and an often-corrupt police force. He—they were always men—had to live by his wits and his own code against the tide of greed, violence, and exploitation that ruled the dark labyrinthine streets of the city, or as Jarold J. Abrams more poetically frames it:

> This dark maze of the night is everywhere and nowhere, and the only one who knows it clean is the hard-boiled detective, who investigates it's thousand hidden passageways. Sam Spade, Philip Marlowe, and Mike Hammer—these are the classic noir detectives, each one stoic and detached, a cold Cartesian spectator with no hope of redemption and no reason to care [69].

Detachment and control are key to the hard-boiled detectives code, all very masculine qualities in this schematic, and which is further qualified by the character's ability to suffer yet carry on, as noted by Jopi Nyland, "In general, the men in hard-boiled narratives are subject to pain which threatens their ability to cope and survive … the character's degree of masculinity is gauged by their ability to control themselves" (109). Pain here is often both physical and emotional, with the former usually being caused by run-ins with thugs and hired hands of the mob and the latter with the inevitable, often duplicitous, female lead. Morality, at least in terms of that seen with the vampire detective, is rather more slippery to define, but is intimately linked to the main character's code in terms of what he has been hired to do, or what he sees as his responsibility; right and wrong often depend more on whether murder was involved and the relationship of the detective to the victim. As Nyman further comments, "Morality does not disappear from hard-boiled fiction but is twisted into a self-centred form of morality" (240). For the vampire detective, this moral responsibility often circles around his connection to the local vampire community, almost directly comparable to the mob or organized crime and as such any outcomes to his investigations will always bear in mind the cardinal rule of not revealing either the existence of said community or even vampires in general.

This is often complicated by the vampire's sire, i.e., the vampire that made him, which quite often is a female. She, more often than not, tries to lure the vampire detective back to the old life, be it the mob, or killing humans for fun, and which is always oppositional to his new moral code of self-control and restraint. Resultantly, the normally never-ending maze of plots and landscapes of the noir detective often become internalized for the vampire sleuth. As Abrams and Cooke observe, about similarly cerebral detectives in *The X-Files,* "The labyrinth theme is also extended from the external world of space to the internal one of the mind" (Abrams and Cooke 182). The vampire detective is then often investigating and uncovering the details of its own past as much as any current case it is working on. Sires in particular bring up these aspects and unwanted, unwarranted memories of deeds the "new" detective would rather keep hidden. Indeed, the preference of a world of darkness and shadows seen in film noir is the natural terrain of the vampire detective and the twilight world of his past. For the vampire, this past, or what we might term his "pre-code" days are represented as times when there was no restraint and only the excess of self-indulgence and bloodlust. There, the vampire is seen to be literally drunk on blood, and the horrors of violence and death that fuel it. This corresponds very neatly to the kinds of non-sobriety that are part and parcel of the noir sleuth, as Abrams further notes, "Intoxication is essential to the detective's method" (81). For the vampire, even more than an alcoholic detective—though the noir detective code forbids continual inebriation—blood is a necessary means of survival, so the precariousness of his relationship to alcoholism is even greater, though back-sliding is often cathartic to his investigation, if costly to those who get in his way. The code of the vampire detective often allows for restrained and specific killing, for survival purposes only, of those deemed to not have their own code, or those that purposely break it: crooks, thieves, villains, and, in particular, those that take the innocence of others. There is of course one quite important difference between the vampire detective and the "hard-boiled" one described in Abrams' quote above, is that the main impetus for the vampire to find redemption is because of or for the love of a human woman.

In many ways this search for redemption actually helps to intensify one of the other main features of the noir detective: suffering and coping with emotional pain. This was especially shown in *Angel*, where the eponymous lead renowned in the show for his glum, pain-fueled demeanor, became a detective as he was looking for a "means of ridding himself of his load of guilt … with the many people he has killed, and … some future redemption" (Melton 2011, 14). As such, his masculine prowess and commitment to his code are reinforced by a quest for salvation that would ordinarily work against that. This is also the main reason for choosing *Moonlight* to look at as, not just does the show purposely cite the hard-boiled detective genre, but its main protagonist, detective Mick St. John exemplifies all of these traits.

Moonlight premiered February 19, 2007, and was set in, then, present-day Los Angeles. It tells the story of Mick St. John (Alex O'Loughlin), a musician, and later a detective, who was turned into a vampire by his wife on their wedding night 50 years prior. However, 20 or so years after that, he killed his now ex-wife after she kidnapped a young girl Beth Turner, who Mick now feels bound to protect. A new case brings him and Beth (Sophia Myles), who is now an investigative journalist, together and, the more they work with each other, the more emotionally entangled they become. Mick's ex-wife Coraline (Shannyn Sossoman) reappears claiming that, although over 340 years old, she has a cure for vampirism, which the detective becomes obsessed with as it means he could have a human life with Beth. After many twists and turns, Mick manages to regain his humanity, but later realizes it has consequences he is unwilling to accept and returns to his former undead self. As noted earlier, he is very much constructed in the mold of the hard-boiled detective, and so it is worth looking more closely at how this works in the series and how Mick's supernatural abilities and his quest for identity often seem to undermine that.

"Am I a cop?"[5]

The dissonance between the vampire and noir detective recur through the series but most notably begin with the very first scene of the pilot episode of the series, with a voice-over narration. The voice-over is a classic element of the hard-boiled detective genre, supplying the true version of the tangled web of intrigue and deception he has entered in to (Altman 166). A street-wise narrator describes the action but also the mental state of the protagonist. Equally, as M. Christine Boyer notes, it is the thread that holds everything together while guiding us through the labyrinth (Boyer 341). Curiously, this first scene is of Mick being interviewed by an unseen reporter—we assume it is a reporter as the lighting suggests a television interview rather than one with the police, or a quest for information by a gangland boss—and rather than looking world weary and crumpled, as most noir detectives are, he looks relaxed, casually dressed, and even coy in front of the camera. One suspects it is more inline with the vampire genre than the detective one. As such, it more obviously references *Interview with the Vampire*, a seminal text in the vampire genre by Anne Rice from 1976, as well as a popular 1994 film of the same name by Neil Jordan, where a young reporter thinks he is questioning a delusional figure only to realize that they really are a vampire. Of course, the scene in *Moonlight* also references the setting for the series, Los Angeles, which is the beating heart of the film industry, but disconcertingly it undermines the seriousness of what follows; one would not expect to see noir icons such as Philip Marlowe or Sam Spade in such a scene. This starts to express the ways in which the references to two separate genres, the noir and the vampire, do not always overlap neatly and can work against each other. One assumes the writers of the series realized how out-of-place this setup was as it only occurs at the start of the pilot episode and never happens again, yet it rather disturbs the expected straight-talking, off-the-hip tough guy of the voice-overs in classic detective noirs, and it indeed takes until the second episode of the season to regain something of an edge. That said, the voice-over by itself becomes increasingly important through the series and especially because Mick is a vampire detective.

For noir detectives such as Philip Marlowe, the voice-over provides an invaluable look inside the detective's mind for the audience, not just in terms of his character but in the ways his personal intuition and instincts lead him to connect clues and ultimately solve the case. With Mick St. John, the explanatory narrative becomes even more important as nearly all his "instincts" come via his vampire senses and, without his voice-over, we would have no idea what he has uncovered. Much of this revolves around his ability to smell blood, often indicating whether humans or vampires are present, which is very useful in a city like L.A.—while vampires are the only supernatural creatures seen in *Moonlight* it very much constructs the city as a magnate for such creatures in the same way that *Angel* did before it—and even allows Mick to discern how old the vampire is, supposedly by the increasing stench of decrepitude. Mick's sense of smell also allows him to discover what the blood type is at the scene so he knows exactly who it comes from.

Alongside this is what appears to be an even more mysterious ability to sense a residue of strong emotions or intense struggles, so that, when he enters certain crime scenes, he seems able to replay in his mind exactly what occurred.[6] In part, this seems linked to the genre idea of blood memory where a vampire drinking or tasting someone's blood relives that person's past (this was a feature of the *Underworld* series of films that began in 2003). But, in *Moonlight,* it also provides a convenient way to condense the plot at strategic points. It is interesting to note that when Mick temporarily becomes human again in "Fated to Pretend" his abilities to sense things at the crime scene abruptly stops, as do his voice-overs when searching for clues—Beth suddenly takes the lead when searching for evidence. As such, it is not surprising that Mick does not remain human for long. Without his powers, he is little more than an average sleuth who knows too much about the dark underworld of L.A.

This underworld is of course a natural habitat for the undead, and there is much about the twilight world of light and dark that the noir detective inhabits that is just like that of the vampire. Indeed, the kind of Expressionist camera work that inspired F.W. Murnau's *Nosferatu* (1922) with its literal autonomous shadows makes the very world of the noir detective inherently vampiric.[7] As such, Mick's world of nighttime L.A. should perfectly fit that mold, and more so because of his connections to the widespread vampire community. In many ways, this does make a direct correlation: the vampire network is easily correlated to that of organized crime; a large, secretive society with an extensive group of members and acolytes that seems hugely wealthy and influential. So much so that they even have a dedicated "clean-up" division to help them remain undetected.[8] Mick's best friend Josef (Jason Dohring) is an important and very wealthy member of it and, as a result, not unlike the average hard-boiled sleuth, Mick has connections to what the series constructs as the mob and even uses them to help crack cases. In fact Josef quite often seems to act as his assistant on cases that are more intricately linked to either of their pasts. Unsurprisingly, many of the cases he solves are committed by rogue members of "the mob," who have broken its code, so that Mick not only needs to solve a crime but also help the vampire community.

With this, noir detectives usually have connections within the police force, being in-between creatures with their own individual code. Unlike many noir detectives, Mick is not a former cop or associate of current law-enforcement officers and so gets to maintain this through his connection to Beth, who, as an investigative reporter, is in a relationship with the Assistant D.A. However, Beth is very problematic for Mick in terms of his being a hard-boiled detective. On one hand, she helps to reinforce Mick's noir credentials, assisting in positioning him between the forces of law and the mob, but also in providing ongoing psychological pain that he needs to control. But his obvious emotional attachment to her seems as much of a liability as it is a benefit, mainly as she does not really fit the normal noir model and resultantly becomes a point of dissonance rather than affirmation. In part, this is because Beth is somewhat of an innocent compared to the usual love interest of the noir detective, the femme fatale, but more importantly he is substantially older than she is, a troubling feature, whose implications the series tries to avoid. This is not to say that detective noirs have not shown much older men having relationships with very young girls, but with Mick, who is potentially 60 years her senior, this is complicated by him being the one that rescued her when she was a prepubescent child, adding a darkness to their relationship that the series struggles to nullify with its worry aspects of stalking and/or pedophilia.[9]

Because Beth does not fill the role of femme fatale the series is in constant search of one. The role is an important one that normally acts as an equal, if opposite, foil to the noir detective, often mirroring each other with the fatale substantiating the latter's claim to be considered the "hero" (Jaber 2). Consequently, in noir films, this mirroring between the two allows them to talk as though following "a script they've likely uttered a thousand times before, [and] with an attitude borrowed from Ladd and Lake, Bogart and Bacall" (Darghis 64).[10] *Moonlight* lacks this and tries to cover this up with the reappearance of Mick's ex-wife Coraline, but she is not in the series long enough or given enough dialogue with her former husband to establish such a significant relationship. In fact, in many respects much of this role is filled by Mick's long term friend Josef, who seems much more of a mirror to the detective and shares a greater amount of dialogue with him—there is even an awkward "penetration" scene between the two men when Josef turns the newly human Mick back into a vampire again.[11] Yet, the series does not want to promote that relationship and so forces it back onto the connection between him and Beth, increasingly becoming a point of weakness for him, and emphasizing the dissonances between his own code and that of the noir detective.

The hard-boiled detective's code, as intimated above, usually centers on himself but inevitably contains a measure of morality, though not one that is necessarily inline with the judiciary. Indeed, with the speed of unfolding events, he is forced into the role of both judge and avenger (Cawelti 1976, Grella 1988) at a moment's notice. This tends to mean that each detective has their own code but, in general, there is always a sense of right and wrong (honorable and dishonorable), which can be problematic in a world that is created as overwhelmingly corrupt and again complicated when actions are often evaluated on context. More straight-forward is the rigid application of this code over and above any personal emotional attachments. Mick's code aligns with some of that but more often tries to navigate a path between the police, generally viewed as not corrupt, and the world of vampires, who seem to provide the biggest source of corruption in the series but who St. John is honor-bound to protect. Beyond this, his views on whether someone is good or evil is curiously based on his own culinary preferences. An odd rule to use to be sure, but Mick refuses to kill (drink the blood of) children, women, and innocents and so anyone that does not follow that same rule is usually seen by him to be bad—though in actuality the series only ever shows Mick getting blood from his contact at the morgue—again excepting vampires unless they are seen to threaten the wider vampire community.

This, however, is then superseded by his emotional attachment to Beth which comes before all other concerns. Taken together, these factors combine to make Mick's code a rather different moral guide than that of the usual noir detective. Firstly, it is heavily weighted to the protection of, what is to all intents and purposes, organized crime with the solving of his cases and catching killers. always affected by his need to protect the vampire community. More so, his emotions for Beth push into this dynamic as well, not quite usurping the place of the mob, but certainly that of seeking justice. In terms of the hard-boiled and hard-bodied detective, this makes him rather soft. A point reinforced by his problematic relationship with sunlight, one of the few traditional vampire weaknesses that the series utilizes.

Sunlight seems to have varying results when it strikes Mick St. John. In his voice-over, he states that it is not dangerous but affects his powers, not unlike Bram Stoker's Count Dracula, but what is shown in the series rather complicates this assertion. Though at times it would seem to cause little reaction in the vampire sleuth, at other times it seems to send him scampering across the street with a newspaper over his head—rather belying his supposedly stoic noir status. More than this, in "Fever," Mick gets stuck in the desert trying to protect a witness, and this not only causes him discomfort but pushes him to the verge of death and where only human blood can save him—to keep himself in a form of stasis he has to lay in a bath full of ice water. This rather undermines the kinds of (hyper) masculinity expected of the noir detective who almost wishes to suffer as a badge of courage and appear "manly" in all situations. Subsequently, Mick's reactions to sunlight tend to be somewhat emasculating and reveal what should be a "hard body" as soft and easily damaged. In fact, this rather sums up the dichotomies throughout the series where an undead and, virtually, unkillable creature who lives outside mortal needs and desires is consistently shown as being all too human.

Noir or Not?

Ultimately, all these conflicting points come to a head when Mick becomes human again. Coraline, who it now turns out is an 18th-century French courtesan, has a special recipe from her family that allows for vampires to become human for a limited time. Mick takes it thinking it will mean he can finally be with Beth, but it ultimately does exactly the opposite. Beth is kidnapped by a vampire, but the newly human Mick realizes that he is unable to save her and keep her safe. He also understands that the very core of his code as a vampire detective, indeed his very identity as Mick St. John, is the ability to protect those he cares for. This is very important moment in terms of his search for redemption and his place as a hard-boiled detective. In regard to the former, redemption would not only kill his vampire self, but also his own self-identity—if he's no longer undead he's no longer alive. For the latter, he has also disavowed his attempts to be a noir detective by giving his emotions full sway and placing his love for a woman above all other considerations. After this moment, and understandably, the narrative seems to run out of steam as it tries to re-establish the noir credentials it gave up earlier but can never claim back while Mick is happy. This sentences Mick to live in an never-ending undead goodbye, where he will always try but will never be a true hard-bodied noir detective because, rather than ensuring the happiness of others by embodying the gallant who slays the dragon to save the "innocent and helpless" (Phillips 52), he will always put Beth, and therefore himself, first.

Notes

1. Though in *Blood Ties* the vampire, Henry Fitzroy, is more a vampire assistant than the lead investigator. It is worth mentioning the British miniseries *Ultraviolet* (Aherne: 1998) in this context as it involved a vampire policeman (Stephen Moyer in his first role as a vampire) and government secret agencies.
2. *Angel* and *Moonlight* were both set in Los Angeles, and *Forever Knight* and *Blood Ties* in Toronto.
3. This also informs the later remake *Nadja* (Almereyder: 1994)
4. Though narratives such as *I Am Legend* (Matheson 1954), *Daughters of Darkness*, *Daybreakers* (Speirig Brothers: 2009) point to other more hybrid options than a straightforward return to the human condition.
5. Opening line of the first episode of *Moonlight* spoken by Mick St. John to an unseen interviewer.
6. As such it is very similar to the sixth-sense that the detective Will Graham has in the film *Manhunter* (Mann: 1986) taken from Thomas Harris' book *Red Dragon* (1981).
7. Slavoj Žižek claims that film noir is itself vampire-like, particularly modern interpretations (Žižek, 1993: 199).
8. Obviously styled upon The Wolf (Harvey Keitel) from *Pulp Fiction* (Tarantino: 1994) though in *Moonlight* they are led by PVC clad female vampires.
9. In this aspect Moonlight almost prefigured The Twilight Saga with its highly problematic feature of 'imprinting' where Werewolf males imprint on much younger girls as their 'predestined' partners for life, in particular Jakob, who is in his 20s and Renesmee who is still a baby. See Schwartzman 2010, 134.
10. Alan Ladd and Veronica Lake starred together in 3 noir films, *This Gun for Hire* (Tuttle: 1942), *The Glass Key* (Heisler: 1942), and *The Blue Dahlia* (Marshall: 1946), and Humphrey Bogart and Lauren Bacall also starred in 3, *The Big Sleep* (Hawks: 1946), *Dark Passage* (Daves: 1947), and *Key Largo* (Huston: 1948).
11. The series quite astutely avoids and non-heteronormative relationships even though that is an innate part of the vampires inherently transgressive nature and sexuality.

Works Cited

Abrams, Jerold J. "From Sherlock Holmes to the Hard-Boiled Detective in Film Noir," *The Philosophy of Film Noir*, edited by Mark T. Conard, UP of Kentucky, 2006, 69–90.
Abrams, Jerold J., and Elizabeth Cooke. "Detection and the Logic of Abduction in the X-Files." *The Philosophy of TV Noir*, edited by Steven M. Sanders and Aeon J. Skoble, UP of Kentucky, 2008, 179–202.
Altman, Rick. *A Theory of Narrative*. Columbia UP, 2008.
Bowyer, M. Christine. "The Double Erasure of Times Square." *The Urban Underworld: Formation, Perception, Representation*, edited by Peter Madsen and Richard Plunz, Routledge, 2005, 330–52.
Cawelti, John G. *Adventure, Mystery, and Romance: Formula Stories as Art and Popular Culture*. U of Chicago P, 1976.
Dargis, Manohla. *L.A. Confidential*. BFI, 2003.

Grella, George. "The Hard-Boiled Detective Novel." *Detective Fiction: Critical Essays*, edited by Robin W. Winks, Foul Play Press, 1988, 103–20.

Hibbs, Thomas. "Buffy the Vampire Slayer as Feminist Noir." *Buffy the Vampire Slayer and Philosophy: Fear and Trembling in Sunnydale*, edited by James B. South, Open Court, 2003, 49–60.

Jaber, Maysaa. *Criminal Femmes Fatales in American Hardboiled Crime Fiction*. Palgrave Macmillan, 2016.

Melton, J. Gordon. *The Vampire Book: The Encyclopedia of the Undead*, 3d ed. Visible Ink, 2011.

Nyman, Jopi. *Men Alone: Masculinity, Individualism, and Hard-Boiled Fiction*. Rodopi, 1997.

Phillips, Gene D. *Creatures of Darkness: Raymond Chandler, Detective Fiction, and Film Noir*. UP of Kentucky, 2000.

Roth, Judith. "Suddenly Sexual Women in Bram Stoker's Dracula." *Literature and Psychology* 27 (1977), 113–21.

Schwartzman, Sarah. "Is *Twilight* Morgan?" *The Twilight Mystique: Critical Essays on the Novels and Films*, edited by Amy M. Clarke and Marijane Osborn, McFarland, 2010, 121–36.

Žižek, Skavoj. "'The Thing That Thinks': The Kantian Background of the Noir Subject." *Shades of Noir: A Reader*, edited by Joan Copjec, Verso, 1993, 199–226.

True Resonance

The Intersection of the Noosphere, Spirituality and the Supernatural in True Detective—Season One

PHIL FITZSIMMONS

Set in the petrochemical bound swamplands of Louisiana which in the American psyche is seen as the union's "dark corner" (Romine 44), the premier of *True Detective—Season One* on American cable television in January 2014 was followed by a wave of immediate acclaim. From the moment of the opening credits and the ensuing entrée into the narrative, critics and audiences alike soon realized Nic Pizzolatto's scripts, Cary Fukunaga's directing, and the choice of Matthew McConaughey ("Rust" Cohle) and Woody Harrelson (Marty Hart) as the lead roles had set this eight episode drama markedly apart from the previous raft of American police and detective shows. More importantly, it presented a vastly different sense of the supernatural as compared to contemporary television which at best is "simply a spiritualist discourse where the dead speak" (Allen 133) or an "intrusion or portal fantasy" (Mendlesohn 56).

The series focuses on the investigative journey of two detectives, "Rust" Cohle and Marty Hart as they attempt to solve an apparent string of sacrificial slayings, beginning with a young woman, Dora Lange. Found deliberately posed as if kneeling in prayer, in a remote cane field, with evidence of brutal torture and apparent satanic symbols inscribed on her body the comments made by the first responders all initially point to a "white trash" and "white detective" narrative. Only detective Cohle recognizes Dora Lange's body is both a personal cartographic and cosmological signpost.

This initial *mis-en-scène* as a contained visual space of death and apparent pagan ritual, represents the typical transtextual markers of mythic

Louisiana liminality and its Southern transtextual gothic tropes of sexualized backwardness, deprivation, death and monstrosity (Courtney). *True Detective* never veers away from these themes of seemingly marginalized possibilities in which the human geography is being "undone by category crisis" (Smith and Appleton 8). The latter is another long-held trope that Louisiana is a littoral zone of uncertainty that has both a "strong emotional paranormal past" (Samuel 110) and a supernatural "intertwining of Christian fundamentalism and voodoo" (Arthur).

As stated, the crime scene is littered with icons of the occult as are the emblems and images left on Dora's body. However, for detective Cohle, the blue spiral on her back has a different allegorical meaning in that it is a spiritual connector to all the other elements at the scene. In particular, for Cohle this was a mythical signature of the "red thread" of the labyrinth, the supernatural helix binary that potentially forms the upward convergence of mind with the universe. This marker is emblematic of the intuitive mind path that is a two-way flow and positive connection to a universal understanding that only becomes activated when those who truly seek it become those that truly sense it.

This one facet acts as an entrée into a supernatural *mise-en-abyme* that is gradually unpacked through the beliefs and spiritual praxis of detective Cohle, and the killer's iconic signature. In contrast to the Christian fundamentalism and its underpinning tropes of crime-transgression and creation-fall mythologies that continually surface, Cohle engages with the supernatural through similar icons, but a more holistic and mythical locus. In doing so he shifts the typical histophysiology detective investigations to a nexus with the supernatural that for him is an epistemological and ontological labyrinth, but for the killer of Dora Lange is case study of pure Gothic horror. To understand this evil, Cohle must of necessity recognize how thin the line is between evil and the appearance of morality. In this dualistic engagement Cohle becomes for a time the psychical and symbolic extension of Dora Lange, the killer and the Louisiana worldview. In doing so, and enduring "that which evokes the abyss" (Thacker 105) his worldview eventually becomes a "a site one stays in, clings to even, because it nourishes one's capacity to resist. Thus he offers the possibility of radical perspectives from which to see and create, to imagine new alternatives, new worlds" (hooks 341).

Through its gothic symbolism the American metanarrative was confronted head on as a "natural container of social memories" (Fentress and Wickham 50) that gives rise to "the repetition of privileged narratives" (Nadel 4). Through the use of the two contrasting detective types with a vastly different ideological belief systems, the entwined America archetypal television detective narratives of "category crisis" (Arthur 8) and conservatism were compared and contrasted. This occurred at a time when contemporary popular culture as a whole in the United States, and television in particular was still "experiencing a forensic turn," as an engagement reaction "of a society believed to be increasingly chaotic and dangerous" (Steenberg 1). *True Detective* from its opening frames of ritualistic death launched into the latter but veered away from any forensic underpinning.

For American television audiences, used to the visual semiotic of clinical settings and the meticulous nature of scientific evidence in the "victimized body as autopsy" found in the CSI formats, *True Detective* was confronting. The initial sight of an upright naked young woman bent over a tree root wearing antlers and ritualized patterns drawn on her back immediately contradicted the normalized CSI "access to objective truth" (Jenner 2). While relatively new and innovative in themselves, the ratings of the CSI formats clearly indicated that television audiences were clearly enjoying these series' "saturated visibility of showing and telling" (Kompare 15) as well as the clarity of their detective logico-mathematical discourse and rational scientific method (Yar). More importantly, at a time when the events of 9/11 were still lingering issues related to crime, justice and retribution in the American psyche, the cultural chaos surrounding the apparent satanically posed body of Dora Lange resonated with the concept of what it meant in "establishing a perfect truth in our troubled historical age of catastrophe and cultural unease" (McCabe 95).

With each episode, the narrative content and subtext moved further and further away from the ideal of empirical research methodology, which in detective television has come to represent national American conservatism: "not in terms of Republican Party politics, but in terms of preserving established power structures, social norms and value systems" (Jenner 2).

In *True Detective* "Rust" Cohle unpacks and reveals a deeper perspective regarding this worldview and values, in that the supernatural becomes an "overarching two-way flow of influence: from organisms to fields and fields to organisms" (Sheldrake 109–110). Unlike the typical representation of the supernatural as an external "detection on earth" (Ascari 17), evil proclivities or assistance from angelic hosts, Cohle's developing outlook rests on the perhaps the oldest metaphors of the supernatural as life giving: the labyrinth myth of the noosphere. As defined by Targ (ix), this is "a Vedic concept that corresponds to Plato's field of ideals, Jung's archetypes, and De Chardin's Noosphere. The pinnacle of Vedic thought is the idea that our innermost self (Atman—ever more subtle, ever contracting) is identical to the entire universe (Brahman—ever expanding, cosmic). We are one with everything."

Perhaps the oldest form of ideological belief structures, connecting with the noosphere is based on electing to converge one's choices and mindset with the swirl of the greater universe in regard to time and space. The primary mode of convergence is through resonance with the archetypal narratives and archetypal patterns that speak to "the collector and connoisseur of detail" (Birkerts 165) in everyday life. On a larger scale this resonance leads "to the surveying of space, for it is only in space, in the network of layered particulars, that the successive images of time are concretized. Space exists to take the print of time" (Birkerts 165).[1] However, in doing so, one does not automatically or easily find access to stasis or the peace of the "divine principal within us, which is the thoughts and revolutions of the universe" (Plato 1152). The authentic seeker enters into the pathway of the "spirit paraclete" (Johnston), the "wounded storyteller" (Frank) or the "coincidence of opposites" (Turner 50).

This mythic process of "coincenditia oppistorum" is clearly identifiable in *True Detective*, as Cohle moves into and then out of his "mythic wound" related to death and existential angst, through sensing and resonating with the supernatural. In the same way, the use of symbols reveals this is the same pathway of the "meta-psychotic" monster (*TD* 1:18:30) that Cohle is tracking. Though it appears that like many human beings, the apparently crazed serial killer Childress has remained trapped in "the unassimilable wound or trauma at the heart of existence" (Restuccia 205). As Turner states, "it is only when the symbolic path from the unknown to the known is completed that we can look back and comprehend its final form" (20).

An even closer inspection of this series reveals that the elements that weave Cohle's "wound journey" together are visual and textual supernatural "puncta." To paraphrase, Botting (295) these are "black dots" of connectivity representing the beginning and end of rational thought. These "black dots" or black holes, as Botting also calls these entrée points allow the imagination and creative brain to connect with a transcendent space of both mind and matter. De Chardin believed this transcendent space to be the ultimate evolutionary end of mankind leading out of the encompassing biosphere into a global network thinking, or indeed universal network of connectivity. Although Cohle uses a synonymous term, "psychosphere" ("The Long Bright Dark"), directly drawn from Lumly's sci-fi horror's trilogy, the term noosphere is the oldest definition of this all-encompassing sacred participatory zone "in which all things are substance natural, supernatural, human: and all are related in one way or another to each other" (Malone 131).

As with all who seek to make contact with that "still small voice" within and without, Cohle also has to sort through the significance of conscious and unconscious points of possibilities, and the impact of his own woundedness and that of the killer he and his partner are tracking. Sensing "black dots" to tie them into a cohesive linkage is, as Campbell states, "like a bubble surfacing from the bottom of the sea" ("Primitive Mythology" 18).

Settling Deeper Into the Scene: Topography, Tropes and Types

While murder scenes often have within them some degree of left-over physical markers linked to the killer or killers, the site of the apparent murder of Dora Lange is bereft of any forensic evidence. With her body washed clean and the apparent physical Satanic icons attached to her body devoid of fingerprints, her body truly becomes what criminologists term a "silent witness" (Fuhrman 226). While from the moment Marty Hart and Rustin Cohle arrived at the scene as the CID investigators, the former was content to let her remain this way until there was a clear string of criminological evidence. While not adverse to forensic science or an evidentiary trail, Cohle let Hart wait for the clues while began to immediately focus on the "black dot" signs. In particular, it was his conscious and unconscious connections with the markings on her body, and in particular the blue spiral inscribed by the gloved finger of her killer on her back that grabbed his attention. As the investigation continues, it also becomes clear that this circular motif, a contemporaneous metaphor for the labyrinth (Levi Strauss 428), was also inscribed internally within Cohle. He was just not fully cognizant of it at the time. However, his close scrutiny revealed he was becoming aware that this passageway marking would form the core filament in the case, and direct him into a different conduit of investigation.

While skeptical at times regarding his partner's intellect, Cohle's approach to detective work was on the surface similar to his partner's typical policing logic of detection "as an intellectual problem" (Ascari 2). Cohle differed though as it was clear that he had a default position of intermittently and iteratively shuffling through an increasing emotional connectivity with aspects of the noosphere in general and the "labyrinthine path" specifically. What he termed the "tasting the psychosphere" Eliade sees as engaging with "divine energies" (21). For this particular detective "the cosmos in its entirety became a hierophany" (Eliade 12). While Coomaraswamy contends that this sacred pathway of understanding is a "fusion without confusion" (12), for this detective it was in fact a fusion with confusion. Or as Eliade has also stated, any sacred journey or transcendent path entered into, the human condition "continues to remain what it was before: an object, a creature, a gesture; it participates in the world and yet transcends it" (Eliade 257).

For Cohle, this sacred journey arose out his meditative practice that focused on the symbol of Christ's crucifixion. "I contemplate the moment in the garden, the idea of allowing your own crucifixion" ("The Long Bright Dark"). Although he had internalized some of the sacrificial aspects of Christianity, it was the symbolic meaning of the "cross as a labyrinth" (Jerome qtd. Dodd 64) and the accompanying existential connotation of the "cry of the lost soul" (Ashton 171) searching for the connection with the noosphere, that became the central core of his personal journey. "success is a natural consequence of the path's design; the walker is guided to the center by the existing framework" (Kern 316). The finding of self and connection with the power of this symbol and the power of the universe is deeply rooted in one being patient, being prepared to watch, wait, wonder and wander in a naturally unfolding but "complex process that leads from ignorance to enlightenment" (Dodd 65).

For Cohle, the solving of this murder inquiry through the supernatural was a natural all-encompassing dimension or divinity that incrementally allows the painful resonant tapping into of a higher order of awareness. In specific terms, this was a patient process of conjoining his meditative habits, natural tacit awareness and the understandings exuding from within self, with the natural environment and with forces encompassing the immediate setting and the earth itself. "The framing of types and qualities of knowledge means that nature is apprehended in her variety, in her distinctiveness, in her unpredictability, with energies crossing boundaries continually" (Kane 119). Termed "morphic resonance" by Rupert Sheldrake, this process "cannot be accounted for in terms of any known types of resonance, nor would it involve a transmission of energy" (70). Instead it is a gradual increase of sensitivity to certain points of perceived tacit connection. These were not always fully appreciated or immediately understood, as these points of connectivity are always "surrounded by a blur owing to the effect of less common variants" (Sheldrake 71). The gradual, and at times painful evolution of Cohle's connection with these "puncta points" of sensing form the structural flow of the next section. While certain key elements of Cohle's connectivity with the noosphere appeared repetitive or convoluted, this is because these points are components of what Deardorff (47) calls the "cosmo-liminal locus overlap" in which the social-cultural elements "permeate each other." This rhizomatic circular flow also follows the spiraled line on Dora Lange, the circular "time is a flat circle" ("The Secret Fate of All Life") pattern of Cohle's initial ideology and the emergent investigation. "Knowledge, then, has two faces: the confused, pejoratively labyrinthine face turned to the student as yet ignorant of what may be discovered, and the ordered face delineated by the experience of the labyrinth. As the *rota rosa* contains two designs in one figure, so the labyrinth is a dual image of circuitous confusion and concentric circles of order" (Doob 197).

Sensing the Environmental Topography: Source of the Symbolic

The entire series of *True Detective*, which includes the naming of each episode, is clearly paratextually bookended by visual references to the bleakness of the Louisiana environment caused by the petroleum industry. Black contends that the darkness of the industrial desolation of Louisiana is a metaphor for the intersection of the religious schema of the American populace as a whole, and its emphasis on consumerism: "The myth of Petrolia here becomes a grand poem of humanity. The horrors remain as necessary as barrels in which to store the product. In good Protestant order, material gain had to be accomplished at some price" (77). In parallel to this, Cohle and his partner were to find there were other horrors yet to emerge. Cohle describes this "a dream that you had inside a locked room; a dream about being a person, and like a lot of dreams there's a monster at the end" ("The Locked Room").

Cohle's dream and darkness motifs in this series also speak to another viewpoint, in that it also is an overarching design in respect to both the evolutionary development of the noosphere and the evolutionary psycho-sensory facets that allows connection to it. Just as the earthly development of the noosphere supposedly commenced with the first arrival of humankind on the planet and their primitive state of abjectness, with a corresponding evolutionary prospect of ending with entry into a "fullness of knowing" (Ritchie 214). This cycle of awareness is reflected in the first scene of female desecration and the final scene of night-time darkness. It is in the last episode that both detectives emerge damage and wounded but into a personal transcendent reference to light and a "transrational understanding" (Ashton 57) for.

Drilling into this cyclical connection even further, prior to arriving in Louisiana Cohle's two-year-old daughter Sophia has been killed in a car accident, more than likely as a result of his inattention. In contrast to the meaning of her name defined as "knowledge," Cohle fell into the unknowing pit of depression and self destruction through alcoholism. When Cohle finds Dora Lange's body on the same date as Sofia's birthday, and with

Dora meaning "gift" the pain of both them possibly becoming the ultimate "abject" through death surfaces. As is often the case in this series, Cohle describes this sense of darkness to Hart through the Nietzsche's notion of the abyss: "She went straight into a coma, and then, somewhere in that blackness she slipped off into another, deeper kind" ("Seeing Things"). However, in tacitly recognizing the connection between these deaths and the abussos he begins to make connections to this landscape swathe of "southern dysfunction from race to sexuality" (Courtney 130). Although telling Hart that: "Fuck, I don't want to know anything anymore. This is a world where nothing is solved" (The Secret Fate of All Life), he begins to realize that in order to find and confronting the landscape that produced the psychotic terror he must accept the pain and depth of the abyss. As Frank (1995:202) contends: "The wound is a source of stories, as it opens both in and out: *in,* in order to hear the *story* of the other's suffering, and *out,* in order to tell its own *story.*" Hence, Cohle he is also allowing the wounds of Dora Lange to speak, but this initial wound provides his particular "other within" to emerge and also speak for both of them.

Cohle's comment concerning his daughter's "slipping into darkness" and the visceral connection to the landscape was further expressed to Hart in the language peculiar to the Biblical apocalypse, creation and end of the noosphere. "I get a bad taste in my mouth out here. Aluminum, ash, like you can smell the psychosphere" ("The Long Bright Dark"). As Kristeva states (1991:187) this kind of primeval sensory experience is a dark and liminal spatial "encounter with the other-whom we perceive by means of sight, hearing, smell, but do not 'frame' within our consciousness."

While the apocalyptic-like landscape, and Lange's death scene both haunt and guide Cohle as not only "becomes what he sees and a way of seeing," it also forces him to enter the mythic "beast within paradigm" (Bourgault du Courdray 5). As a holistic symbol, the spiral motif is one of the most fundamental of archetypal patterns representing resonance of the physical world with an existential disturbance in a culture. This cycle of cultural disorder and a sense of spiritual loss develops giving rise to an ongoing surfacing of darkness and the monstrous. Cohle becomes a key component of overcoming the bleakness of this disharmony as the archetypal and metaphorical repeat of Theseus and the Minotaur narrative. Like this mythic character, he ultimately enters a symbolic Knossian darkness to destroy a monstrous serial killer, as both the intended sacrifice and the victor.

Just as Dora Lange was initially a "silent witness" emerging from the darkness of night, so Cohle's first point of tacit resonance with the spiral marking on her back was in the same vein. While first thought to be satanic signs by those at the crime scene, this emblem has multiple meanings, one of which is the "brilliant darkness of hidden silence" (Dionysius in Eco, 151). This oldest of human markers also represented Cohle's initial point of entry into the killing of young woman who lived on the dark side of Louisiana life, and the primitive state of Cohle's personal and investigative connectivity with the noosphere. As an integral component, this association and the visual voice of the environment is inferred through the constant insertion of visually bleak and dark referents to the petrochemical industry, and the destruction of the Louisiana littoral zone. Described by Black (62) as "the sacrificial landscape of Petrolia," these bleak locus points reveal the particular subliminal mythic power of this particular landscape, which has become imbued with the sense of darkness beyond and below the surface of the seen. This aspect of how a landscape can seep into one's sense of being is not restricted to this investigative landscape. As Taylor believes, all the landscapes in which humans live are "a storehouse of cultural values, … and not only what we see but a way of seeing. It is not a dead history but history which is with us now" (25, 26).

However, in another way Cohle had already connected to the bleakness of this landscape and become conditioned "to a way of seeing" and to the concept of "seeing within" through his topographical meditative practice of focusing on the cross above his bed. While the cross is often deemed to be Christian, it is in fact one the oldest pagan symbols with numerous forms, but it is often represented as a tree, which in turn extends the symbolism as creation, the sign of life or life giving. As Hislop states: "There is hardly a pagan tribe where the cross has not been found" (199). In a mythological sense, the cross is often viewed synonymously with noosphere and the creation of the earth through the "light of the Great Fire" (Bayley 120). However, in order to find this light, one must first suffer the "hollowness of the locked room in the cellar" (Deardorff 167). The locked room experience is a critical theme in *True Detective*.

While similar to Hart's concept of the cross and Christianity, both of which denote a sacrifice of the innocent, vicarious intercessory death and resurrection, for Cohle it also initially symbolized a cry of self-sacrifice, abandonment and death to his own ego consciousness. Thus, this motif was both a representative of the sacrificial landscape of Louisiana and the setting in which Dora Lange was found. The only emblematic relationship with Christianity that Cohle had with the cross symbol that he focused on each day is the notion of death as penultimate abandonment: "My God! My God! Why have you forsaken me?" (*New International Version*, Matt, 27:46).

However, only those who have the determination to "enter the unknown, from the solid ground of the known" (Ashton: 40) can grasp the true meaning and power of both sacrifice and darkness. This "unknown" is more than simply an empty space, as Ashton (7) believes it is the state of also becoming a "void, of being nullified, a state of being made into nothing." It is only becoming as nothing that one's tacit knowledge and awareness of the world outside of this "abyss like state" can spread in all directions. As stated in previous sections engaging with the noosphere and the subtle complexity of the labyrinthine networks of understanding this brings is not an instantaneous experience. This connectivity actually begins with moments "in the rough" (Whitehead 1966:6). These are often simple experiences that appear as unnoticed or barely felt inklings of importance.

From another parallel perspective, arriving as an investigator in this city whose name means "here comes the knower a quick, clever mind capable of grasping and assimilating new ideas," (Kabalarian Philosophy), Cohle firstly had to become "the nullified, a place where nothing is" (Ashton 8). As the unknown detective with "files that were classified or redacted" ("The Long Bright Dark") he entered the state of Louisiana and the murder site as a Melchizadek figure. Just as this biblical figure entered the Biblical world of Abraham "with a revelation of the Divine Voice" (Orlov 44), as a vague and completely unknown "sacrificial saviour type," so to Cohle "came from Texas and nobody knew him" ("The Long Bright Dark"). Through his arrival, this mythical Melchizadek figure linked the distant past with the present manifesting a distinction between light and darkness through the "apocalypse of Abraham" (Orlov 110). This mythic apotelesmatic intersection, or cyclical repetition of possibility finality, not only allowed for the development of a new "convergence of probabilities" (Sheehan 127) but also heralded a final eschatological battle for those willing to authentically sense the "beyond," "which obliterates emptiness" (Ashton 13). In the same way Cohle entered the murder site as the unknown, earning the nickname of the "tax man" ("The Long Bright Dark"), which has a strong Biblical reference of transcending darkness to light as found in the Gospel of Luke. In similar ways to all of these Biblical figures his life was connected to, Cohle was able meld the unseen psychical world of the psychosphere with the physical evidence of the murder scene. As well, just as Melchizadek's appearance triggered deep emotional reflection and reaction in Abraham the patriarch, leading ultimately to a sacrificial offering, so too Cohle's murder investigation of the sacrifice of Dora Lange became an emotional investigation in which "one sense triggers another sense" ("The Locked Room").

Through the circular refocusing of Cohle's psyche and constant connection to the landscape within episode and through the series, it becomes clear that his connection to the murder and the events in his life began to crystallize as he and Hart drove up to the initial crime scene. With Dora Lange's body positioned at a crossroad, where "the unvillaged" gather "to find a sense of self and community" ("The Hero with a Thousand Faces" xxxvi); and under a tree, the latter an ancient symbol of crucifixion, and both death and the resurrected life (Ashton 35), Cohle begins to simply circle the scene and look extremely closely. As indicated by the title of the second episode, "Seeing Things" and in contrast to the laissez faire approach by Hart, Cohle he has begun to step out of simply seeing and is ready to perceive "the vague beyond, waiting for penetration in regard to its detail" (Whitehead 6).

Hence, at the Lange crime scene, after commencing his investigation Cohle stares into the center of the tree, which is the same ancient symbol of the cross as a bifurcated place understanding and sacrifice. Explaining this further, Campbell believes this particular semiology represents a "crisis of conscience, illumination and delusion, where *A* is not *A* as what is mirrored is one's own inward reality and truth" ("The Mythic Image" 58). There is a deep resonance in this place and symbolism with the "vague beyond," which in one sense stares back at Cohle, the true detective, further asking what is truth? He returns to this tree years later with deep uncertainty regarding the actual killer, and again at the site finds a wreath similar to the "crown" which had been placed on Dora Lange's head in the same spot in which she has been posed. This time he squats down and peers into the center of the twisted wreath. Cohle realizes that the wreath is not a representation of flat time but as a spiraled symbol of a multicursal universe. While this symbol can reflect the noosphere as a multifaceted maze of "contraries—art and chaos, comprehensible artifact and inexplicable experience, pleasure and terror" (Doob 24), in this context it is the embodiment of a place where every possibility and outcome "must be exhausted before one reaches the heart of the labyrinth: 'Where, mind, the Minotaur waits with two final possibilities: defeat and death or victory and freedom'" (Barth 75).

For Cohle, the original rose crown found on Dora Lange has now become superimposed into his psyche and his investigation by deeper facets of symbolism. With the rose being emblematic of the feminine, and the wreath a three-dimensional representation of the noosphere as labyrinth, this crossover linkage would certainly speak to Cohle about the intersection of Dora Lange's murder and this investigation. Rather than being part of "ghetto in space" her death was a parallel to his "moment in the garden contemplation" ("The Long Bright Dark"). While her death mirrored his daughter's death, and indeed his own bleak ideational propensity, the symbols surrounding her final posed death site and his meditative site, speak more to the possibility of self awareness than the mind being simply and "accretion of sensory experience" ("The Long Bright Dark"). Indeed, the labyrinth is also considered to be a mirror, which we find later in the series, and which will also be dealt with in the next section. "This rise of the symbolism related to the Noosphere also directs Cohle to trust in the development of his hyperconsciousness. the adequation of mind to things, the belief that the mind, given enough time, can understand everything. There are no mysteries, there is only incorrect reasoning" (Holquist 141).

Sensing the Victim's Topography: Unfolding of the Symbolic

Just as this investigation commences in the darkness of night as a monstrous killer carries Dora Lange's body to the tree, Cohle is also coming undone because of category crisis, as it was the anniversary of his deceased daughter's birthday. So too his initial contact with the body of Dora Lange adds to his of pessimism, and his belief that "human consciousness is a misstep in evolution" ("The Long Bright Dark"). His general nihilist philosophic underpinning is confirmed at the Lange crime scene with later comments to Hart that it's "all one giant gutter in space" ("The Long Bright Dark"). However, his embodied responses at the crime scene also tell another unfolding side to his story. With Dora Large bound in a face down prayer position under a tree, bound to "the very symbol of the universe" (Aivanhov 25) her overall embodiment could also denote an archetypal connection of "wholeness, ... once the external or mask aspect is no longer identified with" (Ashton 35). Just as Dora's "false mask" behind which she has been hiding had been removed through the release of death and the touch of the tree in death, so too for Cohle this site is rich in symbolism and represents the possibility of still being able to remove "the mask of the persona veiling the true Self" (Seifer and Viewig 216). For Cohle, his investigation becomes entwined with an intensely personal connection to the ideal of rebirth and the "knowledge of eternal release while living" ("Myths to Live By" 90).

Moving forward into the investigation, Cohle's later comment that this murder is "some kind of archetype" ("The Locked Room") not only reveals his existential resonance to the scenes of carnage he comes across, but also resonance with the existential and mythic patterns that emerge. In contrast to Dora Lange's downward death gaze, arriving at the initial crime scene and at the site of the Reggie Ledoux's killing grounds, a pattern of looking to the heavens has begun to develop. Indeed, before Marty Hart shoots him in the head after finding the captive children, Ledoux also looks up. His with his final words to Cohle are: "Black stars rise" ("The Secret Fate of All

Life"). Just as at this time the stars are not visible at both sites, it is only at the end of this intuitive investigative stream that he also looks to the heavens and realizes the inverse is actually the truth, and that the now visible stars are the "brain of heaven" (Forster 76, 77).

There are other instances at Dora's death scene that indicate that Cohle is experiencing an existential shift away from "time is a flat circle" to one in which the universe is multifaceted, multi-dimensional and rich in "nodes and spiral" (Eco 37). While a tree itself is a symbol of the universe as a labyrinth (Eco), the devil traps hanging from the trees above Dora Lange and found in key investigative points are also symbols of a multi faceted universe. While in this instance the killer has used them as a marker of what Cohle later learns is the territory of the Yellow King, he is also becoming aware that this is also a perversion of their original meaning. The foundational meaning of these pyramids relates directly to the noosphere view of the time-space continuum in which the "sovereign rules over space because he is master of time" (Maheu et al 44). Related to this concept, they also have spatial meaning implying "that which reaches to heaven" (Morgan 43). Given the philosophy that Cohle discusses with Hart regarding meditating on the cross event also a symbol of reaching to heaven, it is reasonable to assume he is also aware of the transgressive ideals and the "inversion of symmetry" practices (Morgan 25) of those who seek to subvert this universal ideal. As well, Cohle later confesses to Hart that he doesn't sleep but dreams, and "like a lot of dreams, there is a monster at the end of it" ("The Locked Room"). The monster's role is to transgress, destroy and invert the status quo. In other words, Cohle clearly could see the "devil traps" found around Dora Lange as markers of a monstrous inversion that are markers of an ideal that instead of reaching up, signifies that which is reaching down. "When contained by geographic, generic, or epistemic marginalization, the monster can function as an alter ego, as an alluring projection of (an Other) self" (Clark 48). Indeed, at the end of his hunt for Childress, he finds himself underground in the heart of an actual labyrinthine structure, and at the depths of human depravity.

More importantly, while the devil traps are defining a monstrous space and a monstrous act, they are also defining the number of the members who perpetrate these kinds of deaths. As will be seen in comments in ensuing sections of this chapter, the metaphoric markers in this space reveal a reflexive shift in Cohle's thinking, and reflexive shift towards the symbolic meaning of this space also symbolically travels with him. Just as there are five "devil traps" there are five points of crucifixion in Cohle's immediate sight in his daily mediation, five people around the dinner table on Cohle's first visit to the Hart home, Audrey and Maise are seen playing with five Ken doll standing over a lone Barbie, five hooded men on horseback as seen in Dora Lange's family home and there are five human ("The Locked Room"). Cohle mentions, or experiences all five of these in his investigations, but more importantly in these synaesthesia episodes all of these senses become heightened, and according to Cohle interconnected. "One sense triggers another sense" ("The Long Bright Dark"). Commencing in the very first episode in relation to his connection to the environment and repeated towards the end of his investigation, "…aluminum, ash. I've tasted these before" ("The Long Bright Dark"), these episodes are often attributed to insomnia, PTSD and drug use as part of his time as an undercover agent. However, for those like Cohle who are becoming attuned to the noosphere, hyper-sensory experiences are not medical or mental health issues but rather entry into "flickering modes of timeless schema" ("Primitive Mythology" 18). These experiences in fact appearing over the immediate horizons of time and space allowing a shift from the myopia of the supposed real world in which seeing is actually "blindness … and thinking means to grope one's way" (Eco 82). While Cohle was not sure of the reliability of these experiences, he certainly felt at times he "was mainlining the secret truth of the universe" ("Seeing Things").

His alternate noosphere blasts of synesthesia experiences, and return to the reality of the immediate reveal a developing understanding that the symbols in his investigative world originating from the Lange site and are pinpointing the murderers. This is no more revealed than in his high degree of resonance with the number five. All the subtle indicators related to this number is made clear when in Cohle's interrogation with Papania and Gilbrough, he cuts five male figures out of the beer cans he has been drinking and places them in a circle. Clearly done in their sight they are unable to access any of his clearly symbolic actions or motifs. Hart had recognized Cohle's ability and later tells these two investigators: "Well, if you two talked to Rust, you weren't getting a read on him. He was getting a read on you" ("The Locked Room").

Sensing the Internal Geography: A Connection with the Symbolic Core

It becomes abundantly transparent through Cohle's explicit comments, and his ellipsis remarks both oral and visual that his mind and investigation had begun a synchronous expansion as well as telescopic reflective introspection with respect to all the symbolic aspects embedded in his investigation. The "red thread" (Fitzsimmons and Lanphar) that was woven as a multicursal symbolic connector throughout *True Detective* was the symbolism of the cross and the garden crucifixion. While not having the vestiges of the religion, the ideals of Cohle's meditation, and his connection to the Christian pilgrim entering the labyrinth of the world, "being in the world but not of it" (*New International Version*, John 17.16) is a long standing spiritual metaphor. This pathway is never smooth or singular in direction, and as seen in *True Detective* follows a circuitous, and at times inverse revolving and intersecting pathway to a central core. "Only the curved, crossed or knotted line can be a sign making the line simultaneously something intelligible, conveying meaning standing for something else, and at the same time repeatable, already a repetition, so imposing on the sign the aporias of repetition, the blind alleys in thought to which repetition leads" (Miller 8).

Just as the labyrinth of investigation Cohle had embarked on was focused on a central core of finding the mass murderers, so too it ended in a psychophysical central core of a Corcosian labyrinth. Cohle's focus on finding an existential stasis through the cross motif followed the same repetitious pattern of his investigation, "which seeped to the surface" (Levi-Strauss 443). Experience in this labyrinth pathway of criminal investigation paralleled life itself, to the point where Cohle found himself looking at himself.

The critical instance where Cohle fully exposed his attempts to find himself, is revealed in his comments to Marty Hart: "I contemplate the moment in the garden, the idea of allowing your own crucifixion" ("The Long Bright Dark"). The central thrust of Cohle's premise is that Christ his crucifixion and willingly allowed himself to be killed rather than being part of a divine plan, or as an ordained or redemptive act. In that sense, it was more akin to suicide. However, Cole realized he was unable to follow "this through to this completion." "I tell myself I bear witness, but the real answer is that it's obviously my programming, and I lack the constitution for suicide" ("The Long Bright Dark"). Cohle reflective praxis regarding the cross event was simply seen as a component of following one man's historical pathway to crucifixion, and the conditions that allowed one to fully give over to the pull of the cosmos. As he was drawn to a propensity of pessimism, the idea that time is flat circle, and the labyrinthine ideal that "the wanderer in the labyrinth" ("From Tree to the Labyrinth" 76) as naturally on a cross focused pathway initially fitted with his statement: "The truth wills out, and everybody sees. Once the strings are cut, all fall down" ("The Locked Room"). In essence his daily cross experience was a rejection of the Christian concept of a divine plan where one divine being from on high was an intercessory "ransom for many" (*New International Version*, Mark

10.45), which lead to a final resurrection. Despite his synathaesic episodes, which were transitory markers of subjective knowing, reflectively falling into the circular heart of the noosphere was "the only sensory experience that gives meaning" ("The Long Bright Dark").

Seemingly arising from his past experience that had coalesced into a distinctive points of memory with the death of his daughter, and his subsequent undercover work within a motorcycle gang, he came to the conclusion that the disposition to accept psychical suffering provides the means to authentic understanding. Following on from these experiences his worldview now includes a willingness to accept his fate, his place in the universe and the guilt arising from his daughter's death. "To realize that all your life—you know, all your love, all your hate, all your memories, all your pain—it was all the same thing" ("The Locked Room").

However, this nihilist perception of reality began to change when he realized through the labyrinthine graphics left on the body of Dora Lange, the deserted church wall and their own dwellings that they were trapped in a never-ending cycle of repetition. This notion of cyclical entrapment of the killers, and the corresponding possibility that Cohle can emerge from his own cycle of psychical ensnarement is also prefigured before entering this church, when Cohle again looks up and sees a bird murmuration in the form of a spiral ("Seeing Things"). "The myth grows spiral wise until the intellectual impulse that originated it is exhausted" (Levi-Strauss 443). This particular scene acts as a connection to the noosphere spiral as does the constant repetition of related spiral images amplifying and reordering Cohle's inner vision. This constant subliminal repetition can be seen when for example Cohle visits Kelly in the mental institution ("Haunted House") and in the drawing by one of Hart's daughters seen on a paper plate on the Hart's kitchen wall.

This understanding of being trapped in someone else's vision of a universal cycle is further fleshed out in the episode entitled, "The Locked Room." Endlessly pouring through case notes because of his insomnia Cohle realizes he has come upon a suspect, the meth dealer Reggie Ledoux, who skipped bail. While Ledoux has become a primary suspect who both detectives realize they must catch him before it kills again, it is in a retort to Hart that Cohle's cross reflection has begun to shift his thinking. "See, we all got what I call a life trap, this gene-deep certainty that things will be different, that you'll move to another city and meet the people that'll be friends for the rest of your life, that you'll fall in love and be fulfilled. Fucking fulfillment, heh, and closure, whatever the fuck those two … fucking empty jars to hold this shitstorm, and nothing is ever fulfilled until the very end, and closure" ("The Locked Room"). The last phraseology reveals his realization that he too has been trapped in a locked room, and that rather than life's pathway being a never-ending circle there will be a point of closure. In a linkage to an earlier episode where he admitted to Hart that he didn't sleep but simply dreamt, Cohle comes full circle and states "like lots of dreams there's a monster at the end of it" ("The Locked Room"). While this is a reference to Ledoux, Cohle also links himself to the entrapped psyche of this serial killer. Although bound within his own locked room meditating on the cross, a reference to the locked tomb of Christ, this has enabled him to search the depths of his soul. It also has left him with the possibility that just as Christ was deemed to be a criminal and died with criminals he may suffer the same fate. However, more importantly there is a possibility that a form of personal resurrection may also be an ending. Willingness to accept an alternate fate, a shift in his place in the universe and a resolution stands in direct contrast to the killers he has been hunting.

Cole's cross experience in his own locked room becomes fleshed out in real life when, in the final scenes of the series as he chases Childress into a labyrinth of underground tunnels, we hear the killer call out: "This is Carcosa.... Come die with me, little priest" ("Form and Void"). Cohle also finally is given proof that his reflexive rites of contemplation are now given full voice as he sees the cosmic spiral above him. While Childress has a false sense of this place and the actions in this symbolic vortex, he does understand the death of Christ as both sacrifice and high priest, and extends this to a cosmic role of the cross-death. Like the Christ figure, Cohle is also now both the sacrifice and the high priest who has willingly entered the site of sacrificial death. Childress then stabs him in much the same way the centurion pierced the body of Christ, and in Biblical terms, lifts him up between the heavens and earth as an intermediary sacrifice. However, Childress' claim to his sister prior to Cohle's arrival that his "ascension removes me from the disc and the loop. I'm near final stage" ("Form and Void") does not pan out as he expected. He is shot and killed by Hart and Cohle, and they are the ones who survive to see the meaning of the "infernal plane" ("Form and Void"). Cradled by Hart, and in all respects similar to the "La Pieta" paintings of the dying Christ, Cohle is also seen with a cross emblazoned on his forehead. Thus, he had completed the meaning of the labyrinth and "raised his eyes from the confusion and limited perceptions of earth to the concentric circles of divine order and justice in the rose which portrays the wounded Christ at the last judgment" (Doob 132).

However, it is only in the symbolic light of the stars as they leave the hospital after their experience in the depth of Carcosa, that both realize that the circular windings of the labyrinth are internal (Bloom xvi). More importantly just as Cohle initially entered the void of death through his cross-contemplation, he also completed the "point of atonement with the voice of the universe, and the other realms" (Ashton 149). He conjoined the "disc and loop" in his death experience in the hospital. In this death sleep he gave voice to his own daughter, and that of Dora Lange and to his final realization of his overall metaphysical journey. As seen in the following final interaction between these two he condenses his thinking, the anguish of his experiences and his cross reflections into a Manichean binary. This labyrinthine "ending sends us back to the beginning in order to work out what the story may be about, as distinct from what, at first sight, it seems to be about" (Borge 33).

Just as Theseus emerged from the Knossian labyrinthine darkness into the light of day as a victor of "self-awareness," so too Cohle has emerged from the psychological high walls of apparent indecipherable unknowing. The environmental, personal and spiritual darkness that once enveloped him is now gone and he can loosen the reflective grip of the "red thread" of his cross reflection. His initial foci of looking up, looking into and looking through at the murder scene of Dora Lange had reached fruition.

As is the case with all metaphysical narratives, and metaphysical detective narratives in particular, the focus on Cohle's approach to solving the murders in Louisiana, the epitome of the Southern myth is more about weaving through and away from "problems of knowing to problems of modes of knowing" (McHale 10). Both of these epistemological and ontological points are the very cultural concerns embedded in the metanarrative of American culture, if not Western society. In an actual world of chaos and spiritual confusion, as represented by the seeing, envisioning and reflection of Rustin Cohle, *True Detective—Season One* steps ahead of embedded and underlying cultural concerns and issues, "as to model the discontinuity between our own mode of being and that of whatever divinity we may wish there were" (McHale 13).

Notes

1. It should be noted that Birkerts had drawn on, and paraphrased the writing of Walter Benjamin

Works Cited

Aivanhov, Omraam. *Angels and the Other Mysteries of the Tree of Life*. Prosveta, 1990.
Allen, Michael. *Reading CSI: Crime Television Under the Microscope*. Taurus, 2007.
Arthur, Kate. "The True Detective Creator Debunks Your Craziest Theories." *Buzzfeed*, 16 January 2017, 5:30a.m., wwwbuzzfeed.com/kateaurthur/true-detective-nale-season-1-nic-pizzolatto#.nxVI0vgnP.

Ascari, Maurizio. *A Counter History of Crime Fiction: Supernatural, Gothic, Sensational*. Palgrave Macmillan, 2007.

Ashton, Paul. *From the Brink: Experiences of the Void from a Depth Psychology Perspective*. Karnac Books, 2007.

Barth, John. *Further Fridays: Essays, Lectures, and Other Nonfiction 1984–1994*. Little, Brown and Company, 1995.

Bayley, Harold. *The Lost Language of Symbolism, Vol. 2*. Citadel Press, 1990.

Becker-Leckrone, Megan. *Julia Kristeva and Literary Theory*. Palgrave Macmillan, 2005.

Bierce, Ambrose. "An Inhabitant of Carcosa." *The Complete Short Stories of Ambrose Bierce*. U of Nebraska P, 2005, pp. 51–53.

Birkerts, Sven. "Walter Benjamin, Flâneur: A Flanerie." *The Iowa Review*, Vol. 13, No. 3 (1982): 164–179. Feb 2017, ir.uiowa.edu/iowareview/vol13/iss3/42.

Black, Brian. *Petrolia: The Landscape of America's First Oil Bloom*. Johns Hopkins UP, 2000.

Bloom, Harold. "Into the Living Labyrinth: Reflections and Aphorisms." *The Labyrinth*, edited by Harold Bloom and Blake Hobby, Infobase Publishing, 2009, pp. xv–xvii.

Boldt-Irons, Leslie. "In Search of the Archaic Mother: The Space of the Abject in Bataille's *My Mother* and Baudelaire's *Flower of Evil*." *Beauty and the Abject: Interdisciplinary Perspectives*, edited by Leslie Boldt-Irons, Corrado Federici and Enersto Virgulti, Peter Lang, 2007, pp. 43–58.

Borges, Jorge Luis. *Labyrinths: Selected Stories and Other Writings*, edited by Donald A. Yates and James E. Irby, New Directions, 1964.

Botting, Fred. "Technospectrality: Essays on Uncannimedia." *Technologies of the Gothic in Literature and Culture: Technogothics*, edited by Justin Edwards, Routledge, 2015, pp. 17–34.

Bourgault du Courdray, Chantal. *The Curse of the Werewolves: Fantasy, Horror and the Beast Within*. Taurus, 2006.

Caldwell, John. *Televisuality: Style, Crisis, and Authority in American Television*. Rutgers, 1995.

Campbell, Joseph. *The Hero with a Thousand Faces: Commemorative Edition*. Bolligen, 2004.

_____. *The Inner Reaches of Outer Space*. New World Library, 2002.

_____. *The Masks of God: Creative Mythology*. Condor Press, 1968.

_____. *The Masks of God: Primitive Mythology*, Martine, Secker and Warburg, 1960.

_____. *The Mythic Image*. Princeton UP, 1974.

_____. *Myths to Live By*. Bantam Books, 1993.

_____. *Primitive Mythology*. Martin Secker and Warburg, 1960

Chambers, Aiden. *Tell Me—Children Reading and Talk with the Reading Environment*. Thimble Press, 2011.

Chevalier, Jean, and Alain Gheerbrant, editors, *The Penguin Dictionary of Symbols*, translated by John Buchanan Brown, Penguin Books, 1996.

Clark, David. "Monstrosity, Ineligibility, Denegation: De Man, Bp Nichol and the Resistance to Post Modernism." *Reading Culture*, edited by Jerome Cohen, U of Minnesota P, 1996, pp. 40–73.

Collins, Christopher. *Homeland Mythology: Biblical Narrative in American Culture*. Pennsylvania UP, 2007.

Conty, Patrick. *The Genesis and Geometry of the Labyrinth*. Inner Traditions, 2002.

Cook, Michael. *Detective Fiction and the Ghost Story: The Haunted Text*. Palgrave Macmillan, 2014.

Coomaraswamy, Ananda Kentish. *Time and Eternity*. Artibus Asiae Publishers, 1989.

Coomaraswamy, Rama. *The Door in the Sky: Coomaraswamy on Myth and Meaning*. Princeton UP, 1997.

Courtney, Susan. *Split Screen Nation: Moving Images of the American West and South*. Oxford UP, 2017.

Davies, Michael. *The Order of Melchisedech: A Defense of the Catholic Priesthood 2nd Edition*. Roman Catholic Books, 1993.

Deacon, Terence. *Incomplete Nature. How Mind Emerged from Matter*. Norton, 2012.

Deardorff, Daniel. *The Other Within: The Genius of Deformity in Myth, Culture, and Psyche.* White Cloud Press, 2004.
De Chardin, Pierre Teilhard. *The Phenomenon of Man.* Harper Perennial, 1959.
Doob, Penelope Reed. *The Idea of the Labyrinth.* Cornell UP, 1990.
Durgnat Raymond. *Films and Feelings,* MIT P, 1971.
Eco, Umberto. *From Tree to the Labyrinth: Historical Studies on the Sign and Interpretation.* Translated by Anthony Oldcorn, Harvard UP, 2014.
_____. *Postille a Il Nome Della Rosa,* Bompiani, 1984.
Eliade, Mircea. *The Sacred and the Profane: The Nature of Religion.* Harcourt Brace, 1987
_____. Translated by Mac Ricketts. *Autobiography Volume 1: Journey East, Journey West, 1907–1937,* Harper Row, 1983
Faris, Wendy. *Labyrinths of Language: Symbolic Landscape and Narrative Design in Modern Fiction,* Johns Hopkins UP, 1988.
Fentress, Kames, and Chris Wickham. *Social Memory,* Blackwell, 1992.
Fetterman, David. *Ethnography Step by Step.* SAGE, 2009.
Fitzsimmons, P., and Edie Lanphar. "Jumping Gaps, Buildings and Bridges: Making Meaning Across Transmedia Narratives." *Worlds, Words and Narratives: Transmedia and Immersion,* edited by Eric Forcier and Tawnya Ravy, Interdisciplinary Press, 2014, pp. 1–11.
Forster, E.M. *Aspects of the Novel.* Edward Arnold, 1974.
Francis, Andrew (2014) "Creature of Water." *Deep Blue: Critical Reflections on Nature, Religion and Water,* edited by Sylvie Shaw and Andrew Francis. Routledge, 2014, pp. 89–106.
Frank, Arthur. *The Wounded Storyteller: Body, Illness and Ethics.* U of Chicago P, 1997.
Fuhrman, Mark. *Silent Witness: The Untold Story of Terri Schiavo's Death.* HarperCollins, 2005.
Genette, Gérard. *The Architext: An Introduction.* U of California P, 1992.
Hills, Matt, and Schneider, Stephen J. "The Devil Made Me Do It!: Representing Evil and Disarticulating Mind/Body in the Supernatural Serial Killer Film." *The Changing Face of Evil in Film and Television,* edited by Martin F. Norden, Rodopi, 2007.
Hislop, the Rev. David. *The Two Babylons: Or the Papal Worship Proved to Be the Worship of Nimrod and His Wife.* S.W. Partridge, 1984.
Holquist, Michael. "Whodunit and Other Questions: Metaphysical Detective Stories in Post-War Fiction," *New Literary History,* Vol. 3, No. 1, Johns Hopkins UP, 1971, pp. 135–156. Scribd, https://www.scribd.com/document/245339641/Whodunit
The Holy Bible: New International Version. Zondervan, 1984.
hooks, bell. "Marginality as Site of Resistance." *Out There: Marginalization and Contemporary Cultures,* edited by Russell Ferguson et al., The New York Museum of Contemporary Art, 1990, pp. 341–343.
Hornsby, Teresa. "The Annoying Woman: Biblical Scholarship After Judith Butler." *Bodily Citations: Religion and Judith Butler,* edited by Ellen T. Armour and Susan M. St. Ville, Columbia UP, 2006, pp. 71–92.
Houston, Jean. *The Search for the Beloved: Journeys in Mythology and Sacred Psychology.* G.P. Putnam's, 1987.
Howe, Irving. "What's the Trouble? Social Crisis, Crisis of Civilization, or Both?" *A Voice Still Heard: Selected Essays of Irving Howe,* edited by Nina Howe, Yale UP, 2014, pp. 139–160.
Jenner, Marieke. *American TV Detective Drama: Serial Investigations.* Palgrave Macmillan, 2016.
Johnston, George. *The Spirit Paraclete in the Gospel of John.* Cambridge UP, 1970.
Johnston, Jessica, and Cornelia Sears. "The Stepford Wives and the Technoscientific Imaginary." *Extrapolation,* vol. 52, no.1, 2011, pp. 75–93.
Jung, Carl. *The Archetypes and the Collective Unconscious.* Princeton UP, 1959.
Kabalarian Philosophy Available https://www.kabalarians.com/index.cfm
Kandinsky, Wassily. *Concerning the Spiritual in Art.* George Wittenborn, 1955.
Kane, Sean (1994) *Wisdom of Mythtellers.* Broadview Press, 1994.
Kant, Immauel. *Perpetual Peace and Other Essays.* Translated by Ted Humphrey, Hackett, 1983.
Kern, Hermann. *Through the Labyrinth: Designs and Meaning Over 5,000 Years.* Prestel, 2000.
Kojpare, Derek. *CSI.* Wiley-Blackwell, 2010.

Kristeva, Julia. *Powers of Horror: An Essay on Abjection.* Columbia UP, 1982.
Lam, Anita. *Making Crime Television: Producing Entertaining Representations of Crime for Television Broadcast.* Routledge, 2013.
Lawrence, Samuel. *Supernatural America: A Cultural History.* Greenwood Publishing, 2011.
Levi-Strauss, Claude. "The Structural Study of Myth. Myth: A Symposium." *The Journal of American Folklore,* vol. 68, no. 270, 1955, pp. 428–444.
Lumly, Brian. *Psychosphere.* Tor Doherty, 1984.
Logan, Elliot. *Breaking Bad and Dignity: Unity and Fragmentation in the Serial Television Drama.* Palgrave, 2016.
Maheu, René, et al. *Science and Synthesis: An International Colloquium Organized by Unesco on the Tenth Anniversary of the Death of Albert Einstein and Teilhard De Chardin.* Springer Verlag, 1971.
Malone, Thomas. "Global Change." *Biosphere and Noosphere Reader: Global Environment, Society and Change,* edited by Paul Sampson and David Pit, Routledge, pp. 131–133.
Mann, Jocelyn. "Traversing the Labyrinth: The Structures of Discovery in Eco's *The Name of the Rose*." *Naming the Rose: Essays on Eco's the Name of the Rose,* edited by Thomas Inge, UP of Mississippi, 1988, pp. 130–145.
McCabe, Janet. "Mac and Monotheism—Remembering 9/11, Surviving Trauma and Mourning Work *CSI: NY*." *The War on Terror: Post 9/11 Television Drama, Docudrama and Documentary,* edited by Stephen Lacey and Derek Paget, U of Wales P, 2015, pp. 95–108.
McHale, Brian. *Postmodernist Fiction.* Methuen, 1987.
Mendlesohn, Farah. *Rhetorics of Fantasy.* Wesleyan UP, 2008.
Milestone, Kate, and Anneke Meyer. *Gender and Popular Culture.* Polity, 2012.
Miller, Hillis. *Ariadne's Thread: Story Lines.* Yale UP, 1992.
Morgan, Diane. *From Satan's Crown to the Holy Grail: Emeralds in Myth, Magic and History.* Prager, 2007.
Nadel, Alan. *American Narratives, Post-Modernism, and the Atomic Age.* Duke UP, 1995.
Nemme, Kori, and Phil Fitzsimmons. "The 'Hero's Journey: Personal Resonance as Response to Narrative. December 2–5, 2004." *Australian Association for Research in Education,* March 2016, aare.edu.au/04pap/nem04361.pdf
Nietzsche, Friedrich. *The Gay Science (1882).* Translated by Walter Kaufmann, Vintage, 1974.
Orlov, Andrei. *Heavenly Priesthood in the Apocalypse of Abraham.* Cambridge UP, 2013.
Ozouf, Mona. "Fraternity." *A Critical Dictionary of the French Revolution,* Translated Arthur Goldhammer, edited by Francois Furet and Mona Ozouf, Harvard UP, pp. 694–702, 1989.
Plato. "Timaeus," translated by Benjamin Jowett. *The Collected Dialogues of Plato,* edited by Edith Hamilton and Huntington Cairns, Princeton UP, 1980, pp. 1151–1211.
Pizzolatto, Nic, writer. *True Detective—Season One.* HBO, 12 January 2014.
Porter, Dennis. *The Pursuit of Crime: Art and Ideology in Detective Fiction.* Yale UP, 1981.
Restuccia, Frances L. "Black and Blue: Kieslowski's Melancholia." *Revolt, Affect, Collectivity: The Unstable Boundaries of Kristeva's Polis,* edited by Tina Chanter and Ewa Plonowoska Ziarek, SUNY P, 2012, pp. 193–208.
Richer, Jean. *Sacred Geometry of the Ancient Greeks: Astrological Symbolism in Art, Architecture and Landscape.* Translated by Christine Rhone, SUNY P, 1994.
Ritchie, Daniel. *The Fullness of Knowing: Modernity to Postmodernity from Defoe Gadamer.* Baylor UP, 2010.
Rollason, Christopher. "The Detective Myth in Edgar Allan Poe's Dupin Trilogy." *American Crime Fiction: Studies in the Genre,* edited by Brian Docherty, Macmillan, 1988, pp. 4–22.
Romine, Scott. *The Narrative Forms of Souther Community.* Louisiana State UP, 1999.
Roszak, Theodore. *The Cult of Information: The Folklore of Computers and the True Art of Thinking.* Lutterworth, 1986.
Savage, William. *Cowboy Life: Reconstructing an American Myth.* U of Colorado P, 1993.
Seifer, Nancy and Martin Viewing. *When the Soul Awakens: The Spiritual Evolution and a New World Era.* Gathering Wave Press, 2009.
Selby, Nick. "Mythologies of 'Ecstatic Immersion': America, the Poem and the Ethics of Lyric in Jorie Graham and Lisa Jarnot." *American Mythologies: Essays on Contemporary Literature,* edited by William Blazek and Michael Glenday, Liverpool UP, 2005, pp. 202–225.

Sheehan, John. "Melchisedech in Christian Consciousness." *Catholic Priesthood: Biblical Foundations*, edited by Fr. Thomas Lane, Science Ecclesiasioues 18, 2016, Emmaus Road, pp. 127–38.
Sheldrake, Rupert. *The Presence of the Past: Morphic Resonance Residence and the Habits of Nature*. Park Street Press, 1988.
Smith, John David, and Thomas H. Appleton, Jr. *A Mythic Land Apart: Reassessing Southerners and Their History*. Greenwood, 1997.
Steenberg, Lindsay. *Forensic Science in Contemporary Popular Culture: Gender, Crime and Science*. Routledge, 2012.
Stern, Daniel. *The Interpersonal World of the Infant: A View from Psychoanalysis and Developmental Psychology*. Karnac Books, 1998.
Tacey, David. *The Spirituality Revolution: The Emergence of Contemporary Spirituality*. Brunner-Routledge, 2004.
Tait, R. Collin. "The HBO-ification of Genre." *Cinephile*, No. 4, pp. 50–57, June 2017, cinephile.ca/archives/volume-4-post-genre/the-hbo-ification-of-genre/
Targ, Russell. *Limitless Mind: a Guide to Remote Viewing and Transformation of Consciousness*. New World Library, 2004.
Taylor, Ken. "Reconciling Aesthetic Value and Social Value: Dilemmas of Interpretation and Application." *APT Bulletin*, vol. 30, no. 1, 1999, pp. 51–55. JSTOR, www.jstor.org/stable/1504627.
Thacker, Eugene. *Tentacles Longer Than Night: Horror of Philosophy Vol. 3*. Zero Press, 2015.
Thomson, Kirten. *Apocalyptic Dread: American Film at the Turn of the Millenium*. SUNY P, 2007.
Tillich, Paul. *Dynamics of Faith*. Perennial, 2001.
Torben, Grobal. *Moving Pictures: A New Theory of Film Genres, Feelings and Cognition*. Clarendon P, 1999.
Turner, Victor. *The Ritual Process: Structure and Anti-structure*. Cornell UP, 1991.
Verndasky, Vladimir. *The Biosphere*. Springer Verlag, 1998.
Vest, Jason. *The Wire, Deadwood, Homicide, and NYPD Blue* Praeger, 2010.
Wagner-Martin, Linda. *A History of American Literature: To the Present*. Wiley-Blackwell, 2012.
Whitehead, Alfred North. *Modes of Thought*. The Free Press, 1968.
Wilson, Andrea. *Biopoetics: Towards an Existential Ecology*. Springer, 2015.
Wilson, Scott. "The Nonsense of Detection: Truth Between Science and the Real." *True Detection*, edited by Edia Connole, Paul J. Ennis, und Nicola Masciandaro, Schism Press, 2014, pp. 146–163.
Yar, Majid. *Crime and the Imaginary of Disaster: Post Apocalyptic Fictions and the Crisis of Social Order*. Palgrave Macmillan, 2015.
Yates, Donald, and Irby, James, E. *Labyrinths, Selected Stories & Other Writings, by Jorge Luis Barges*, edited and translated by Donald Yates, James E. Irby et al., New Directions Publishing, 1964.

Pushing Daisies, Forensic Fairy Tales and Supernatural Crime Procedurals

SCOTT ROGERS

There are a number of features that define the typical—and wildly popular—police procedural. Broadly speaking, the genre focuses on the process of solving a crime, and the reveal of both the criminal and the motive usually serves as the denouement of the story. Typically, the shows focus on the law enforcement officers—or on individuals or groups operating as detectives in some capacity. Often, and especially so in the early days of the genre (with *Dragnet* [1951–59] or *The Untouchables* [1959–63]), the shows were episodic and did not require viewers to follow much—if any—plot from episode to episode. Later series, such as *Hill Street Blues* (1981–87), *Cagney and Lacey* (1981–88), and *Miami Vice* (1984–90), sometimes threaded B-plots and character development through multiple episodes. The popularity of this genre is unquestionable. The original *Law and Order* (1990–2010) series ran 20 seasons (tying it with *Gunsmoke* [1955–75] for the longest-running scripted television show). Its first spinoff, *SVU* (1999–present), is, at the time of this writing, poised to equal its parent series' 20-year-run. Similar series that followed, such as *CSI* (2000–15) and *NCIS* (2003–present), continued to capitalize in this police procedural structure to great success.

Significant modifications to the genre are a relatively recent phenomenon, and many seem to have emerged from a period of fairly remarkable experimentation (or, perhaps more accurately, rampant copying) in the 1990s. The origins of the supernatural procedural lie in that period of experimentation. *Forever Knight* (1992–96) presented viewers with an 800-year-old vampire police detective in Toronto. *The Sentinel* (1996–99) focused on a police officer with mystical powers and duties. *The X-Files*

(1993–2002, 2016–18) set the buddy-cop police procedural in a rogue office of the FBI investigating unexplained phenomena (and shows that followed, such as *Fringe* [2008–13], largely followed the same structure where the partners were one believer and one skeptic). The 2000s saw a proliferation of police/crime procedurals that fully embraced these supernatural additions to the genre. Shows such as *Medium* (2005–11), *Supernatural* (2005–present), *Torchwood* (2006–11), *Moonlight* (2007–08), *Sanctuary* (2008–11), *Warehouse 13* (2009–14), *Lost Girl* (2010–15), *Haven* (2010–15), *Grimm* (2011–17), *Once Upon a Time* (2011–18), *Sleepy Hollow* (2013–17), *Constantine* (2014–15) fully embrace their supernatural components.

Perhaps the most curious addition in this list is Bryan Fuller's beloved—and, tragically, prematurely canceled—series, *Pushing Daisies* (2007–09).[1] At first glance, *Pushing Daisies* may seem an odd entry in this list of supernatural crime procedurals. Structurally, each episode contains at least an A- and a B-plot, with the A-plot serving as the crime procedural and the B-plot often focusing on other characters or on the larger mystery of Chuck's (Anna Friel) murder (there are subsequent subplots involving Olive's [Kristin Chenoweth] love life, Ned [Lee Pace] and Chuck's relationship, Chuck's aunts' [Swoosie Kurtz and Ellen Greene] mental health and career, and Cod's [Chi McBride] various hobbies). Early episodes in season one focus particularly on worldbuilding, presenting us with relatively straightforward crimes for the team to solve while slowly building the various other plot threads that will occupy the peripheral characters in their respective subplots. In some ways, then, *Pushing Daisies* offers two layers of procedural crime narrative, one of which focuses on the mercenary activities of Ned and Cod, while the other attempts to solve the mystery of Chuck's murder—which, we learn at the end of the first episode, carries a $50,000 reward. Its primary distinction is that it is neither a drama nor is it horror-based in any way; at its core, it is a comedy whose throughline concerns two lovers kept apart by terrible circumstances. Despite these distinctions, ABC explicitly promoted *Pushing Daisies* as a show about crime: the initial teaser trailer for *Pushing Daisies* described it as a "forensic fairy tale," thus marking it clearly as a kind of procedural crime drama.[2]

In her review of "Dummy" for *The AVClub*, Genevieve Koski wondered about the show's genre:

> The big question after last week's episode seemed to be "how in the hell are they going to sustain this for a whole season?" and this episode basically laid out the formula. Despite the candy colors and musical numbers (more on that in a minute), it looks like *Daisies* is basically shaking out as a procedural of all things, with [a] couple of extended arcs to tie the season together. It's a workable enough hybrid, though the weirdness of this week's mystery overshadowed any meatier developments [Koski "Dummy"].

Later, Koski would note that the series was deploying familiar elements in unconventional ways:

> As the weeks go by, it's becoming more obvious that *Pushing Daisies* is not going to be about head-scratching, *Lost*-esque twists in the name of advancing an ongoing, unwieldy plot. Rather, the name of the game seems to be appropriating familiar, comfortable material and tweaking it with unexpected details and imagery [Koski "Girth"].

What leads *Pushing Daisies* to occupy a special place in this genre, however, are its "fairy tale" elements. The show focuses on Ned, who discovers as a young boy that he has the ability to bring dead things back to life merely by touching them—the first touch brings them to life; a second touch returns them to being dead.[3] To highlight this fantastic dimension, showrunner Bryan Fuller and his team present the show in hyper-saturated color (which reinforces the surreality of what we are seeing), idealized sets, and rapid-fire—and often deadpan—delivery of dialogue. As Shannon Carlin puts it in a 2017 piece for *Bustle* (written a decade after *Pushing Daisies* was canceled), much about the show marked it as unlike anything else on television at the time:

> Back in 2007 when *Pushing Daisies* premiered it would have been easy to write it off as an Amélie homage. Especially since Fuller and his cinematographer Michael Weaver never denied *Amelie*'s influence over *Pushing Daisies*. "We decided it should feel somewhere between *Amelie* and a Tim Burton film," Weaver told *Variety* in 2007. "Something big, bright and bigger than life."
>
> And that's what it was. From the color palette to the narrator to the fanciful design—Ned's pie shop The Pie Hole is literally shaped like a giant pie…. But, to make the *Amelié* comparison takes away from *Pushing Daisies*' charming originality.
>
> It was a fairytale that wasn't quite a fairytale; a murder mystery that wasn't quite a murder mystery; and a love story that wasn't quite a love story. After all, Ned and Chuck can't even touch due to his condition and hers. It was a will they won't they relationship with deadly consequences [Carlin].

However much the show may have been visually inspired by *Amélie*, Carlin's larger point about the show's complexity is important. As she points out, *Pushing Daisies* makes a number of generic gestures as it builds its world. The most significant of those generic touches, I want to suggest, is that it is a crime procedural.

The show's pilot establishes its procedural conceit. After local private investigator Emerson Cod witnesses Ned revive and then un-revive a dead man, he hatches a plan to use Ned's abilities to solve crimes and collect rewards by waking up the dead and simply asking them how they died. The series wastes little time establishing itself as a crime procedural. In the pilot episode (cleverly titled "Pie-Lette"), we see private detective Emerson Cod chasing a man across a rooftop. Cod watches as the man accidentally falls to his death by landing on a dumpster, only to bounce into Ned, whose accidental touch brings the man back to life. Cod watches as Ned chases him down and returns him to being dead. As the narrator explains, "Mr. Cod proposed a partnership. Murders are much easier to solve when you can ask the victim who killed them" ("Pie-Lette"). Cod's proposal is not altruistic; they are not solving crimes for the greater good; they focus their efforts on crimes for which there is a substantial reward.

The show's first crime is a simple one. A local businessman appears to have been mauled to death by his dog, Cantaloupe, and there is a $20,000 reward to clear the dog's name and find the real killer. After gaining access to the corpse by pretending to be a canine expert examining the body, Ned and Cod quickly learn that Cantaloupe has been falsely accused and that the victim's secretary sicced her Rottweiler on him. Later episodes in the first season take on crimes associated with corporate scandals. The second episode, "Dummy," concerns the hit and run death of a scientist working on a car powered by dandelions. When Ned revives him, he says his murderer was a crash test dummy. Because the murderer was disguised, the detectives must therefore solve the crime the old-fashioned way, during the course of which we learn that the car is, in fact, fatally flawed in a way that makes it explode. The victim, a safety tester named Bernard Slaybeck, confronted CEO Mark Chase about it, and Chase covered up the story by murdering Bernard and making it look like an accident at the facility. In episodes such as this, *Pushing Daisies* functions almost identically to any other procedural crime drama. In the end, Ned's ability serves no more remarkable function that any other seemingly magical power of one of the team of (modern) investigators.[4] Such a move by a supernatural procedural is perhaps unsurprising. As much as the show may offer the promise of certainty by tapping into the knowledge of a supernatural authority, the overuse of its central conceit would render such shows fairly uninteresting.

In the third episode, "The Fun in Funeral," Ned must confront the implications of his choice to keep Chuck alive again. When Ned raises her from the dead in the "Pie-Lette" and refuses to touch her again to return her to the dead, his "gift" takes the life of the funeral director, Lawrence Schatz, in exchange. This episode is, essentially, the only time that the series grapples with the moral implications of what Ned can do (although Chuck, as an act of kindness, does insist on asking the victims if they would like to have any last words). As we learned in the "Pie-lette," Lawrence Schatz was guilty of grave robbing—stealing valuables off of corpses once the family has completed its visitation and the coffin will not be opened again. In "the Fun in Funeral," Lawrence's twin, Louis, hires Cod to investigate his brother's death—his ulterior motive is that he believes his brother stole more valuables than he admitted, and he hopes that Cod will locate the stash. Like "Dummy," Ned's gift here proves largely useless; he refuses even to revive Lawrence Schatz, and even admits that he caused Schatz's death. The result is that these episodes function largely as conventional procedural crime dramas and less as supernatural ones.

Other episodes rely on Ned's ability more strongly. In "Pigeon," the widow of a pilot who has crashed into a building hires Cod to prove to the insurance company that her husband's death was not a suicide—there is a $500,000 insurance payout on the line. Ned reanimates the pilot, who explains that his death was caused by a man in a prison jumpsuit hijacking his plane. The owner of the apartment the plane crashed into, we later learn, was murdered and stuffed in a trunk in the living room; the person impersonating him, Cod learns, is an escaped convict named Lemuel Weingar. Ned's gift becomes useful again when our detectives exhume the prisoner's cellmate, Jackson Lucas, so that Ned can reanimate him. Lucas explains that Weingar is after diamonds Lucas stashed in a windmill. In typical mercenary fashion, Cod captures Weingar and collects the reward. This episode is remarkable for its reliance upon Ned's power as a crucial element in the development of the plot. Few other episodes rely so heavily upon Ned's abilities. Even more, whereas other episodes have negated Ned's power (in the same way that any superhero's abilities must eventually be rendered useless in order to keep the narratives consistently interesting—Superman must have his kryptonite, after all) in order to establish its *bona fides* as a procedural, this episode relies heavily on Ned's ability to advance the plot and solve the crime.

One other way the show cements its status as a crime procedural is through the narrator (voiced by Jim Dale), whose voiceover—*noir*-like—sets the stage for us and often clearly explains connections that the viewer may not have made—or could not have made. The narrator, who seems to operate as a lawyer presenting the facts of a case to a jury, also performs another crucial function in every episode: he serves as an omniscient narrator who both allows us access to the thoughts of the characters and, most importantly, connects the dots for the viewer by supplying information previously unrevealed. For instance, in "Pie-Lette," the narrator explains the specifics of Ned's powers, the background of his relationship with Chuck, Ned's childhood in a boarding school, Chuck's childhood living with her aunts (one of whom, we eventually learn, is her mother), Ned's obsession with pie, how Ned's powers connect to his business model (he revives dead fruit), and Emerson Cod's connection to Ned. In other episodes, he functions similarly. The narrator provides us the facts of each case in the episode.

It is perhaps unsurprising, then, that every episode announces the details of both the crimes and of any particular situation with Jim Dale's declaration of the specifics. Indeed, the show's voiceover consistently tells us the specific dates that events transpire. The first words we hear in "Pie-Lette," for instance, are these:

> At this very moment in the town of Coeur d'Coeurs, Young Ned was 9 years, 27 weeks, 6 days and 3 minutes old. His dog Digby was 3 years, 2 weeks, 6 days, 5 hours and 9 minutes old. And not a minute older.

Similarly, when we encounter Chuck for the first time, the narrator tells us "Her name was Chuck. At this very moment, she was 8 years, 42 weeks, 3 hours and 2 minutes old" ("Pie-Lette"). As we move out of the backstory and into the present, the narrator explains that ' [i]t's 19 years, 34 weeks, 1 day and 59 minutes later, heretofore known as now" ("Pie-Lette"). While these oddly specific details are certainly humorous, it is important to realize that they function as part of a set of facts presented to the show's viewers. This concern over facts does not end there. Indeed, in nearly every episode, Jim Dale's voiceover presents the case to the viewers by explaining "the facts were these," as if he were a lawyer presenting a case to a judge and jury.

In later episodes, the narrator often clearly explains the conclusion of the episode's plot by connecting the dots for the viewer. In "Dummies," the narrator explains the conclusion:

> Murder was not new for Mark Chase. The facts were these: through a series of crash test experiments, Bernard Slaybeck had learned that the Dandy Lion was a deadly dud. Bernard begged the president to cancel the car's launch. But Mark Chase had other plans. Like a smoking gun, the smoking dummies would have to be buried. The company had invested millions in the Dandy Lion and he knew that keeping this terrible secret would still be cheaper than halting production of the car. And so Mark Chase, big dreamer and secretkeeper, perfected his stain-free slaughter style on Bernard Slaybeck, erstwhile lover of models and automotive safety. The Dandy Lion SX would bloom on time and no one would stop him.

In "The Fun in Funeral," the narrator provides information that only an omniscient narrator could know:

> Wilfred Woodruff was not adopted. On a hot day in the summer of 1863, Wilfred Woodruff's great-great-great-great grandfather, Fambing Woo, was laying track for the Central Pacific Railroad. The decision was made to find a better life. As the Civil War was still raging, the other men chose to go Northwest. Why Fambing Woo chose to run Southeast is not known. Some said it was the hand of destiny, others felt it was heatstroke. Eventually, Fambing was forced to steal the clothes off a fallen soldier. Returning to his journey, he soon realized he was not alone. Fambing immediately realized he did not belong in this place at this time, but this time and place seemed more than

happy to have him. Decorated for his bravery in the Battle of Missionary Ridge and the second Battle of Murfreesboro, Fambing went on to found his own branch of the Woodruff family tree.

In "Pigeon," the narrator provides essential backstory that the viewer has not been privy to:

> There was a bitter chill in the air the night Jackson Lucas found refuge in the VonRoenn windmill. Already five days on the lam, he knew the police were closing in. To preserve his dreams of one day owning an art gallery in Mexico, Jackson decided to bury his stolen treasure in the staircase of the seemingly-abandoned property. His heart stopped, however, when he saw an angelic creature descending the stairs. Her name was Elsa. And this was her windmill. It was love at first sight. Knowing he had very little time left he kissed her. It was a perfect moment. The next moment was not. Elsa kept true to her word. For the next 20 years, she and Jackson continued their love affair by correspondence. Letters sent to and fro with the help of her virtually-untraceable carrier pigeon. Until the day Jackson knew he would no longer be able to keep his promise. Someone else would have to do it for him.

Consistently, as the A-plot of each episode resolves, Dale's voice emerges like an omniscient narrator from Fielding or Dickens to reveal some bit of information that we have not been provided and thus to connect the dots for the viewer in a way that is authoritative. This use of the omniscient narrator sets *Pushing Daisies* apart. Where other series obtain their authority primarily through their reliance on the supernatural, *Pushing Daisies* relies on a combination of Ned's ability to raise the dead and its narrator's omniscience. This desire to present omniscience suggests certain anxieties that both the genre and the shows may be addressing.

As a genre focusing literally on law and order—and more specifically on the solving of crimes and the catching of criminals—crime procedurals appeal to a desire to see justice meted out and for criminals to be punished. In this sense, they are similar to Westerns or superhero stories—both of which have at their heart a desire to see the heroes triumph over the villains. In episode after episode, viewers watch as the system *usually* works: criminals are caught and punished through the methodical and competent actions of the institutions designed to do just that.

There are any number of explanations for the popularity of the crime procedural. Almost certainly, the genre presents certain benefits both in terms of production and reception. Its reliance on series (as opposed to serial) storytelling allows viewers to consume the show in a desultory fashion; missing an episode or two here and there will have little to no impact on the viewer's ability to follow the story. The absence of emphasis on character development removes the need to follow characters' growth from episode to episode.[5] Similarly, the self-contained nature of each episode places little requirements on the viewer to follow a story arc from week to week. All of this, of course, also means that these kinds of shows perform exceedingly well in syndication. Given these consistent features, it is unsurprising that the genre is among the most popular in the West— if not in the world.

Supernatural crime procedurals in particular suggest another anxiety. As much as viewers may hope to see competent and responsive institutions, the possibility also exists that these institutions may be inadequate to the task and fail—or be corrupt. These anxieties are certainly not particular to crime procedurals. From David Simon's representation of the ways talented detectives can be stymied by the institutions they are a part of in *Homicide: Life on the Street* to the trope in Westerns of the corrupt or incompetent lawman, anxieties about the reliability of our legal institutions runs deep in American life and art.[6] The transformation of the supernatural crime procedural from shows such as *Forever Knight*—where a Canadian vampire detective solves crimes—to something like *Grimm* or *Sleepy Hollow*—where supernatural individuals use their powers to combat other supernatural creatures or to receive revelations about the crimes they are investigating—is in some ways unsurprising. If one of the functions of the crime procedural is to assure us that our institutions work and that justice is not a myth (but with the acknowledgment that, *sometimes*, those institutions may fail us), the addition of a supernatural element suggests the presence of an otherworldly certainty about whatever conclusions the investigations reach. The answers that such procedurals provide are not subject to the vagaries of institutional or individual weaknesses; they come directly from, or with the aid of, some supernatural authority who possesses a knowledge that does not derive from investigative or scientific methods and does not hinge on the ability of a jury to convict. The answers that these supernatural crime procedurals provide are, it seems, unassailable *facts*—something quite different than the sense of justice being served that a traditional procedural crime drama provides.

The reliance on the supernatural such series, whether deliberately or not, necessitates some kind of mythology. As it builds its world, *Grimm* must explain the ancient history of the Grimms and the Wesen. This is no easy task. The various wikis on fandom.com serve to make this point. The *Grimm* wiki entry for the Wesen on fandom.com runs 5400 words and contains sections on Wesen history, characteristics, behavior, genetics, hybrids, and species. Indeed, the main page for *Grimm* on the fandom wiki boasts that it contains 1750 articles (the *Pushing Daisies* wiki only contains 509). *Sleepy Hollow*, with its need to explain not only the legend of the horsemen but also the Witnesses and Moloch, is similar. The fandom wiki for *Once Upon a Time* contains 3135. The entry for *Supernatural* contains 4663.

Shows such as these must explain what are often enormous elements of mythology in order to provide a context for the supernatural elements of the series.

Additionally, many supernatural crime procedurals—such as *Grimm*, *Sleepy Hollow*, *Once Upon a Time*, *Constantine*, *Lucifer*—have some kind of literary origins. What these series do with those literary origins is, of course, world-build and create a new set of narratives that are retrofitted to the existing narrative. This tendency is particularly interesting, considering these series began as works of literature. *Grimm* taps into the legacy of Brothers Grimm, who compiled the German folktales that dominate Western popular culture. *Sleepy Hollow* is based on Washington Irving's 1820 short story, "The Legend of Sleepy Hollow." *Once Upon a Time* focused on fairy tales from around the globe (although primarily the West).[7] *Constantine* is based on the DC comic series *John Constantine Hellblazer* (later simply *Constantine*). *Lucifer* is based on a character in Neil Gaiman's *Sandman*. In other words, these series take literary sources and locate them in the world of a procedural crime drama.

In turn, the pre-existing supernatural framework in these shows necessitates that they construct some kind of mythology to house that supernatural framework. Shows grounded in Christian mythology typically accept that framework. But shows like *Grimm* or *Once Upon a Time* or *Supernatural* must manufacture an elaborate mythology to contain the enormous number of narratives it will work with. In effect, as shows such as these create their worlds, they take a work of literature and transform it into essentially a mythology. In contrast, Ned's ability to raise the dead is such a crucial element of the series, *Pushing Daisies* has to devote a significant amount of time in almost every episode to explaining Ned's powers and how they relate to the basic plot of the series. Despite this need to reiterate the show's conceit, however, *Pushing Daisies* never actually explains the origins of Ned's powers—nor does it make any effort to locate those powers within some broader mythological or religious context. Ned simply has these abilities, and as with other examples of magical realism, we must simply accept that this is the case in the world of the series.[8] The narrator explains the matter-of-fact nature of Ned's gift in the pilot episode:

> This touch was a gift given to him, but not by anyone in particular. There was no box, no instructions, no manufacturer's warranty. It just was. The terms and use weren't immediately clear, nor were they of immediate concern.

The narrator invokes the religious or supernatural—"a gift given"—but immediately undermines any expectations about a giver. By refusing to explain Ned's gift, the show obviates any need to develop an elaborate mythological context for the series, which in turn keeps the magical conceit of the show simple and without any need for lengthy explanations. Unlike other series that might encourage viewers to study the minutiae of the mythology of the show's world, *Pushing Daisies* merely asks viewers to accept a magical concept and reject any notion of a larger mythological context.[9]

The absence of any mythology to contextualize Ned's powers means that there is no acknowledgment of an afterlife—at all. The characters Ned raises from the dead simply wake up and carry on as if nothing had happened. Their only supernatural authority is that they can, often, remember the particular circumstances of their deaths. *Pushing Daisies* does not construct an elaborate mythology or religion to explain Ned's powers; instead, our omniscient narrator explains, Ned's ability "was a gift given to him, but not by anyone in particular"—thus using its godlike omniscient narrator to dismiss mythology in favor of magical realism and an omniscient narrator. In this sense, where other supernatural crime procedurals transform literature into religion, *Pushing Daisies* transforms the religious into the literary.

Notes

1. Despite its positive reception and critical acclaim, very little scholarship on *Pushing Daisies* exists. At the time of this writing, the MLA bibliography returns only five articles on the series. Three of them focus on the show's treatment of death and sex: Rebecca Feasey's "Beekeeper Suits, Plastic Casings, Rubber Gloves and Cling Film: Examining the Importance of 'No-Sex' Sex in *Pushing Daisies*," Elinor Levy's "Pushing Up Daisies: Death and American Culture," and my own "Nobody Wants to Be Un-Anything: *Pushing Daisies* and the Problem of a Kinder, Gentler Undead." Kasey Butcher's "New Beginnings Only Lead to Painful Ends": "Undeading" and Fear of Consequences in *Pushing Daisies*' focuses on the show's treatment of hope and redemption. Jeanetta Vermeulen's "Pushing Boundaries; Introversion and Social Commentary in *Pushing Daisies*" concerns itself with the show's representation of introversion. This, sadly, is currently the extent of the scholarship on this show.
2. See "Pushing Daisies First Look." *YouTube*, uploaded by ezazusernamefoglalt, 15 July 2007, www.youtube.com/watch?v=WEayMH7X3sc.
3. If Ned brings something back to life and does not return it to being dead, something of apparently equal value nearby must die. As the Narrator explains in "Pie-Lette," "Young Ned's random gift that was came with a caveat or two. It was a gift that not only gave... it took. Young Ned discovered he could only bring the dead back to life for one minute without consequence. Any longer and someone else had to die."
4. Following *The X-Files*, which presented us with two investigators with expertise in their respective fields, crime procedurals often present us with partners (or groups) of individuals with different skills or abilities, which sometimes appear magical to the viewers. There are many examples of this trope, but a few examples serve to make the point. In *The X-Files*, Mulder possesses a seemingly limitless knowledge of alien conspiracy theories. In *Law and Order: Criminal Intent*, detective Goren's encyclopedic knowledge of seemingly every subject serves as a crucial element of nearly every episode. In both *Profiler* and Fuller's own

Hannibal, Sam Waters' and Will Graham's respective ability to empathize so perfectly that they can figuratively see through the eyes of the killers they are searching for plays a key role in almost every episode. Finally, Spencer Reid on *Criminal Minds* slowly transforms from an autistic savant into a character with seemingly magical intellectual powers (his character biography indicates that he holds 3 BAs and 3 PhDs). There are many other examples.

 5. Certainly, there are any number of examples of character development in crime procedurals. The transformations of Mulder and Scully in *The X-Files*, the attention to character in *Law and Order: Criminal Intent* or *Special Victims Unit*, attest that there is room for character development in the genre. Regardless, character development in the genre usually takes a back seat to the particular demands of each episode's plot.

 6. I would argue that the longstanding interest in superheroes reflects the same profound and deeply rooted anxiety that the institutions designed to protect us may fail or be inadequate, and so both Westerns and other representations of vigilante justice (such as with superheroes) address this concern.

 7. *Once Upon a Time* actually has a doubly literary origin, since it is widely regarded as having brazenly copied Bill Willingham's multiple Eisner award-winning graphic novel series, *Fables*.

 8. This is no different than accepting that hunger artists exist in Kafka or that angels may fall out of the sky in Marquez.

 9. There is another important element to the show's magical realism that connects in interesting ways to my contention that the genre of the crime procedural and the supernatural crime procedural. If, as I have suggested, one of the more significant effects of the crime procedural is that it reassures viewers that institutions of the system of justice are competent, and that supernatural crime procedurals improve upon that assurance by adding to it a supernatural authority that is immune to the possibility of the mistakes that the human institutions are susceptible to.

WORKS CITED

Abrams, J.J., Alex Kurtzman and Roberto Orci, creators. *Fringe*. Bad Robots Productions and Warner Brothers Television. 2008–13.
Armer, Alan A., Desi Arnaz, Leonard Freeman, Quinn Martin, and Jerry Thorpe, creators. *The Untouchables*. Desilu Productions, 1959–63.
Attanasio, Paul, creator. *Homocide: Life on the Street*. Reeves Entertainment, MCEG Sterling Incorporated, Fatima Productions, NBC Productions, and NBC Studios, 1993–99.
Avedon, Barbara, and Barbara Corday, creators. *Cagney & Lacey*. Mace Neufeld Productions, Filmways Television, Orion Television, 1982–88.
Bellisario, Donald P., and Don McGil. *NCIS*. Belisarius Productions, Paramount Network Television, CBS Paramount Network Television, CBS Television Studios, 2003–present.
Bilson, Danny and Paul De Meo, creators. *The Sentinel*. Pet Fly Productions and Paramount Network Television, 1996–99.
Bochco, Steven, and Michael Kozoll, creators. *Hill Street Blues*. MTM Enterprises, 1981–87.
Butcher, Kasey. "'New Beginnings Only Lead to Painful Ends': 'Undeading' and Fear of Consequences in Pushing Daisies." *Time in Television Narrative: Exploring Temporality in Twenty-First-Century Programming*, edited by Melissa Ames, UP of Mississippi, 2012, pp. 139–150.
Carlin, Shannon. "Why Pushing Daisies Is Still Unlike Anything You've Ever Seen on TV." *Bustle*. https://www.bustle.com/p/why-pushing-daisies-is-still-unlike-anything-youve-ever-seen-on-tv-2741608.
Caron, Glenn Gordon, creator. *Medium*. Paramount Network Television, CBS Paramount Network Television, CBS Television Studios, Picturemaker Productions and Grammnet Productions, 2005–11.
Carpenter, Stephen, Jim Kouf, and David Greenwalt, creators. *Grimm*. Universal Television, GK Productions, Hazy Mills Productions, and Open 4 Business Productions, 2011–17.
Carter, Chris. *The X-Files*. Ten Thirteen Productions, 20th Television and 20th Century–Fox Television. 1993–2002, 2016–18.

Cerone, Daniel, and David S. Goyer, creators. *Constantine*. Ever After Productions, Phantom Four Films, DC Entertainment, and Warner Bros. Television, 2014–15.
Cohen, Barney, and James D. Parriott, creators. *Forever Knight*. Glen Warren Productions, Paragon Entertainment Corporation, Tele München, TriStar Television, USA Network, 1992–96.
Davies, Russell T., creator. *Torchwood*. BBC One, BBC Two, BBC Three, and Starz, 2006–11.
Davis, Jeff. *Criminal Minds*. The Mark Gordon Company, Entertainment One, Touchstone Television, ABC Studios, Paramount Network Television, CBS Paramount Network Television and CBS Television Studios, 2005–present.
"Dummy." *Pushing Daisies*, season 1 episode 2, ABC, October 10, 2007.
Ernst, Sam, and Jim Dunn, creators. *Haven*. Big Motion Pictures Productions, Entertainment One Television, Piller/Segan/Shepherd, Universal Networks International, Canwest Global, and Shaw Media, 2010–15.
Espenson, Jane, and D. Brent Mote, creators. *Warehouse 13*. Universal Cable Productions, 2009–14.
Feasey, Rebecca. "Beekeeper Suits, Plastic Casings, Rubber Gloves and Cling Film: Examining the Importance of 'No-Sex' Sex in Pushing Daisies." *Television, Sex and Society: Analyzing Contemporary Representations*, edited by Basil Glynn et al., Continuum, 2012, pp. 65–77.
Fuller, Bryan K., creator. *Hannibal*. Dino de Laurentiis Company, Living Dead Guy Productions, AXN Original Productions, and Gaumont International Television, 2013–15.
_____. *Pushing Daisies*. The Links/Cohen Company, Living Dead Guy Productions, and Warner Brothers Television, 2007–09.
"The Fun in Funeral." *Pushing Daisies*, season 1 episode 3, ABC, October 17, 2007.
Gaiman, Neil, Sam Kieth, and Mike Dringenberg, creators. *The Sandman*. DC Comics and Vertigo, 1989–1996, 2009, 2013–15.
Kapinos, Tom. *Lucifer*. Jerry Bruckheimer Television, DC Entertainment, and Warner Bros. Television, 2016–present.
Kindler, Damian. *Sanctuary*. The Beedie Group, Bell Media, My Plastic Badger, Sanctuary 2 Productions, Sanctuary 3 Productions, and Sanctuary 4 Productions, 2008–11.
Kitsis, Edward, and Adam Horowitz, creators. *Once Upon a Time*. ABC Studios and Kitsis/Horowitz, 2011–18.
Koski, Genevieve. Review. "Dummy." https://tv.avclub.com/pushing-daisies-dummy-1798203246.
_____. Review. "Girth" https://tv.avclub.com/pushing-daisies-girth-1798203406.
Koslow, Ron, and Trevor Munson, creators. *Moonlight*. CBS. 2007–08.
Kripke, Erik, creator. *Supernatural*. The WB and The CW, 2005–present.
Kurtzman, Alex, Roberto Orci, Phillip Iscove, and Len Wiseman, creators. *Sleepy Hollow*. Mark Goffman Productions, Sketch Films, K/O Paper Products, and 20th Century Fox Television, 2013–17.
Levy, Elinor. "Pushing Up Daisies: Death and American Culture." *Ghosts, Ghouls & Gravestones: The Trades of Burial*, edited by Siobhán Fitzpatrick, Museum of Early Trades & Crafts, 2013, pp. 7–22.
Lovretta, Michelle, creator. *Lost Girl*. Prodigy Pictures, 2010–15.
Moore, Alan, Stephen R. Bissette, and John Ridgway, creators. *John Constantine, Hellblazer*. DC Comics, Vertigo, Titan Books, 1988–2013, 2013–present.
"Pie-Lette." *Pushing Daisies*, season 1, episode 1, ABC, October 3, 2007.
"Pigeon." *Pushing Daisies*, season 1, episode 4, ABC, October 24, 2007.
"Pushing Daisies First Look." *YouTube*, uploaded by ezausernamefoglalt, 15 July 2007, www.youtube.com/watch?v=WEayMH7X3sc.
Rogers, Scott. "Nobody Wants to Be Un-Anything: Pushing Daisies and the Problem of a Kinder, Gentler Undead." *Romancing the Zombie: Essays on the Undead as Significant "Other,"* edited by Ashley Szanter and Jessica K. Richards, McFarland, 2017, pp. 32–41.
Saunders, Cynthia. *Profiler*. NBC Studios, Three Putt Productions, and Sander/Moses Productions, 1996–2000.
Vermeulen, Jeanetta. "Pushing Boundaries; Introversion and Social Commentary in Pushing

Daisies." *An Introvert in an Extrovert World: Essays on the Quiet Ones*, edited by Myrna Santos, Cambridge Scholars, 2015, pp. 89–103.

Warren, Charles Marquis, creator. *Gunsmoke*. CBS Productions, Filmaster Productions, Arness and Company, The Arness Production Company, 1955–75.

Webb, Jack, creator. *Dragnet*. Mark VII Productions and Mark VII Limited. 1951–59.

Willingham, Bill, creator. *Fables*. Vertigo, 2002–15.

Wolf, Dick, creator. *Law and Order*. Wolf Films, Universal Television, Studios USA, NBC Universal Television Studio and Universal Media Studios, 1990–2010.

———. *Law and Order: Criminal Intent*. Wolf Films, Studios USA, Universal Television, NBC Universal Television Studio, Universal Media Studios, and Universal Cable Productions, 2001–11.

———. *Law and Order: Special Victims Unit*. Wolf Films, Universal Television, Studios USA, NBC Universal Television Studio and Universal Media Studio, 1999–present.

Yerkovich, Anthony, creator. *Miami Vice*. Michael Mann Productions and Universal Television, 1984–90.

Zuicker, Anthony E., creator. *CSI: Crime Scene Investigation*. Jerry Bruckheimer Films, Jerry Bruckheimer Television, Alliance Atlantis, CBS Productions, CBS Paramount Network Television, and CBS Television Studios, 2000–15.

"Magic's a nasty game"
John Constantine as the Trickster Detective
Shawn Edrei

In determining a baseline for the generic definition of fantasy, Rosemary Jackson claims that "a characteristic most frequently associated with literary fantasy has been its obdurate refusal of prevailing definitions of the 'real' or 'possible,' a refusal amounting at times to violent opposition" (Jackson 14). Indeed, Jackson positions fantastic literature as practically antithetical to any pretense of realism in a given text, pointing out that the former does in fact "disturb 'rules' of artistic interpretation and literature's reproduction of the 'real'" (Jackson 14). Even a cursory glance at the transmedia oeuvre of fantasy works may confirm this perspective, bearing in mind the innate flexibility of the genre's ontological requirements: a concept as fundamental as "magic" can be constructed and depicted in a myriad of ways, leading to frequent contradictions and inconsistencies within the corpus. Some authors, for example, put forth an ironclad "rule" that the casting of magical spells requires the use of wands, while others establish the need for blood or consorting with otherworldly entities. As these concepts have no corresponding parallels in our reality, they can be imagined in vast, practically limitless combinations, with minimal need for intertextual fidelity.

The crime procedural, on the other hand, follows a much more defined structure, one which leaves little room for ambiguity. In tracing the literary ancestry of the 2008–2013 television series *Fringe*, Amy Sturgis characterizes the modern detective story as springing "from a common idea born of the Enlightenment: that the Universe could be understood through reason, and that using the proper investigative method would uncover the answer—whether the question was how to reach outer space or who killed the victim" (Sturgis 27). Sturgis' analysis of the detective story reveals an underlying impetus which the crime procedural shares: "At the heart of the investigative enterprise—whether scientific research or crime detection—is the Enlightenment's faith in an orderly universe. It follows that if we ask the right questions in the right ways, we can find the truth" (Sturgis 28). Thus, the format of the realistic crime procedural is clearly oriented towards affirming that same faith in order and rationality: the process of investigation, the temporal arrangement of plot, and the cyclical representations of the investigators as actants tend to be broadly consistent.

The past decade has seen a rise in juxtapositions of crime procedurals onto supernatural worlds across a multitude of narrative media; these hybrid genre works are, in essence, attempts to weld the innate variability and mutable ontology of fantasy onto the precise, explicable format of the procedural. Given the ubiquitous presence of these hybrids in television—from *Grimm* to *Lost Girl*, from *Haven* to genre flagship *Supernatural*—it is clear that the supernatural crime procedural has taken root in popular culture. One such example is the CW's 2014–2015 series *Constantine*, an eponymous adaptation of the DC Comics magician/con artist/antihero John Constantine—in many ways the progenitor of the supernatural detective. Constantine's exploits in print, television and film paint a compelling picture of the ways in which magical elements, introduced into crime procedurals, distort and reshape basic tropes and conventions of the genre. This essay will discuss Constantine's first appearances in DC Comics, his short-lived television show, and 2018 animated feature film *City of Demons*, in order to illustrate the transformation of the crime procedural investigator into a quintessential "trickster detective," an archetype warped by the presence of magic and indefinable supernatural elements. This shift is mandated by the need to construct a fictional reality in which the standard deductive processes of crime-solving are complicated by the presence of magic and supernatural entities which do not conform to any one set of ontological rules.

John Constantine was introduced to readers of DC comics as a supporting character in another title; Roz Kaveney claims that "the scruffy trench-coated magus John Constantine is not a character around whom an infinite number of stories can usefully be told, which is why, when Alan Moore invented him, he was a foil to Swamp Thing, his Virgil through the Gothic world of the real America and through his own powers" (Kaveney 58). The titular protagonist of Moore's *Saga of the Swamp Thing* was indeed too laconic and alien to serve as an efficient detective, and so a proxy was required to help solve the increasingly prevalent mystical crimes and supernatural riddles presented by Moore and his collaborators. First appearing in issue 37 (June 1985), Constantine's introduction clearly positions him as an investigator of some sort, interviewing old acquaintances in order to piece together the nature of an impending magical threat. While each interviewee points to a different source of the event (a black hole, Cthulhu, Satan), Constantine immediately deduces the true perpetrators are a cult known as the Brujeria, who intend to increase superstition and paranoia across America: "Yeah, well, that's what they're going to do, isn't it? It's obvious. They'll use all the classic frighteners … werewolves, vampires, haunted houses, dreams" (Moore 70). What follows is an extended set of misadventures informally known as the "American Gothic" storyline, in which Swamp Thing largely serves as Constantine's enforcer, providing the brute strength necessary to resolve various crises while the mysterious magus directs his efforts. Here we see an early indicator of how supernatural elements distort the narrative structure of the crime procedural: because Swamp Thing is not knowledgeable in matters pertaining to magic, Constantine is forced to play the role of distant guide rather than conduct the investigation himself. As a practitioner of the occult arts, Constantine already knows the ontological laws which govern his world—the emphasis of this inaugural storyline is on his attempts to bring Swamp Thing up to speed on those very laws, their meanings, and how the Brujeria intend to subvert them. As these rules had not previously been clearly defined, they are as unknown to the reader as they are to the protagonist; thus Constantine's teachings double as clarifying exposition on what magic can and cannot accomplish in this particular fictional world. However, Moore ensured that the full extent of the character's experience and expertise were held at a distance from the reader: "I'm too busy to sit explaining things to you. If you want answers, you'll have to keep up with me. No promises, mind. Maybe I'll give you the answers, maybe I won't … we'll let it be a surprise" (Moore 76).

As the storyline progresses, it becomes evident that contrary to the Swamp Thing's positive and heroic characteristics (contrasting his monstrous appearance), Constantine is a far closer match to the definition of the comic book antihero, as established by Michael Spivey and Steven Knowlton: "There are many comic book characters whose personalities cluster around this difficult-to-define prototype: partly good, partly evil, partly likeable, and partly repellent. As we discuss these wrecked souls, it will become clear that sometimes a good guy does more than *dress like a bad guy*. Sometimes he *does bad things*. And yet those bad things that the anti-hero does are often arguably … the right thing to do" (Spivey and Knowlton 52). The solutions Constantine proposes during the American Gothic storyline are frequently amoral at best, not at all typical of the invariably benign resolutions produced by rational investigation. For example, upon eliminating an underwater infestation of vampires, Swamp Thing is chastised by Constantine for not completing the task at hand: "A kid and his parents survived. They got out to tell the story. The whole point was to stop that from happening. You see, the story will get bigger in the telling. Fish stories do. Before you know where you are, everybody within fifty miles believes in vampires a little bit more … just as they planned it" (Moore 130). Tellingly, "American Gothic" concludes in a cosmic stalemate, with Constantine's interference ultimately playing a very small part in ensuring the continued survival of humanity—an understated subversion of the catharsis typically depicted during the climax and resolution of detective stories.

In 2014, television network the CW launched *Constantine* as part of its slate of live-action adaptations for DC Comics. The series was a hybridized adaptation of two storylines drawn from the comics: the aforementioned "American Gothic" (sans Swamp Thing), and "Original Sins," the first arc of Constantine's solo series *Hellblazer*. Per the usual format of the crime procedural, *Constantine* split its time between a primary plotline which ran the length of the season, concerning the Brujeria's attempt to harness the forces of darkness (per "American Gothic"), and smaller-scale, self-contained mysteries such as a gramophone that kills anyone who listens to it in episode 3, a resurrected priest granted the power to heal the injured in episode 7, and the kidnapping of an infant by a sister of Eve in episode 8. When examined on their own merits, the individual mysteries featured in each episode provide clear indications of how supernatural elements distorted the format and inherent *raison d'être* of the crime procedural.

"Danse Vaudou," the fifth episode of the series, serves as a perfect demonstration of this complex juxtaposition, and its effect on the procedural narrative. The episode begins with a significant diversion from the standard process of crime investigation, as a murder occurs in the opening scene in contradiction of Tsevtan Todorov's basic definition of modern detective stories: "We might further characterize these two stories by saying that the first—the story of the crime—tells 'what really happened,' whereas the second—the story of the investigation—explains 'how the reader (or the narrator) has come to know about it.' … The first, that of the crime, is in fact the story of an absence: its most accurate characteristic is that it cannot be immediately present in the book" (Todorov 123). In the case of *Constantine,* the audience witnesses this first event, followed by Constantine (Matt Ryan) and his allies Zed (Angélica Celaya) and Chas (Charles Halford) being directed to the scene of the crime through a magical map (in other words, an inexplicable mystical power). Only then are they informed as to the particulars of the case, concerning a female murderer who can apparently deflect bullets. But "Danse Vaudou" is of particular interest due to its guest star, as the episode pits Constantine against police detective Jim

Corrigan (Emmett Scanlan)—who DC readers will recognize as the future host for divine entity the Spectre. In the context of *Constantine*, however, Corrigan represents the episode's coded, implicit rejection of orderly investigation and deduction. When Constantine's magical aptitude allows him to reach conclusions Corrigan can neither comprehend nor follow, the rational detective initially arrests him: "Anyone who calls the police about an accident before it happens isn't a psychic, he's a murderer" ("Danse Vaudou"). Moments later, Constantine has divined not only the nature of the threat at hand, but the identity of the perpetrators: "See, the police, they're looking for a living killer in that alleyway stabbing, and they're not gonna find it. Based on what I saw in the alleyway and out here on this road, you got two perps on the loose, and they're very possibly dead. Or undead" ("Danse Vaudou"). The mystery put forth at the end of this scene is why two unrelated ghosts have risen up—a matter ultimately resolved between Constantine and another practitioner of magic, Papa Midnite (Michael James Shaw). Corrigan ends the episode a "convert," having been undeniably exposed to the supernatural world and acknowledging it as such: "I'm the one who's crazy. Running after a ghost with a gun. Won't make that mistake again" ("Danse Vaudou"). Constantine, on the other hand, solves the murders not by deducing motives or collecting evidence, but by performing a vague mystical ritual with Papa Midnite that releases the undead from their terrestrial bonds. Because the rules of magic are as subject to author's fiat in this narrative as in any other work of fantasy, the arbitrary and intangible nature of this solution does not prevent the audience from accepting it as a positive resolution.

The transformative effect of magic in Constantine's world is especially pronounced when comparing the television series to its source material. While the primary threat of the Brujeria was never resolved due to the series' cancellation, the presence of Mary "Zed" Martin as a supporting character is a direct reference to Constantine's first storyline as a solo protagonist in *Hellblazer*. Christopher Knowles offers the following summation of the series, which began with Jamie Delano replacing Moore as Constantine's writer: "Constantine is an antiheroic rogue in the hard boiled tradition, with his signature disheveled suit, trench coat, and cigarette. He is an outsider figure who is often pitted against the forces of both Heaven and Hell on behalf of humanity. His friends and allies in the occult world frequently end up sacrificed to these forces, usually also through Constantine's own self-preservation efforts" (Knowles 177). Even this brief description is somewhat at odds with the predominantly heroic and moral character seen in the television series—yet Zed's participation serves as an intertextual reference to a story that firmly defined Constantine as a trickster detective.

1988's "Original Sins," in which Zed made her first appearance, finds Constantine trapped between two supernatural factions: the Damnation Army, condemned souls enslaved to the will of the demon Nergal, and the Resurrection Crusade, a militant group of fanatic Christian zealots who intend to use Zed as their new Mary, coupling her to an angel in order to produce a new Messiah on Earth. The standard process of investigation and deduction is once again disrupted, as Nergal simply informs Constantine of the threat in order to conscript him against the Crusaders: "The agents of Heaven were not slow to seize their chance. The Resurrection Crusade is their net, cast wide to scour the world of souls and set them on God's table.... There has been a prophecy. Incontrovertible—engraved on a stone dredged up from Hell" (Delano 210–211).

This revelation fast-tracks Constantine's comprehension of the mystery at hand: the impending "crime" to be committed by the Resurrection Crusade. But where a realistic crime procedural would have the investigator either prevent the crime or arrest the perpetrator after the fact, the laws of magic inherent to this ontological system allow Constantine to directly interfere with the Crusade's plans, albeit in a reprehensible fashion. He seduces Zed and claims her virginity, knowing full well this will render her unworthy of the divine plan. Because she herself is unaware of this fact, the act of sexual intercourse—though consensual—takes on a sinister undertone, with Constantine left despondent by his actions: "The enormity of what I've done appalls me. If not for me, she could've been the mother of God. Christ, that demon's devious. He knew I'd never kill her. He healed me with his blood just so that, loving her, I'd taint her—knowing that no angel would ever come where I'd spilled poisoned seed" (Delano 238). While this course of action conforms to Constantine's persistent characterization as a trickster detective, his manipulation of the victimized Zed is atypical of crime procedurals, particularly as a means to resolve the threat at hand. While it is unclear whether the CW's Constantine would have taken the same course of action had the series continued past its first season, Jackson's framing of moral ambivalence in fantasy makes it a likely possibility: "Because of this progressive internalization of the demonic, the easy polarization of good and evil which had operated in tales of supernaturalism and magic ceased to be effective.... A loss of faith in supernaturalism, a gradual scepticism and problematization of the relation of self to world, introduced a much closer 'otherness,' something intimately related to the self" (Jackson 56). The presence of Zed, and subsequent appearances of both Nergal and the Resurrection Crusade, suggest the series may have attempted to push Constantine closer to his antihero origins; both Moore's work in *Saga of the Swamp Thing* and Delano's work in *Hellblazer* ensured the threats

Constantine faced were dangerous and ruthless enough to justify amoral responses:

> When analyzed in a continuous state space, it becomes clear that the anti-hero concept is flexible enough to accommodate some rather intriguing variations on a theme. By having the guts and moral ambiguity to commit astounding acts that require anything from intimidation to mass murder as the means to an end, anti-heroes blaze trails in the uncharted territory between the categories of obvious goodness and unmitigated evil. Thus, any attempts to categorize them (including those presented here) are best treated as an affiliation with regions along a continuum, rather than as a set of discrete classifications that are either applied or not [Spivey and Knowlton 61–62].

Despite its more heroic tone, *Constantine* pits the character against predatory entities such as the Brujeria, Lamashtu and the Coblynau, all of whom take an adversarial role towards humanity in general and Constantine in particular; thus, Constantine is "permitted" to take actions such as inviting demonic possession in episode 9, cursing his angelic supervisor Manny (Harold Perrineau) with a deep and painful well of human emotion in episode 12, and more. Resorting to extreme measures is quite often depicted as the correct course of action.

The 2018 animated film *City of Demons*, tangentially canonical to the CW television series, follows a similar pattern of distortion and disruption both in terms of narrative progression and characterization of the protagonist. A loose adaptation of the *Hellblazer* graphic novel *All His Engines*, *City of Demons* distinguishes itself from the previous examples by beginning with a mystery centered on Constantine (Matt Ryan) himself: upon awakening from a drunken stupor, he finds his apartment swarming with miniature imps dressed in his own attire. After they identify themselves as projections of his own "inner demons," Constantine reabsorbs them only to note the unprecedented nature of this attack: "Something opened a door between my conscious and unconscious mind and let them out. That's never happened before" (*City of Demons*). This threat is sidelined when Chas (Damian O'Hare)—another character who appears in *Constantine*—arrives seeking aid for his comatose daughter Tricia (Laura Bailey). Chas' assumption regarding the allegedly magical nature of Tricia's illness is based on his past experiences with Constantine, and upon summoning the Nightmare Nurse (Laura Bailey)—a spirit who serves as analogue for a forensics expert in a realistic crime drama—Constantine confirms these suspicions: "It's not possession, because there's nothing here to possess. Her physical form is here, but her essence? Her soul? It's gone" (*City of Demons*).

Following a prophetic dream, Constantine finds his way to the lair of the demon Beroul (Jim Meskimen), who claims responsibility for Tricia's abduction. However, Beroul freely admits his victimization of Chas' daughter was simply a means to lure in Constantine himself, in order to facilitate the demon's plan: "I had what you Brits would call a brainwave. A branch office of Hell, right here. A franchise operation, like fast food, but with the added benefit of eternal damnation. So many souls just begging to be corrupted and consumed. So much power for a demon to absorb. The sky is the limit for the entrepreneur who gets in first" (*City of Demons*). This constitutes a unique subversion of the crime procedural format, as the investigator is rarely the direct target of criminal activity. The twist is compounded by the later revelation that Beroul is an alias of Nergal (Robin Atkin Downes), the same demon seen in "Original Sins"—and, in *City of Demons*, the entity responsible for Constantine's initial mystical traumas. Having briefly appeared in obscured flashbacks during *Constantine,* Nergal's presence in *City of Demons* is no coincidence; Max Nestorowich's "Sifting Through the Ashes: Analyzing *Hellblazer*" positions this character as a recurring nemesis to Constantine:

> The demon blood infusion, alongside the events of Newcastle, both of which directly involve Nergal, are two defining events of John Constantine's life, and from which many future storylines would build off either directly or indirectly. They are his origin events, his Crime Alley and his radioactive spider bite, every comic character has something like them, and to an extant most fictional characters have some sort of event driving them on some sort of quest, Captain Ahab lost his leg hunting Moby Dick, King Arthur is given Excalibur by the Lady of the Lake and so forth [Nestorowich, "Sifting Through the Ashes" #7].

The notion of a returning villain is almost antithetical to the standard format of the crime procedural, as investigations typically conclude with the arrest and prosecution of the perpetrator—and, in a world defined by order and rationality, justice would be done, the criminal incarcerated. But supernatural entities such as demons, ghosts or witches are able to transcend the constraints of physical imprisonment and mortality, and thus return to engage the investigator again and again. Given these factors and his pre-existing relationship with Constantine, Nergal's persistence across narrative media comes as little surprise.

City of Demons concludes with Nergal defeated through a trick of Constantine's, and—just as in "Original Sins"—the use of magic exacts a price: "In order for the curse to work, I had to channel Renee and Trish's love for you into and through Nergal. Every last bit of it. It's gone, Chas. All their love for you is gone…. Renee won't have any memory of you now. Oh, she'll recall a drunken one-night stand eight years ago, but your face, your name…. Trish has never known her father. There's always a price to pay, Chas" (*City of Demons*). Chas' anger towards Constantine is short-lived, as the latter continues to explain the fallout of the magical resolution:

The Camdever is big magic. And Renee and Trish, no matter how much they loved you, it wasn't enough, Chas. So, I had to throw in some extra juice to put the spell over the top. I had to throw in us. You'll have a vague memory of an arrogant sod who saved your girl and ruined your life. But the memory of those two kids who grew up together in the pool.... Gone [*City of Demons*].

Thus, though Tricia is rescued, the cost incurred is a personal loss to the investigator. In this, the film ultimately aligns itself with the themes and tropes that have defined Constantine since *Saga of the Swamp Thing*, through creative team changes, relaunches, reboots and adaptations—the same conventions which tend to carry over into more contemporary supernatural crime procedurals.

If we consider the narrative structure of the realistic crime procedural as a basis for comparison, we see that every stage of the magical/supernatural detective story is altered by those same ontological forces that define the work in question. First, the crime that triggers the investigation is directly depicted more often than not, due to the fact that in a supernatural system questions pertaining to the killer's identity and motive are secondary to discovering the method by which the crime was committed (e.g., which supernatural creature or magical tool was used to achieve that particular result). Like most standalone episodes of *Constantine*, "Danse Vaudou" begins with a ghost committing the instigating murder that draws the protagonists' attention. Every element of that initial crime is portrayed: the audience sees the killer, the victim, the murder weapon. The identity of the killer and the method of the murder are secondary to a more immediate, pressing question: how is the killer able to ward off Detective Corrigan's bullets during her escape? The same can be said for *City of Demons*, which begins with a direct attack on Constantine that is only resolved at the very end of the film. While the subsequent theft of Tricia's soul is not depicted in real-time, her incidental relevance to Nergal's agenda again redirects the audience's attention away from "whodunit" and towards more complex questions.

Likewise, the traditional archetype of the investigating detective is almost completely inverted in the character of John Constantine. His moral alignment varies, echoing Jackson's claim regarding the increasing proximity of the demonic in modern works of fantasy—though this is largely dependent on the platform in question (the CW would not be likely to permit an approved protagonist killing a stray teenager in order to serve the greater good). Beginning with his mentorship of Swamp Thing through to his current television incarnation, Constantine's key advantage as an investigator is not his deductive reasoning, but his knowledge of mystical lore and supernatural phenomena. As the ontological definition of "magic" varies from one fictional world to another—and, indeed, even within Constantine's own milieu of stories and adaptations—the audience is typically excluded from the standard process of investigation: the search for evidence, the interviewing of witnesses, verbal expressions of deduction and so on. Instead, Constantine's detective work is fueled by dreams, visions, half-remembered myths and conjured spirits who lead him from one step to the next. Nestorowich notes that even within the framework of the ostensibly coherent DC Universe, Constantine's magical abilities hardly guarantee any kind of supreme advantage in his chosen profession: "Whereas the magic of characters like Zatanna, and Doctor Fate employ bright displays of power, Constantine's magic is more subtle and underwhelming. Instead of blasts of lightning and balls of fire, Constantine opts for wards and divinations, a style of magic some perceive as boring as it lacks the flash, bang, and immediate discernible effect" (Nestorowich, "Sifting Through the Ashes" #1). Because key information is provided to him rather than acquired by him, this sub-genre compensates by redefining the detective as a trickster whose true talents lie in manipulation rather than rational thought. Unable to defeat powerful supernatural entities through brute force, Constantine and his successors must seek victory through deception, outsmarting and outmaneuvering their opponents. This approach, in turn, enables the creation and sustaining of personal vendettas against the investigator himself, with the recurring appearances of Nergal constituting but one example of how the protagonist of supernatural crime procedurals may become directly involved in the crime itself, either as an indirect cause or its intended target—Zed's presence in both "Original Sins" and *Constantine* is a deliberate means of tying the future victim of a supernatural conspiracy to the protagonist either through romance (as seen in the comics) or friendship (as seen in the television series).

As one of the earliest examples of the supernatural crime procedural, *Hellblazer* establishes certain narrative patterns one can find in abundance throughout the current landscape of television fiction. Flagship CW series *Supernatural*, in its fourteenth season as of 2019, features the Winchester brothers as trickster detectives who overcome superior demonic and mythological foes through wit, manipulation and exploitation of lore, and are frequently opposed by enemies whose immortality permits them to recur throughout the series; 2010–2015 Canadian series *Lost Girl* empowered the detective figure (in this case, a sympathetic succubus) yet maintained the power imbalance by pitting her and her supernatural allies against far greater magical foes such as the Morrigan, the Garuda and Druids; and so on. Constantine himself currently appears on CW television series *Legends of Tomorrow*, the resident expert on magic within a larger superhero ensemble, while a rebooted version co-stars in DC Comics' *Justice League*

Dark along with several other staples of the DC Universe's supernatural cast. Given the apparent ease with which the archetypal trickster detective can be integrated into other genre content, one may assume that the supernatural crime procedural is not only here to stay, but may soon begin crossing into other ontological systems.

Works Cited

Constantine: City of Demons. Written by J.M. DeMatteis, directed by Doug Murphy. CW Seed, 9 October 2018.
"Danse Vaudou." *Constantine*. Written by Christine Boylan, directed by John Badham. The CW Network, 21 November 2014.
Delano, Jamie, and John Ridgway, Alfredo Alcala, Rick Veitch & Tom Mandrake. "Shot to Hell," originally published Sept. 1988. *Hellblazer Vol. 1: Original Sins*. DC Comics, 2011.
Jackson, Rosemary. *Fantasy: The Literature of Subversion*. Methuen, 1981.
Kaveney, Roz. *Superheroes! Capes and Crusaders in Comics and Films*. I.B. Tauris, 2008.
Knowles, Christopher. *Our Gods Wear Spandex: The Secret History of Comic Book Heroes*. Weiser Books, 2007.
Moore, Alan, Stephen Bissette and John Totleben. *Saga of the Swamp Thing Book 3*.
Nestorowich, Max. "Sifting Through the Ashes: Analyzing *Hellblazer*" #1, #7. Sequart Organization. http://sequart.org/magazine/51389/analyzing-hellblazer-part-1/
Spivey, Michael, and Steven Knowlton. "Anti-Heroism in the Continuum of Good and Evil." *The Psychology of Superheroes*, edited by Robin S. Rosenberg and Jennifer Canzoneri, BenBella Books, 2008.
Sturgis, Amy H. "In Search of Fringe's Literary Ancestors." *Fringe Science: Parallel Universes, White Tulips, and Mad Scientists*, edited by Kevin R. Grazier, BenBella Books, 2011.
Todorov, Tsvetan. "The Typology of Detective Fiction." *Narrative Reader*, edited by Martin McQuillan, Routledge, 2000.

Runnin' with the Devil
The Procedurals from Hell

Cynthia J. Miller *and*
A. Bowdoin Van Riper

Criminal procedural dramas have introduced viewers to many unlikely pairings: Rick Castle and Kate Beckett, Temperance Brennan and Seeley Booth, Don and Charlie Epps… and supernatural procedurals have continued this trend with characters such as Ichabod Crane and Abbie Mills, Nick Burkhardt and the Wesen Monroe, among others. Each of these pairings, in its own way, carries out the basic functions of the procedural—with human/supernatural partners reinforcing social norms and values and reaffirming the effectiveness of systems of law and order—at least until the Devil enters the picture.

When the Devil becomes part of a procedural's mix of characters—whether as a CIA-like "handler" in *Brimstone* (1998–1999), an exasperated boss in *Reaper* (2007–2009), or an eccentric partner in *Lucifer* (2016–2018)—the narrative landscape changes considerably. These characters violate norms and upend values, encouraging other characters to do the same. But more than that, they attempt to knock "procedure"—the glue that holds these dramas together—right out of the picture (and often, at least temporarily, succeed). Hedonists, nihilists, bad boys, and bullies, they chafe at the procedural tradition in which they play a key role, continually asking of their counterparts and audiences alike, "Why? Why play by earthly rules when you now know how inconsequential they are? Why not just have a little *fun*?"

Even as the Devil's presence disrupts the procedural's defining (and thus, paradoxically, least-examined) element, however, it also calls into question the genre's underlying moral framework. Procedurals take for granted the integrity and efficacy of the criminal justice system. Even those that, like *Law & Order* (1992–2010), acknowledge the power of prejudice, influence, and ambition to corrupt the result of individual cases treat the system as a whole as fundamentally sound. The Devil is also an agent of punishment, however, and thus part of a system of divine justice that operates outside, and independent of, that administered by human law enforcement agencies, court systems, and prisons. Bringing the Devil—the ultimate agent of corruption—to Earth and involving him in the pursuit of justice by all-too-fallible humans invites viewers to contemplate the profound limitations of temporal, earthly justice by contrasting it with the effortless perfection of the eternal, divine justice of which the Devil is an agent.

This essay, then, will explore the portrayals of the Devil—as trickster and tempter, playful antagonist and deadly serious agent of divine justice—in these three series, examining the characters' strategies for blurring the line between duty and pleasure, the varying roles they play in the familiar lineup of procedural stock characters, and the ways in which their presence in the series' narratives complicates and plays with the notions of good and evil that animate other forms of procedurals, without fully undermining those series' underlying moral messages.

Three Takes on the Devil

Procedurals, as a genre, are defined by the intersection of process and personality. They are about "how things are done" in the methodological sense—standard procedures, limiting conditions, and ways to overcome them—but also about the ways in which all three are shaped by the personality of the investigator(s). *Dragnet* (1951–1959) and *Hill Street Blues* (1981–1987), for example, are both procedurals saturated with insider detail and flecked with police jargon, but their vast differences in tone derive from the gulf between the robotic dourness of Sgt. Joe Friday and the earthy humanity of the *Hill Street* cops. Similarly, more contemporary series such as *Bones* (2005–2017), *Castle* (2009–2016), *NCIS* (2003–present), and *Criminal Minds* (2005–present) pivot on the quirks and idiosyncrasies of their primary investigators, from near-compulsive attention to detail to technological wizardry to stoic masculinity. These intersections of process and character allow procedurals, as a genre, to be far more varied than their relatively rigid formula would suggest. The three series considered in this essay—despite their shared supernatural elements and the presence of the Devil as a main character—approach it from three distinct angles.

Brimstone, which ran for thirteen episodes on the Fox network from 1998 to 1999, wraps the procedural in the trappings of film noir. Its central character, Ezekiel Stone (Peter Horton), is a decorated New York City police detective who, in 1983, took justice into his own hands when his wife was raped and her assailant acquitted for lack of evidence. He hunted down her assailant, killing him in cold blood, only to be killed himself two months later, when a suspect in an unrelated crime shot him in the face aboard a deserted subway train. Sent to Hell for his sins—not committing the murder, but taking pleasure in it—he is paroled by the Devil (John Glover) fifteen years later, in the series' present, for a special mission. One hundred and thirteen of "the most vile creatures" in Hell have broken out and returned to Earth as seemingly human, but virtually un-killable, monsters. The Devil, knowing that his powers are severely limited on Earth, enlists Stone to recapture the fugitive souls, promising him "a second chance at life" (and, presumably, Heaven) if he rounds up all of them.

Relocated to Los Angeles, Stone becomes a cross between a classic noir hero and Raymond Chandler's "knight in tarnished armor": psychologically scarred, morally compromised, but stubbornly righteous. The damned (including Stone himself) are nearly invulnerable—they can be dispatched, the Devil explains, only by piercing their eyes—and nearly all (due to their longer tenure in Hell) are more powerful than he is. Most episodes end in brutal hand-to-hand fights that leave him badly battered and tempt him to embrace the savagery he unleashed on his wife's rapist. Even victory leaves a mark: Stone's body is covered with 113 tattooed symbols, one of which painfully, spontaneously burns away each time he returns a damned soul to Hell.

Produced nearly a decade later (2007–2009), and aired on the youth-oriented CW network, *Reaper* swapped the darkness of *Brimstone* for the cheery eccentricity of a slacker comedy. Where Ezekiel Stone is a tortured loner-hero whose deal with the Devil was part of a desperate search for redemption, Sam Oliver (Bret Harrison) of *Reaper* is an amiable college dropout who becomes a servant of the Devil (Ray Wise) because of a deal made by his parents before he was even born. A low-paid clerk at a home-improvement warehouse store, content to socialize with his even-less-ambitious friends Ben (Rick Gonzalez) and Sock (Tyler Labine) and nurse an unrequited crush on his co-worker Andy (Missy Peregrym), Sam is initially resentful of—and barely competent at—his new side job as a "Reaper." He gradually reconciles the mortal and supernatural sides of his life, however, enlisting his friends to help him recapture escaped souls, and finding the work more meaningful than ringing up two-by-fours and gallons of semi-gloss enamel. The broad comic-fantasy tone of *Reaper*, which mirrors that of contemporary series such as *Pushing Daisies* (2007–2009) and *The Middleman* (2008), means that violence is relatively muted. Supernatural technology in the form of "vessels"—ordinary looking objects endowed with magic that enables them to draw in and contain the souls of specific escapees—take the place of hand-to-hand combat and pierced eyes.

Another decade, and another shift in tone, separates from *Reaper* from *Lucifer*. Built—like *The Mentalist* (2008–2015) and *Castle* (2009–2016)—on the partnership (and unresolved sexual tension) of a by-the-book female police detective and an eccentric male "civilian consultant" to the department, it is explicitly a *police* procedural. The cases that drive each episode involve mortal criminals rather than damned souls in human form, and end with them dead or in the hands of the criminal justice system. Lucifer Morningstar (Tom Ellis), as the Devil styles himself in the series, is fully immersed in the human world. Bored with ruling in Hell, he gives up his throne and (before the events of the series) establishes himself as the owner of an exclusive Los Angeles nightclub: a sleek, sexually omnivorous figure with a British accent, a taste for tailored suits, and a reputation for throwing parties that celebrate hedonism in every imaginable form. Ellis approached the character, according to one online commentary, as "the love child of Nöel Coward and Mick Jagger, with a touch of actor Terry-Thomas" (Dowling).

The supernatural elements of *Lucifer* remain comparatively muted in the week-to-week mystery plots. The title character's superhuman strength, speed, and healing ability are used sparingly, and his ability to read mortals' innermost desires and subtly "encourage" them to act functions, in the context of the show's police work, as a supercharged version of the mind games played by mortal characters in series ranging from *Mission: Impossible* (1966–1973) and *The Rockford Files* (1974–1980) to *The Mentalist* and *White Collar* (2009–2014). Detective Chloe Decker (Lauren German) is, significantly, the only mortal character immune to Lucifer's powers, something so remarkable to him that it draws her immediately to his attention and, by the end of the first episode, leads to their unlikely professional partnership. Lucifer, despite his reputation as the "Father of Lies" (John 8:44), is steadfastly honest about his true identity, despite mortals' equally steadfast refusal to believe him. Those closest to him are gradually forced to accept it, however, as his decision to abandon Hell begins to have repercussions on Earth, and his mother (Tricia Helfer) and brother, the fallen angel Amenadiel (D. B. Woodside), come to Los Angeles to persuade him to return "home" and rule again in Hell.

The Devil for a Partner

The Devil may be one of film and television's most enigmatic characters. In motion pictures, as Nikolas Schreck observes, he is equally at home in both the arthouse and the grindhouse (6). Since his first portrayal on screen by George Méliès in 1896, the Devil has been represented across genres as great deceiver and tragic hero, purveyor of evil and comic stereotype. Variously associated with such diverse arenas as Nazi Germany, heavy metal music, the hippie counterculture, and the legal profession, the Devil has proved that, when it comes to popular entertainment, he is nothing if not flexible (Schreck 6).

Regardless of the vehicle in which he appears, certain satanic identity points remain fixed, among them: subversiveness, ego, and eroticism. As Hans-Joachim Neumann observes, "the cinema Devil is ... a thoroughly polyglot, often elegant, urbane and, above all, well-spoken apparition. His terror is the terror of a provincial public before the seductions of the great wide world" (Schrek 10). Satan is the great seducer; the embodiment of the inner human battle between social mandate and individual will; in other words, the antithesis of law and order. And yet, the figure of the Devil seems to have an affinity for procedurals—or we have an affinity for him, and what he brings to the earthly realm of law and order. In each of the series discussed here, the figure of the Devil is a complex character that brings chaos in the name of order, fun in the line of duty, and punishment—both institutional and supernatural—because, that is, after all, a satanic specialty. In so doing, however, he asks us to think again about both the process and intent of systems of law and order, the circumstances under which they function, and just how often we subconsciously wish for an alternative. Like F.W. Murnau's Faust, our protagonists make their deals with the Devil, and as in every rendition since that that early tale, the telling aspect is whether—and how—the Devil holds up his end of the bargain.

Procedurals featuring the Devil oblige us to consider the role he fills: What, if any, shifts are made in traditional genre formulas to accommodate the overlord of Hell? Does his presence complicate procedurals in ways that other supernatural elements do not? How does his presence for us to reconsider our notions of crime, punishment, and justice? The answers to these questions, of course, tell us more about ourselves—our fears and frustrations—than they do about our actual concern with who's minding Hell.

As historian Jeffrey Burton Russell notes, "a central thesis of the New Testament ... is that the powers of darkness under the generalship of the Devil are at war with the powers of light" (227). Within this context, the Devil's stance toward humans—whose souls are framed as the ultimate prize in the war between good and evil—is thus one of the most complicated aspects of his procedural characterization. In each, Satan is only marginally portrayed as a figure that thrives on evil (as Judeo-Christian lore would suggest), and rather, as a character that relishes *punishing* that evil. While retaining many of his devilish ways, and with them, links to ancient fears of death and the unknown, the Devil of police procedurals has, following Mircea Eliade, been mainstreamed.

In each of the series, the Devil displays an intimate, if periodically antagonistic, relationship with his earthly "partner." While outwardly living up to his reputation as "the big bad," he has a soft side that is betrayed by bending the rules, displays of fondness, and occasionally, envisioning a different way of being. In *Brimstone*, for example, the Devil is a cocky and self-serving trickster figure: nominally the hero's "client" but seemingly more interested in discord for its own sake. He complains, in "Encore," when he finds Zeke enjoying breakfast in a diner rather than chasing after escaped souls, but in other episodes taunts Zeke by deliberately throwing obstacles in his path: withholding potentially useful information, or giving him needlessly cryptic clues. There remains, however, a bond between the two—a grudging recognition of kindred dispositions—that owes more to traditional procedurals and film noir than to satanic cinema.

A decade later, in *Reaper*, the Devil is similarly mercurial—debonair, sarcastic, egotistical—and yet, behaves paternally toward Sam, bonding with him over ice cream and hockey games and covertly suggesting that their relationship runs even deeper than Sam realizes. The Devil thus splits the difference, in *Reaper*, between two stock procedural characters. He functions, within the mechanics of the weekly plots, as the long-suffering Chief who gives the hero his assignments and expresses exasperation at his (in)ability to fulfill them. At the same time, however, he also functions like a veteran breaking in a rookie, grudgingly proud beneath the exasperation. "For all your whining and complaining, lack of fashion sense, you always get the job done," the Devil grumbles to Sam, at one point. "You want to do the right thing. I hate that about you. But I guess that's the quality that makes you so effective" ("The Favorite").

This deepening of the "buddy" relationship between Satan and his earthly bounty hunters moves beyond the traditional procedural template, but power still rests firmly with the supernatural. The Devil's primary affiliation is with Hell, and his human partners serve, first-and-foremost to further his ends (and provide a bit of amusement). "Since when did you care if people get killed?" Sam asks the Devil, after being cautioned that more deaths are inevitable if he fails to act. "I don't," the Devil retorts. "Good call" ("The Favorite"). The development of the Devil's relationships with humans, and with it the series' interrogations of justice and punishment, is secondary.

Moving into the new millennium, *Lucifer* not only presents a more robust (and increasingly human) articulation of the Devil but shifts his from "overlord" to genuine "partner" as he and love-interest detective Chloe Decker solve the crime-of-the-week. The Devil's power shifts significantly as well. Openly emotionally invested in his relationship with Chloe, Lucifer gradually mutes his pansexual hedonism and uses his satanic powers to serve *her* ends, rather than his own. He often sets aside his role as the punisher of sins in deference to her mandate to uphold law and order and acquiesces (more frequently and compliantly as the series progresses) to her exasperated insistence that he respect the law's limits on police behavior. A Devil who has chosen to walk away from Hell, bored with his role as divine enforcer, he finds a satisfying synergy in the context of a police procedural—all of the punishment, none of the responsibility.

Disturbing the Foundation

Each of these supernatural procedurals turns on elements of mystery. Mystery stories are, as John Cawelti notes, tales of order disrupted and restored (97–98). The need for restoration—formal, public restoration—is particularly acute in police procedurals, which frame the criminal justice system as a kind of meta-hero, and the main characters as extensions of it, heroic because of their service. Procedurals all but demand an ending in which the malefactor is placed in the hands of the system—not summarily executed, turned over to vengeful associates, or allowed to walk free—in preparation for an (offstage) process of trial and punishment that will complete the restoration of the social order. The malefactor's patent, unambiguous guilt is also a foundational trope in police (though not legal) procedurals, and for similar reasons. Any other outcome would leave the system's efficacy—its reason for being—in doubt (Winston and Mellerski 6–8).

On one level, placing the Devil at or near center-stage in a television police procedural firmly reinforces both tropes. It introduces a divine justice system that, though it parallels and occasionally intersects the criminal justice system of traditional procedurals, transcends not only human laws but earth itself. The presence of the Devil, which entails the presence and involvement of God, implies that the judgments made within the divine justice system are, by definition, infallible: that those remanded to Hell for an eternity of punishment under the Devil's oversight ("the iniquitous and the vile," as he calls them in the pilot of *Reaper*) patently and unambiguously deserve their fate. Agents of the system—the Devil himself, or those who, like Ezekiel in *Brimstone* and Sam in *Reaper*, partake of his powers—can do things that investigators in ordinary procedurals can only dream of. They can manipulate space and time at will, overpower enemies with superhuman strength or magical weapons, and (in Lucifer's case) draw out the deeply buried, barely acknowledged innermost desires of anyone they meet.

The Devil initially appears, in both *Brimstone* and *Reaper*, to be as deeply committed to the smooth functioning of the cosmic justice system as mortal police-procedural captains are to the efficiency of their assigned precincts. He explains to Ezekiel in the pilot episode of *Brimstone* that escaped souls represent a threat to the stability of the system, and tells Sam in the pilot episode of *Reaper* that "you'll be doing the world a favor, sending bad guys back where they belong." Both series, however, gradually introduce the possibility that the recapture of escaped souls—though important—is merely a pretext for a different, more personal agenda that the Devil is concealing or actively lying about.

In *Brimstone,* for example, the Devil repeatedly taunts Ezekiel by making his assignments unnecessarily difficult, or steers him toward souls whose character flaws are dark mirrors of Ezekiel's own. The implication—never fully explored because of the series' early cancellation—is that he is actually setting Ezekiel up to fail, ensuring that he will spend eternity in Hell. In *Reaper,* on the other hand, the Devil spends inordinate time and energy acting as a mentor—almost a father-figure—to his epically unfocused, unmotivated protégé, Sam. The plot arc of *Reaper*'s abbreviated second season all but confirms that he *is* Sam's father, but the cancellation of the series left the idea unexplored. Unlike the heroes of conventional procedurals, the Devil is not only willing, but eager, to put his own needs (temporarily) ahead of the imperatives of the system.

The Devil's rejection of the system, and its demands, in favor of his own desires receives its most complete and explicit treatment in *Lucifer*. The series' premise depends on Lucifer walking away from the throne of Hell and its attendant responsibilities, and flatly rejecting God's demand that he return. This outright defiance—an echo of the earlier rebellion, chronicled in *Paradise Lost*, that made him Lord of Hell in the first place—sets in motion an arc that stretches across two seasons of and into a third. It pits Lucifer not only against God (who remains offstage, and who he sardonically refers to as "Dad"), but against his mother and his elder brothers Amenadiel (D.B. Woodside) and Uriel (Michael Imperioli), all four of whom use the utterly innocent, wholly virtuous Chloe as a pawn in their cosmic power struggle. Lucifer's own manipulation of the humans around him is, in keeping with his personality, on a smaller and more intimate scale. He encourages Chloe's daughter Trixie (Scarlett Estevez) to indulge her eight-year-old appetites for chocolate cake and staying up past her bedtime, tells his psychotherapist that they can "have as much naked cuddle time as you desire, but you're gonna have to listen to me, too. You know, just an existential dilemma or two" ("Pilot") and takes revenge on a street preacher for being "a liar, a charlatan, someone who doesn't believe what they say" by briefly revealing his true, demonic face ("Lucifer, Stay"). He moves freely, throughout the series, between acting as an agent of justice and order (albeit civil rather than cosmic) and as a sower of chaos and temptation.

All three series, in the course of developing these larger stories, also blur the clear-cut certainty with which procedurals typically approach questions of guilt and innocence. "Don't worry," the Devil tells Sam as they examine the victim of a highway accident in *Reaper*, "he was probably a terrible person" who drank to excess and beat his wife ("All Mine"). The darkly comic twist lies in "probably," which suggests that the man's death *may* have been sheer bad luck rather than cosmic justice. The Devil states in the pilot of *Brimstone*, and Ezekiel repeats in the opening narration of every subsequent episode, that the 113 escapees are "the most vile creatures in Hell," but several of those Ezekiel actually meets belie that description. Teenaged Eileen (Karina Logue) was a medieval peasant girl who took revenge on the young nobleman who raped her by burning down his house with him—and his entire family—inside ("Heat"). Da Ming Po (Roger Yuan) was a Chinese poet whose all-consuming adoration for his lover curdled into murderous jealousy ("Poem"). They are, like Stone himself, flawed human beings guilty of terrible acts, but hardly monsters.

Lucifer, audaciously, takes a similar approach with a villain who actually *is* monstrous: forcing his victims to destroy their careers (asking a noted surgeon, for example, to mutilate her right hand) or watch him execute an innocent person. The criminal is revealed as a scientist whose own career was destroyed by his response to a similar Hobson's choice, and his crimes as deranged attempts to show that "anyone" under similar stress might have done the same. He is last seen in Hell: forced, in a punishment uniquely fitted to his crime, to relieve his fateful moment of decision in an endless loop.

Ninth Circle of Hell

> For you, my darlings, freedom to do what you like is the discovery of how unlikable what you like to do makes you. Not

> that that stops you doing what you like, since you like doing what you like more than you like liking what you do…
> —Duncan 78

The figure of Lucifer, as overlord of Hell and punisher of wickedness, is a product of human moral conflict. But that conflict is decidedly *not* one of good versus evil; rather, it is one of evil versus evil—of collective anger, frustration, and resentment at the violation of moral codes—of the desire to punish.

Society has, throughout its existence, struggled with social control and strategies for ensuring that individuals maintain the moral order. Notions of Heaven and Hell, redemption and damnation, represent one ideological aspect of our engagement with the moral order; social institutions of criminal justice represent its practical, mundane enforcement. On the surface then, the incorporation of the Devil in police procedurals is an easy and natural "fit"—agents of punishment joining forces to ensure that the wicked pay for their violations of the social contract—and an eternity in Hell is a far more satisfying resolution to heinous earthly crimes than a prison sentence. But if we look a bit more closely, this superficial allegiance becomes more complex, and reflects our ongoing, and increasingly troubled relationship with the question and nature of punishment, leaving us to ask: "Does conjuring the Devil in police procedurals blur our vision of justice, or make it more clear?"

John McTaggart defines punishment as simply "the infliction of pain on a person because he has done wrong" (129). It is, as he points out, a deliberate intervention in the course of events; it is intentionally enacted and requires justification (130). We find a classic, and enduring illustration of this in Dante Alighieri's 14th-century classic "Inferno," where nine circles of Hell are designed specifically for the punishment of earthly sins, each representing a gradual increase in wickedness: paganism, lust, gluttony, greed, wrath, heresy, violence, fraud, and treachery, with corresponding tortures of the body and soul. We may thus think of punishment as retributive, in that its "ultimate justifying purpose" is to "match off moral gravity and pain," on the principle that "the wicked should suffer pain in exact proportion to their turpitude" (Kadish 421). However, as we unpack the notion of punishment, we find a constellation of links between society and the individual: practical, emotional, philosophical, and ideological, that complicates this formula of crime and punishment.

Particularly troublesome is punishment's emotional side—its "expressive" function—which communicates an individual's (or society's) condemnation, and which may or may not be commensurate with the actual crime. "Moral outrage," a phenomenon familiar throughout history, can significantly influence the interpretation of "justice" and the course of punishment As Joel Feinberg notes:

> Given our conventions, of course, condemnation is expressed by hard treatment, and the degree of harshness of the latter expresses the degree of reprobation of the former. Still, this should not blind us to the fact that it is social disapproval and its appropriate expression that should fit the crime, and not hard treatment (pain) as such. Pain should match guilt only insofar as its infliction is the symbolic vehicle of public condemnation [423].

So while both retributive and expressive punishment are backward-looking, responding to an act that is considered morally reprehensible, retribution aims to apportion suffering to moral deservedness, whereas expression aims to satisfy society's outrage.

In the space between those two, we find the ideological—and imaginative—opening for the work of the Devil. As the failings and limitations of the criminal justice system increasingly become a source of social dissatisfaction, media debates on law and order flourish, and protests intensify, popular culture both reflects and addresses our preoccupation with crime and legal impotence (Donovan; McManus; Clark). Police procedurals abound, and are among the longest-running television series, but more recent supernatural elements in series like those discussed in this collection signal a desire for responses to crime that can only be found outside the boundaries of earthly law and order. As the overlord of Hell, the figure of Lucifer represents not just momentary, but eternal, punishment, promising fire and brimstone, torture and agony, enough to satisfy the deepest rage. Moreover, the Devil delights in punishing, as Lucifer Morningstar gleefully affirms to his crime-fighting colleagues and victims alike: "Punishing is what I *do*! I'm *good* at it!" adding a note of intense satisfaction to the tortures of the damned. His supernatural specialty has apparently filled a void in the contemporary criminal justice system.

A significant by-product of these satanic collaborations is an overarching rehabilitation of the public image of the Devil. While clearly part of a larger trend toward humanizing the supernatural, these portrayals carry an additional layer of importance. Lucifer has traditionally been … demonized … in both classical antiquity and contemporary popular culture as the consummate evil. The series discussed here, however, shift the "horns and pitchfork" image of the Devil to that of a rogue, a dandy, and an entrepreneur, capitalizing on his seldom-embraced "rebel" persona. As author-activist Saul Alinsky argues,

> Lest we forget, at least an over the shoulder acknowledgment to the very first radical: from all our legends, mythology and history (and who is to know where mythology

leaves off and history begins—or which is which), the very first radical known to man who rebelled against the establishment and did it so effectively that he at least won his own kingdom—Lucifer [ix].

The Devil is many things in these procedurals—warden, employer, partner, gatekeeper, Prince of Darkness, punisher, and even deceiver, if clever bargaining counts—but he is not, as lore would have us believe, evil. The title character in *Lucifer* laments:

> Why do they blame me for all their little failings? As if I'd spent my days sitting on their shoulder, forcing them to commit acts they'd otherwise find repulsive. "Oh, the Devil made me do it." I have never made any one of them do anything. Never! ["Pilot"].

The Devil in these procedurals does not bring wickedness into the world, but swiftly, definitively, and eternally addresses it in the hereafter. As poet and philosopher Jami Criss explains, "He loves all wickedness, but only because he loves punishing wickedness" (5).

Never Just a Character

The trope of mismatched partners—whose seemingly irreconcilable personalities are a source of constant friction, yet also their greatest strength—predates, and extends well beyond, the procedural subgenre. Yet, particularly on television, the two have become almost inextricably linked. *Brimstone*, *Reaper*, and *Lucifer* represent three widely divergent takes on that now well-worn trope, but fans of the subgenre, or television viewers with capacious memories, will have little difficulty in finding antecedents for the character dynamics in all of them.

The Devil, however, is never *just* a character. He is the nexus of a complex, sometimes self-contradictory web of cultural associations; theological doctrines; and depictions on paper, canvas, stage, and screen. He is one of a bare handful of characters in Western culture who comes embedded in, and inseparable from, a fully formed view of the world. Introduced into a story, he brings that worldview with him, leaving the storyteller to work out how—and how much—to integrate it into the story. Integrating the Devil into a story about crime and detection is a particular challenge because, ironically, they raise many of the same themes: temptation, transgression, judgment, and punishment. They cannot simply be juxtaposed, but must be deliberately related, deliberately reconciled or, just as deliberately, allowed to clash and collide.

The three series considered here choose the latter path. Juxtaposing the cosmic justice administered out by the Lord of Hell with the earthly justice meted out by the police and courts, they trouble the reassuring, yet unexamined, certainties that we attach to both. Freeing the Devil from his now-archaic horns and pitchfork, equipping him instead with modern clothes and a postmodern attitude, they force us to consider anew what he represents. Setting him—a being who lives to punish—loose amid a system we ourselves have created for that purpose, they force us to confront questions we have, typically, preferred to brush past: "Whom do we punish, how, and to what end?" That the answers may discomfit us should not be surprising. Inconvenient truths have always been the Devil's specialty.

Works Cited

Alighieri, Dante. "Inferno." *Divine Comedy.* www.worldofdante.org.
Alinksy, Saul D. *Rules for Radicals: A Practical Primer for Realistic Radicals.* Vintage Books, 1989.
"All Mine"; *Reaper: Season 1,* written by Jeffrey Vlaming, directed by Michael Rohl, Lionsgate 2008.
Cawelti, John G. *Adventure, Mystery, Romance: Formula Stories as Art and Popular Culture* U of Chicago P, 1977.
Clark, Bianca. "Trump Administration Is Clueless on Criminal Justice." *USA Today,* 19 May 2017. www.usatoday.com/story/opinion/2017/05/19/trump-administration-clueless-criminal-justice/101648606/.
Criss, Jami. *Healogy.* Self-Published, 2016.
Donovan, Paul. "Stoking the Fires of Resentment." *The Independent,* 20 August 1996. http://www.independent.co.uk/news/uk/stoking-the-fires-of-resentment-1310803.html
Dowling, Amber. "The Devil Is in the Detail: 'Lucifer' Star Reveals the Music Behind the Man." *Hollywood Reporter,* 25 January 2016. http://www.hollywoodreporter.com/live-feed/devil-is-detail-lucifer-star-858324.
Duncan, Glen. *I, Lucifer: Finally, the Other Side of the Story.* Grove Press, 2003.
Eliade, Mircea. *Cosmos and History: The Myth of the Eternal Return.* Harper & Row, 1954.
"Encore," *Brimstone: The Complete Series,* written by Scott A. Williams, directed by Felix Enriquez Alcalá, Fabulous Films, Ltd.
"The Favorite," *Reaper: Season 2,* written by Michele Fazekas and Tara Butters, directed by Kevin Dowling, Lionsgate, 2009.
Feinberg, Joel. "The Expressive Function of Punishment." In *Readings in the Philosophy of Law,* edited by Jules L. Coleman, Routledge, 2013.
"Heat," *Brimstone: The Complete Series,* written by Janis Diamond, directed by Jesus Trevino, Fabulous Films Ltd.
Kadish, Sanford H. "Complicity, Cause, and Blame: A Study in the Interpretation of Doctrine." In *Crimes and Punishments,* edited by Jules L. Coleman, Taylor & Francis, 1994.
"Lucifer, Stay. Good Devil," written by Joe Henderson, directed by Nathan Hope, *Lucifer: The Complete First Season,* Warner Brother, 2016.
McManus, Doyle "Despite Recent Law and Order Rhetoric, the Old Lock 'Em Up Mentality Is Out of Favor with Republicans." *Los Angeles Times.* November 15, 2015. http://www.latimes.com /opinion/op-ed/la-oe-1115-mcmanus-candidates-mizzou-yale-20151115-column.html
McTaggart, John. *Studies in Hegelian Cosmology.* Cambridge UP, 2011.
"Pilot," *Lucifer: The Complete First Season,* written by Tom Kapinos, directed by Len Wiseman, Warner Brother, 2016.
"Pilot," *Reaper: Season 1,* written by Michele Fazekas and Tara Butters, directed by Kevin Smith, Lionsgate, 2008.

"Poem," *Brimstone: The Complete Series,* written by Ethan Reiff and Cyrus Voris, directed by Felix Enriquez Alcalá, Fabulous Films, Ltd.
Russell, Jeffrey Burton. *The Devil: Perceptions of Evil from Antiquity to Primitive Christianity.* Cornell UP, 1997.
Schreck, Nikolas. *The Satanic Screen.* Creation Books, 2000.
Winston, Robert P., and Nancy Mellerski, *The Public Eye: The Ideology of the Police Procedural.* St. Martin's, 1992.

Amateur Hour

Professional Competency in Supernatural Crime Procedurals

Lynn Kozak

In a genre already known for its fluidity (Nichols-Pethick 3), and promiscuous hybridity (Turnbull 147), supernatural crime shows offer exciting new representations of professionalism, teamwork, and morality to traditional criminal procedurals. This essay will focus on how *Lucifer* (FOX, 2015–8; Netflix 2019–present) flaunts its generic hybridity in order to produce complicated dynamics between its protagonists that lead to meaningful character arcs. In featuring a supernaturally gifted protagonist who has little, if any, natural connection to crime-solving, *Lucifer*, like other supernatural crime shows, demonstrates how its protagonists must learn to be professional in their crime-solving capacities and must find their own moralities and forge their own crime-solving teams outside of standard institutional frameworks.

These three strands are inextricably linked, as supernatural protagonists often pair with criminal justice professionals to solve crimes, and slowly assimilate ways of speaking and behaving standard to those working in criminal justice, along with more recognizable moral values. Like other supernatural crime shows, *Lucifer* fundamentally stretches the question of "who can police?" (Brundson 223), and breaks out of its "traditional" murder-of-the-week formulae (Nichols-Pethick 7) as its protagonists learn to work together and assert their own roles in solving crimes.

As Derek Kompare notes, "television professionals typically embody normative, attractive societal ideals. We can only hope that cops are as driven as *Homicide*'s Frank Pembleton..." (56). Crime shows are such because they show crime-solvers, whether police officers or detectives, private eyes or amateur sleuths, using their professionally honed skills, their various "methods of detection" to solve crimes (Jenner 5). Kompare sees in *CSI* a

> sense of dedicated professionalism and even social duty ... as hybrid episodic-serial drama ... (it also traces) the impact these expectations of professionalism have on the protagonists both in the moment and over time [57].

This kind of serial exploration becomes much more marked when the protagonists are not starting on a job that they have chosen and trained for, but rather from another profession entirely, thrust into crime-solving because of their supernatural skills.

In defying professionalism, the supernatural crime-solving protagonist also necessarily stands outside the professional divide that marks the crime show genre, between the "police procedural" and the "genius detective drama" (Jenner 39; Turnbull 97; Creeber vii). Jenner suggests this dichotomy has already given way in the crime show genre, as

> consultants, private actors who work as a part of a team of specialists.... The somewhat unspecified legal position of these consultants blurs boundaries between private and official actors and their relationship with government institutions [Jenner 36].

Lucifer's titular character is explicitly a "consultant," but not because of some learned skill or professional knowledge that could be construed as naturally contributing to crime-solving, which creates incredulity around his role which we might say is part of the fun of the show. *Lucifer*'s eponymous hero is the devil himself, Lucifer Morningstar (Tom Ellis), whose special powers include getting people to reveal their desires, super-strength, and immortality, while professionally, he runs a nightclub in Los Angeles. So Lucifer stands far from the crime-writers (cf., Jessica Fletcher in *Murder, She Wrote*, CBS 1984–96; Richard Castle in *Castle*, ABC 2009–16), forensic psychologists (Dr. Cal Lightman in *Lie to Me*, FOX 2009–11; Dr. Edward "Fitz" Fitzgerald in *Cracker*, ITV 1993–2006), and private investigators (Sherlock Holmes and Joan Watson, *Elementary*, CBS 2012–present) often associated with police consultancy.

Lucifer's unique skills bring new dimensions to the crime genre's traditional tendency to create teams and distribute skills among their protagonists, whether amongst the institutional teams of "police procedurals," (Scaggs 94; Worthington 147–8) or those who work with the "genius detective" (Piper 30; Jenner 48–9). *Lucifer* also distributes crime-solving skills among its protagonists, including angels, demons, goddess,'lawyers, police, and forensics specialists that change and grow. At its heart, *Lucifer* explores morality through its crime-solving teams that coalesce both within and outside of traditional institutions, over a long arc that transcends the show's "murder of the week" formula.

Lucifer takes place in Los Angeles, where Lucifer teams up with a Los Angeles Police Department homicide detective, Det. Chloe Decker (Lauren German). The pilot introduces Lucifer who, alongside being the Devil, is also a law-breaking, womanizing smooth-talker. In the first season, Lucifer manipulates his way into becoming a full-time "civilian consultant" partner to homicide Detective Chloe Decker, a partnership that raises many questions about professionalism, morality, and teamwork.

Lucifer presents a clear combination of elements from previous iterations of the crime show. Lucifer himself seems cut from the hard-boiled cloth (Lee 43) and operates by his own moral code: apropos of his role as the devil, he almost single-mindedly focuses on punishing the wicked, happily embracing violence and other rule-breaking behavior, including a penchant for sexual harassment, in this pursuit. This code emerges in contrast to that of Det. Decker, who fits the model of "the good cop": she is honest, smart, capable, and the daughter of a policeman, still seeking to right his wrongful death.[1] More, as a female cop, her character has the familiar experience of being belittled and ostracized by her male colleagues (Garland *et al.* 15; Turnbull 2014, 231; Brundson 381); she is also divorced (Garland *et al.* 5) and a mother (Garland *et al.* 13). In some ways, these facts place both Decker and Lucifer outside a traditional institutional team; but at the same time, their partnership creates a fruitful point of tension as they try to assimilate to each other's divergent personalities and crime-solving methods (Jenner 33), maintaining a "will they/won't they" romantic dynamic throughout (Jenner 49). This assimilation, however, feels woefully one-sided: Decker's character does not change at all over the course of the series, except in how she views Lucifer. Meanwhile, the show continuously rehabilitates Lucifer (and other members of the team that I will return to shortly) despite lapses in his professionalism, his relationships, and in his general sense of morality.

In addition to Lucifer and Decker, the show's other protagonists include Lucifer's angel brother Amenadiel (DB Woodside); Det. Decker's ex-husband and colleague Det. Dan Espinoza (Kevin Alejandro); Lucifer's demon sidekick Mazikeen "Maze" (Lesley-Ann Brandt); and Lucifer's psychiatrist, Dr. Linda Martin (Rachel Harris). In the second season, lab-tech Ella Lopez (Aimee Garcia) also joins, as does Lucifer and Amenadiel's mother, the Goddess/Charlotte Richards (Tricia Helfer). The third season sees Charlotte Richards (no longer occupied by the Goddess) return as a lawyer who also helps the team, and Lieutenant Pierce (Tom Welling), who also turns out to be Cain, the first murderer, cursed with immortality. This combination of protagonists obviously throws together diverse skill sets and various degrees of connection to "professional" crime-fighting. While

Decker remains the core of the team, with the strongest detective skills and the clearest morals throughout, many of these other protagonists change quite radically over the course of the show's three seasons, and become involved in helping solve crimes in various ways within and without institutional frameworks.

In its pilot, *Lucifer* introduces its eponymous protagonist as a clear foil both to Det. Decker's honesty and competence as well as to Det. Espinoza's indifference, and, we learn later, corruption. Lucifer himself, first seen getting pulled over and manipulating his way out of a ticket with his super powers, witnesses a murder, so that Det. Decker must question him. Before this interrogation at Lucifer's night club, Lux, Det. Espinoza tries to discourage Decker from rigorously pursuing the case. This beat sets up Lucifer's anti-authority, justice-orientated position in his interview with Decker, as he asks her: "What will your corrupt little organization do about this? Will you find the person responsible? Will they be punished? Will this be a priority for you? Because it will be for me."

The episode's structure doubles down on this dynamic, following Lucifer, not Det. Decker, and so aligning the audience with his unprofessional and dubiously moral pursuit of the killer through the next two beats: in the first, he uses his ability to extract people's desires to get his next clue; in the second, he uses his superhuman strength to dangle a suspect over a balcony to get information. Contrasting their detection methods, Decker only catches up with him two clues later, when she reveals she has found the same suspect by following up on the victim's phone records. As Decker arrests Lucifer for interfering with the criminal investigation, Lucifer once again insists on pursuing justice: "C'mon, we're wasting time. We should be out there, solving a homicide and punishing the ones responsible!" Lucifer sexually harasses Det. Decker throughout these scenes, which the series uncomfortably incorporates into Lucifer's "outside the rules" characterization, while also playing on familiar opposite gender police pairings that starts the "will they/won't they" dynamic between the two.

By the end of the first episode, Lucifer, with his physical invulnerability, saves Decker's life: as he shields her from bullets, he calls her "Chloe" for the first time.[2] When Lucifer tells Maze about this when discussing the case later in the episode, Lucifer tells Maze that Decker is immune to his powers, saying that "she's different." Maze insists that maybe "she's not the one who's different," suggesting that Lucifer is changing, especially amazed at him "saving a human": Dr. Linda Martin, a psychiatrist who was a witness in the case, and who agrees to treat Lucifer in exchange for sex, also confirms this, telling Lucifer that "you are changing, and you don't know what's causing the change. Or who." Lucifer's drift towards a "human" sense of morality continues over the course of the series, and runs in tandem with both his personal and professional relationship with Det. Decker.

Part of Lucifer's lack of understanding a professional police partnership feeds the will they/won't they dynamic between the two, which has threatened or sustained other professional crime-solving duos in past shows (cf., *The X-Files*, *Bones*, *Castle*, etc.; Lucifer explicitly compares he and Decker to Bones and Booth in "The Angel of San Bernardino"). Lucifer persistently and openly talks about sleeping with Chloe ("Pilot," "Manly Whatnots," "Pops," "St. Lucifer," "Vegas with Some Radish," etc.), though at times, she, too, tries it on with Lucifer (while drunk, also "Pops"). What persists through this dynamic is Lucifer's focus on Decker's role as "the Detective," the only name he really ever calls her (exceptions to this are marked, and do not always appear where expected), and his growing respect for her in that role. For Lucifer, despite his misgivings about the Los Angeles Police Department, Decker's role as a police detective stands as a kind of metonymy for her essential goodness that he is so attracted to, a goodness strong enough not only to stand up to his supernatural powers, but even to render them useless: Lucifer discovers his invincibility waning in the show's fourth episode ("Manly Whatnots"), when he encourages Decker to shoot him to prove his own immortality, and she does, and he bleeds. But he only discovers that Decker alone affects his immortality ("St. Lucifer") several episodes later, at the same time that she recognizes her own growing attachment to him: "our thing goes beyond just work, or sex … anyhow, I can let my guard down with you. I don't do that with anyone else. You make me vulnerable. And maybe that's okay." To which he responds, "If it's any consolation to your pride, it appears you make me vulnerable too."

In the second season, Lucifer and Chloe grow closer, both personally and professionally. The show foregrounds this deepening premise in the second season's tenth episode "Quid Pro Ho," where Lucifer and Chloe have to testify about Chloe's father's murderer, where Chloe's actions (for the first time) jeopardize the case, and she is forced to either claim that Lucifer is lying or face her father's killer going free. Lucifer's testimony speaks to his increasingly invested partnership with Decker, and how her goodness, her professionalism, and his attraction to her are all intertwined:

> The LAPD, and Det. Decker in particular, acted impeccably on this case. This whole courtroom-nay, the entire city can rest assured that someone as honest, trustworthy, and reliable as Det. Decker is out there protecting them. She is truly good. And I don't mean in bed-I wouldn't know. That's how good she is.

In contrast, Decker's testimony focuses on Lucifer's lack of professionalism, but also asserts Decker's devotion to him as a crime-solving partner, and the whole exchange is worth noting here for its insistence that Lucifer's moral and practical contributions to crime-solving now outweigh his professional incompetence:

> **CHARLOTTE:** Lucifer Morningstar is your partner. Correct?
> **CHLOE:** Yes, he's a civilian consultant for the LAPD. We work cases together.
> **CHARLOTTE:** And how is he qualified for this role?
> **CHLOE:** He is very intuitive. He understands people's desires.
> **CHARLOTTE:** And in addition to that, I assume he studied law enforcement.
> **CHLOE:** Not to my knowledge, no.
> **CHARLOTTE:** Oh, okay, but he has a professional background which is somehow relevant to law enforcement.
> **CHLOE:** He owns a nightclub.
> **CHARLOTTE:** Ok, then I assume his previous job was more relevant to his role as a civilian consultant for the LAPD, right.
> **CHLOE:** Well, if you believe his claims that he used to run hell … then yes, he's accustomed to punishing bad guys.
> **CHARLOTTE:** I'm confused Detective. Are you suggesting that your partner's delusional? Or just lying?
> **CHLOE:** Lucifer Morningstar is many things, but he is not a liar. Everything that Mr. Morningstar said is absolutely true…. Lucifer is the best partner I have ever had, and I can only hope that he can count on me as much as I count on him.

Lucifer reasserts his views on Chloe in the next episode ("Stewardess Interruptus"), and here, too, he conflates Decker's role as "Detective" with her goodness, as he finally declares he does not want to sleep with her, in the exchange where the two share their first kiss:

> **LUCIFER:** I've changed my mind about that actually. I've realized it would never work between us. So from now on, no more attempts at moments. I'd be honored to simply continue working by your side, if you'll have me.
> **CHLOE:** Of course … it's not like you to give up.
> **LUCIFER:** Oh, I haven't given up. I've had an epiphany of sorts. You deserve someone worthy of you, and that isn't me. … You deserve someone better, because you, Detective, are selfless to a nauseating degree. You always put your daughter first, even though the ungrateful urchin does nothing to contribute to the rent, you deserve someone worthy of that grace. Someone that knows that every crime scene breaks your heart, even though you'd never admit it. Someone who actually appreciates your impossibly boring middle name, Jane. More importantly, Detective, you deserve someone as good as you, because, well, you're special, and I'm, I'm not worth it.
> **CHLOE:** Yeah, you're probably right. (*she kisses him*)
> **LUCIFER:** Detective… (*he kisses her again*)

The scene recombines the pilot's dynamics. Now, rather than using his attraction to her to undermine her professional standing, Lucifer appreciates that his attraction to Chloe depends at least in part on her identity as a homicide cop, which stands, along with her role as a mom, for her goodness. In doing so, *Lucifer* reinforces television's on-going portrayal of idealized police, in their social, institutional, and ultimately, moral roles. At the same time, the show's strong equation of goodness with crime-fighting also gives more legitimacy to Lucifer, and his role as a civilian consultant, despite his lack of professional training. Driven primarily by his relationship to the detective, Lucifer's character seems to continue to change (with lapses) over the course of the series, so that his morality more closely reflects her own, allowing for a more relatable crime-solving protagonist.

The "team" that coalesces around Lucifer and Det. Decker also forms over the course of the series, but also has many missteps along the way. The last few episodes of the first season demonstrate that, with the exception of Det. Decker, all the other protagonists have some moral shortfalls. The easiest of these reveals is with Dr. Linda Martin, who Lucifer gets to assist on their case ("Et tu, Doctor?"). She bonds with Decker over the course of the case, culminating in this conversation about Lucifer that signals not only his growth, under both of their influences, but also shows Martin's own change of heart about her trading Lucifer sex for therapy:

> LINDA: He's grown quite a bit since working with you.
> CHLOE: I'm not sure I'm the reason—I think you've really helped him. I underestimated you before, I'm sorry.
> LINDA: Not needed, but thank you.
> CHLOE: I thought, I thought you were sleeping with him!
> LINDA: Oh, I am.
> CHLOE: Oh. Is that, is that…
> LINDA: …ethical? Nooooo. No it is not. But there's something about him. I can't stop myself. But I think it's time I did. I mean, even I'm starting to feel…

By the end of the episode, Dr. Martin tells Lucifer that she has "realized a few things" and that they "should keep their relationship professional from now on." This change away from Linda's apparently sole vice comes in tandem with her professional usefulness in solving the crime, as later Decker tells Lucifer, "You were right about Linda. She helped me figure out the motive."

These last few episodes bear out more complicated arcs of exposing crime and seeking redemption for the other main protagonists, including Det. Espinoza, Amenadiel, and Maze. First, Det. Espinoza, when he volunteers to help Decker on the Palmetto Case ("Wingman"), the same case that he tells her off about back in "Pilot." Decker had been investigating dirty cop Malcolm Graham (Kevin Rankin) when she witnessed him get shot doing a deal: while not knowing who shot him, she continues to believe that he is corrupt, even while the other cops hate her for it. We only learn in the following episode, "Et Tu, Doctor?," that it was Espinoza who shot Malcolm, and that he has been lying to Decker the whole time. It takes him several episodes of being blackmailed and then kidnapped by Malcolm for him to redeem himself, first by trying to stop Malcolm killing Lucifer ("St. Lucifer"), and finally, in coming clean to Decker and helping her prove Lucifer's innocence for a crime he did not commit ("Take Me Back to Hell").

Amenadiel's arc, too, involves Malcolm, as Amenadiel brings Malcolm back to life from Espinoza's gunshot wound ("Wingman"), so that Malcolm might kill Lucifer and send him back to Hell ("A Priest Walks Into a Bar," "Pops"). It is only in the season finale, "Take Me Back to Hell," that Amenadiel makes up with Lucifer, and helps him find and fight Malcolm: in the course of their investigation, when Amenadiel asks a particularly pointed question, Lucifer exclaims, "Oooh, look at you, Sherlock!," a winking nod to Amenadiel's newfound ability to "detect" alongside Lucifer.

Maze, too, changes through these episodes, making friends with Decker's daughter, Trixie (Scarlett Estevez), and then with Dr. Martin ("Pops"), while betraying Lucifer ("Et Tu, Doctor?"), then trying to kill Amenadiel ("#TeamLucifer"), before finally healing Amenadiel's wounds when Malcolm stabs him ("Take Me Back to Hell"). For Maze, part of this change also comes through her helping Decker find Lucifer in "Take Me Back to Hell," which Lucifer later refers to as their "good cop/demon cop action." Here, in this final episode, Lucifer dies at the hands of Malcolm, and then comes back to life to save Chloe and kill Malcolm again, with the promise to God that he will find his mother, who has escaped hell.

The second season follows much of the fall-out of the first, while also presenting new moral challenges to the show's protagonists. Amenadiel and Dan both pay for their moral failings of the first season: Amenadiel loses his powers for his trying to kill Lucifer, and Dan is demoted at work for his role in the Palmetto case. Meanwhile Lucifer decides not to return his mother, the goddess of creation now inhabiting the body of Charlotte Richards (Tricia Helfer) to Hell, though Amenadiel warns him that this might also have consequences.

Those consequences come in the shape of another angelic brother, Uriel (Michael Imperioli), who appears in "Weaponizer" to collect their mother, or, if Lucifer refuses to give her up, Chloe. With Chloe's life under threat, Lucifer kills Uriel with Azrael's blade. Lucifer's murder of Uriel, like the crimes of Dan and Amenadiel in the first season, have mixed consequences. In the next episode, "Monster," Lucifer consistently acts out, drinking and flirting at a crime scene, stealing food at the precinct, sneaking into the interrogation room to threaten a suspect, stealing Dan's badge and gun, etc. And throughout, though Chloe several times calls his behavior "inappropriate," and threatens to "bench him," keeps asking him "what's going on with you?," seemingly more hurt that Lucifer will not talk about it with her, because "that's what partners do." At one point, Lucifer tries to tell her, "Why are you surprised, Detective? I'm the devil! I'm evil!"; and finally, with Linda, he reveals his true face. The episode raises a number of professional and moral questions. On the one hand, Decker chastises Lucifer's behavior, but still praises him for saving a woman's life in the course of the investigation, and shows a clear desire for him to remain her partner—it is not clear whether Lucifer's increased unprofessionalism (just when Decker thought he "was getting the hang of this") actually impedes the case. Decker also understands his behavior not as evil, but as acting out, realizing that something has "happened." So along with Decker (and, eventually, with Linda), we understand that Lucifer is struggling with feelings of guilt, rather than seeing him as evil for killing his own brother; Decker's literal sympathy for the devil here again allows the audience to excuse his behavior.

The next episode ("My Little Monkey"), though, sees Chloe turn down Lucifer's help, telling him, "You're too *you*," as she works on her father's murder. Lucifer decides to be someone "better, more helpful, more boring" and decides that he should emulate Dan. This is a curious choice: we know that Dan has been a corrupt cop and lied to Chloe, yet still Lucifer understands him as a moral superior. But the fallout from this episode further complicates our understanding of Dan. When Maze captures the man responsible for Decker's father's death, and Lucifer and Maze invite Decker to "punish" him (Lucifer tells Decker to "order off the menu" in terms of torture), Decker does exactly what we expect her to do: she turns him over to the police. But in "Quid Pro Ho," when the man is released, Dan and Maze turn him over to the Russian mob, where he is subsequently killed ("Stewardess Interruptus"); an action that Maze uses to blackmail Dan in the third season ("The Last Heartbreak"). So Dan morally "back-slides" (Ferguson 2016), along with Maze, continuing a moral tension within the team and their approach to "justice."

All of this character work allows for a true team effort in in the middle of the second season, when a professor poisons Decker before killing himself ("Love Handles"/"A Good Day to Die"); this coincides with the aforementioned kiss shared and then processed between Det. Decker and Lucifer, and speaks to a larger sense of teamwork around their increasingly intense professional and personal relationship. In the first half of the two-parter, Decker, Espinoza, and Lucifer track the serial killer, a poisoner professor. Since Decker is trying to process her kiss with Lucifer, and on the advice of Maze, she begins to act more like him, which first draws comment from Lucifer himself: "Detective, what has gotten into you today? Usually you're the one telling me to focus on work!" When the three are deciding on their next move, Decker decides to send a taunting email to the killer, with Lucifer's urging. Dan, meanwhile, responds: "Seriously, insulting the serial killer? That's an awesome idea.... Chloe, don't send this. All right? It's not you. This is, this is a rash move. (*she sends the email*) That's great. I mean, what could go wrong?" The killer then responds directly to Decker with his latest threat, which Lucifer and Decker then go to neutralize, leaving it unclear as to whether Decker's "Luciferian" behavior helped or harmed the case.

When Lucifer and Decker arrive, the professor is holding two young men captive in a room that will fill with poisonous gas. Lucifer, knowing that he is invulnerable to the gas as long as he is not near Decker, tells her that he can save the young men while she goes after the professor: "Don't have time to explain. Do you trust me? Then go." Decker catches up with the professor, who takes his own life, while Lucifer successfully rescues the young men. Decker, relieved that he is all right, then says: "I'm so glad you're okay. I guess we make a good team after all, don't we?" Lucifer then realizes that his feelings for Decker are real, and it is interesting to note that he calls her by her first name when he announces this to Maze and his mother in the next scene: "The detective and I ... sorry, Chloe and I, are real..." That same scene, he realizes that God has engineered Chloe, and somehow put her in his path. When he goes to confront Decker to see if she knows, she turns to reveal that she, too, has been poisoned.

In the second part, as Decker finally falls ill with the poisoning, Lucifer convenes a "celestial planning session," gathering Amenadiel, Maze, and Charlotte to hatch a plan to get Lucifer down to hell to question the poisoner for the antidote. Lucifer also includes Linda, who asks, "So um, what's my part in all this?" And Lucifer says, "Well, you went to medical school, correct? ...So you'll be the one bringing me back from the dead." With this "celestial" team in place, Lucifer then also asks Dan and Ella to track down the ingredients for the antidote. Ella, a former car thief, tells Dan that they will need to break into a shop to get one of the ingredients: "Desperate times ... call for a little B and E." Meanwhile, Lucifer leaves Amenadiel to guard over Chloe while he goes to Hell: "If anyone can stop the detective being moved, it's you." When Trixie comes to visit Decker a few scenes later, her exchange with Amenadiel makes it clear how far these protagonists have come:

> **AMENADIEL:** There might be bad people in the world, but you know what? There's a lot more good people in it.
> **TRIXIE:** Really?

AMENADIEL: Like all the good people helping out your mom.
TRIXIE: Like you?
AMENADIEL: Well um, I'm trying to be good.
TRIXIE: I think you're good.

In the end, Maze and Linda kill and resuscitate Lucifer, Lucifer gets the antidote from the professor, Charlotte helps get Lucifer out of Hell, Dan and Ella get the antidote ingredients, and Amenadiel keeps the detective safe where she is. So when Decker wakes up, and she tells Lucifer, "I heard you saved me," we know it is the truth when Lucifer says, "Well, as much as I like to take all the credit, this one's a team effort."

As the second season wraps up, the team goes through other ups and downs outside of crime-solving, including Lucifer's brief show-marriage ("Candy Morningstar"), Lucifer's run in with God ("God Johnson"), and the Goddess' potential threat to humanity ("The Good, the Bad, and the Crispy"). This last issue, arising in the second season finale, "showcases" (Örnebring 25) how far all the characters have come in their arcs. Charlotte/the Goddess goes on the run, having accidentally killed someone when she's injured, as divine light pours out of the wound: Lucifer races to find a solution for Charlotte while Decker hunts for the murderer, Charlotte. Decker, despite not having Lucifer's full support, has his full confidence, as he tells Charlotte: "The detective is on that case! You don't understand—the detective is good. Annoyingly good!" Charlotte backs this up later, telling him, "Your detective is quite good." Meanwhile, Charlotte hunts down Dr. Martin, first to ask her to patch her up (to which Linda responds: "I am a doctor, but patching things up isn't my thing"), and later to torture her for information about Lucifer, which, judging by her injuries, she does not give up easily (this contrasts to her role in "pilot," where she gives out information about her client because Lucifer promises to sleep with her). As Lucifer races against the detective, he has to hire Maze, now a professional bounty hunter for the police. Maze also comes to the rescue when she hears that Linda is in danger, rushing to protect her friend and asking Amenadiel to help. Amenadiel himself gets his powers back and slows down time, allowing Decker to take down the real killer in the case (not Charlotte), while Lucifer sends his mother to another dimension, saving humans from her impending unleashing of power. This teamwork, while not as coordinated towards a common goal as that of "A Good Day to Die," shows how all the amateur protagonists have found some place in the team: Lucifer has shown he cares not only for the detective, but for the safety of mortals more generally; Maze has found her stride as a bounty hunter, and despite constant ups and downs with Lucifer, a real friendship with Linda; Linda has learned loyalty and a greater sense of ethical purpose within her job; Amenadiel, who lost his powers for trying to kill Lucifer, at least temporarily regains them to save Linda and to allow Lucifer to save the world.

Season three challenges these hard-won roles, though, and brings new challenges to the protagonists' moral and professional standing in relation to one another. As the first episode literally introduces Lieutenant Marcus Pierce (Tom Welling) to our team, their roles are redefined: first he meets Dan, who he calls "that corrupt cop that got off easy," undoing much of Dan's rehabilitation since the first season's revelation of his corruption; then Pierce approaches Lucifer, bringing up his ninety-two sexual partners that were involved in a second season case ("Stewardess Interruptus"); finally, he meets Decker, calling her "Lucifer's partner" before she corrects him: "he's actually my consultant." Much like Dan in the pilot, here Pierce seems to undermine Decker's established role as a great detective, subordinating her professional role to Lucifer's. Later in the episode, when Decker tries to defend Lucifer's unprofessional behavior to the Lieutenant, she ends up defending herself. She confirms that she *is* Lucifer's partner, but insists that he's hers as well, and that with their "unorthodox methods" they make an "effective team," which she thinks will be even more effective once she disinvests personally. While Decker insists to Pierce here that she's "a good detective," she also reveals herself in a rare moment of unprofessionalism, talking about wanting to "see Lucifer's thing ... or whatever."

Pierce's arrival destabilizes Decker's character and role throughout the season, while it also complicates her relationship with Lucifer: but Pierce's role, like much of the third season, is a mixed bag that defies easy characterization. Pierce not only serves as a new model for "who can police" and a contrast to Lucifer for Chloe in both personal and professional modes of partnership; but also, as the immortal first murderer Cain, a sympathetic figure like Lucifer also seemingly suffering at the hands of a self-righteous god ("The Last Heartbreak"); and finally, as "The Sinnerman," the season's "big bad" who points to *Lucifer*'s supernatural genre elements more than its criminal procedural roots (cf., Mittell 2006: 33; 2015: 19). The season balances these roles in sometimes awkward ways.

Ella sets up Pierce's standing as a kind of "super-cop" in the season's first episode before we even meet him, talking about attending a conference presentation of Pierce's and calling him a "total rockstar" and a "sweetie pants to boot," while she's "a big fan." Ella does not want to disappoint the new lieutenant, and Decker's professional drive certainly follows suit—as we saw above, she eagerly works to establish herself as a worthy detective to Pierce. In "What Would Lucifer Do?," Lucifer, explicitly keeping a promise, skips out on pursuing a lead so that he can follow up with a love interest;

this means that Pierce and Decker go together to apprehend the episode's criminal. While out on the case, Decker confronts Pierce about not trusting her professionally, telling him that she's "a badass." Pierce tells Decker that the reason he turned her down for a union rep position was because he did not want to waste "one of his best detectives" attending meetings. As they confront the criminal, Pierce ends up diving in front of Decker and taking a bullet. When Decker visits him in the hospital at the end of the episode to thank him for saving her life, he tells her he "couldn't let anything happen to his best detective." These exchanges slightly undermine Decker's character, as they displace our understanding (and her own) of her as a good cop to Pierce's external source of judgment, one who happens to be not only a man, but also a love interest.

But this same episode draws a stark contrast for Decker in terms of who her real "partner" is: when Lucifer arrives at the scene, Dan reassures him that "Chloe's fine. Lucky Pierce was with her." And Lucifer says, "But I wasn't." Lucifer's flightiness in his partnership with Decker takes on a new dimension when held in contrast to Pierce's dependability: this is true through the season on both a professional and a personal level. In "Vegas with Radish," Decker is disappointed when Lucifer leaves town on her birthday, only to go to Las Vegas without telling her why; but Lucifer finally returns to give her a gift of a necklace made from the bullet she shot him with in season one's "Manly Whatnots." Lucifer tests her trust too far though, in "The Sin Bin," when he kidnaps the man he believes to be the Sinnerman. He tries to explain his actions to Decker, but she shuts him down, telling him: "You didn't follow my lead, and, as usual, you did whatever the hell you wanted."

Much of the rest of the season shows the relationship between Decker and Lucifer trying to rebound from this moment. In "All About Her," Decker does not even call Lucifer to help her on the case, and she calls Lucifer out for his self-involvement and his narcissism. Their rift leaves a space for Decker to become romantically involved with Pierce. Throughout, Lucifer and Decker continue to solve cases together, even those that highlight the essential issues in their own relationship: in "Anything Pierce Does I Can Do Better," Lucifer realizes that the killer killed out of his own inability to admit his feelings to his love interest, just as Lucifer cannot tell Decker about his feelings for her, as she gets engaged to Pierce. In the next episode, "All Hands on Decker," we see how closely the show has intertwined notions of professional and personal partnership. Lucifer tries to figure out why Decker is interested in Pierce by pretending to be her as he works a case with Dan. Becoming Decker, Lucifer becomes the responsible, by-the-books partner to Dan that Decker has been to him, so that Lucifer even saves Dan at the end of the case. As he confronts Dan, Lucifer comes to his own realization: "All I see Daniel is that I can't rely on you as my partner, so perhaps I should find someone steady, someone responsible, someone who can actually be there for me…. I get it now."

But when Decker breaks off her engagement, Lucifer just tries to go "back to normal." with Decker, attempting to recreate "moments" from previous episodes that both highlight his unprofessionalism as well as their personal closeness: he plays the piano at a crime scene (cf., "Pilot"); juggling crime-scene objects (cf., "Off the Record"); he smokes weed at a crime scene (cf., "Lucifer, Stay. Good Devil")—interesting that all of these "unprofessional" moments reference early days in his partnership with Decker—then he tries to play Monopoly with Decker and Trixie (cf., "Chloe Does Lucifer") and he tries to dance with Decker (cf., "High School Poppycock"), more personal moments that speaks to his developed relationship with the detective in the third season and his own character change. Finally, Decker tells him to stop trying to force things to return to normal, and she solves the episode's crime with the help of Ella and Charlotte, which Lucifer acknowledges as "on her own," but not before she, too, has a callback moment to her relationship with him, playing "Heart and Soul" on the piano (cf., "A Priest Walks Into a Bar"). This callback has particular significance because that episode intensely reflected on whether or not Lucifer was evil; now, here, as Lucifer tells Decker that he has feelings for her but he has been afraid she would run away if she knew all of him, the parts of him that were "bad, even monstrous" and finally admits to her again that he is the Devil, Decker tells him, "No, you're not. Not to me." And they kiss, only to be interrupted by the news of Charlotte Richards' death. The episode serves as a blaring condensation of the show as a whole: Lucifer behaves badly and tries to be helpful to a decidedly competent cop who does not necessarily need him but yet still chooses him as a professional and personal partner.

This question of Lucifer's goodness runs throughout the series, especially foregrounded in episodes like "Monster," as we saw earlier, but it takes on new depth in season three, which sees Lucifer struggling with the fact throughout the season that his wings have grown back (and grow back whenever he cuts them off) and that his "devil-face" has disappeared. Lucifer is convinced that this change is his father's work, but, as Linda suggests ("High School Poppycock"), these changes might reflect the character changes that have come through his relationship and work with Decker: as Amenadiel says, "Luci, I'm liking this new you" ("Chloe Does Lucifer").

Lucifer's change of character gets added depth through additional flashbacks and flash-sideways (cf., Mittell 2015: 274), as the third season also begins to experiment more with its episodic form. Stand-alone flashback and fantasy episodes, like "My Brother's Keeper," "The Devil Made Me Do It," and "Once Upon a Time" point to two things: that despite his unprofessionalism, his many flaws, and his being the Devil, Lucifer is "a good man," as Linda tells her ex-husband in "The Devil Made Me Do It" who may just be born to police, as he investigates crimes before/outside of his relationship with Detective Decker in "My Brother's Keeper" and "Once Upon a Time." These points coalesce in his relationship with Decker, who persistently insists on his value, both personally and professionally, as we see Lucifer finally realizes in "Quintessential Deckerstar."

These last two aired episodes of the third season finally reveal Cain/Pierce as "the big bad" who has killed Charlotte Richards, just as she has found her own redemption helping Decker put away a former client in "Quintessential Deckerstar." This revelation allows for the meandering relationships of the third season to come back once again into focus with renewed crime-solving purpose, as everyone works together to defeat him—even Maze, who spends much of the second half of the season plotting *with* Cain, returns to the fold in her desire to save Linda from Cain's thugs. The season ends, however, on an ambiguous note when it comes to Lucifer: on the one hand, he tells Decker that he, like her, does not really think of himself as the Devil lately, but, after he uses his wings to save Decker, he returns to punish Cain and his devil-face returns just in time for Decker to see. If the return of Lucifer's wings throughout the third season comments on his goodness, linked not just with his association with Decker, but with his now-professional purpose (he refers to it as his "job" in both "The Devil Made Me Do It" and "High School Poppycock") with the Los Angeles Police Department, the return of his devil-face suggests that Lucifer's redemptive arc is not yet complete.

Now that *Lucifer* will move to Netflix for a shorter fourth and fifth season, we will have to see what this revelation brings: if "Boo Normal" and "Once Upon a Time" were meant to have been aired immediately after "A Devil of My Word," they give few clues as to how Decker responds, but seem to suggest that their crime-solving partnership continues, as will, no doubt, the ongoing tensions around Lucifer's and the other supporting characters' "goodness" and how it relates to their ability to work together as a team towards a common good.

This essay has sought to show how *Lucifer*, like other supernatural crime shows, plays on traditional tropes while expanding the genre's possibilities, especially when it comes to how its protagonists develop both their skills and their morals in relation to solving crimes, creating partnerships, and working in a team. Lucifer's supernatural skills coupled with his professional incompetence, defocuses institutional "methods of detection," and creates a new space within which the show's other protagonists can find their own crime-solving roles. At the same time, Det. Decker remains a paradigm of a good cop, but, in working with Lucifer, shifts that paradigm outside of institutional morals, broadening the horizon as to "who can police."

With *Lucifer*'s breaking the crime show's mold with what morals and skill sets its protagonists start out with, it subsequently expands traditional models of how team-building happens within its character arcs, demonstrating both a stronger tendency towards seriality and a greater investment in character transformation (Mittell 141) than the crime procedural usually allows. *Lucifer*'s investment in unconventional partnership, with its protagonists often overcoming their own moral failings to join together at key points in its seasons against crime, gives new meaning and flexibility to Jenner's assertion of the strength of the "work family" and the reliability of "us." (158) In doing so, *Lucifer* speaks to the fragmentation of a greater truth (Sparks 16), or a singular mode of criminal justice, but it also challenges and then reinforces ideals of partnership, friendship, trust, and valuing what any individual has to offer to the greater good of society, no matter how unconventional it may be.

Notes

1. For children of cops who are cops in television crime shows, cf., T.J. Hooker (William Shatner, *T.J. Hooker*, ABC/CBS 1982–6); Kenny McLaren (Stark Sands, *NYC 22*, CBS 2012); Kyle Craig (Justin Cornwell, *Training Day*, CBS 2017); Tom Hanson (Johnny Depp, *21 Jump Street*, FOX 1987–91). Tom Turcotte (Jason Gedrick, *Boomtown*, NBC 2002–3); Deborah McKenzie (Bonnie Somerville, *Golden Boy*, CBS 2013); Abby Kowalski (Rachel Carpani, *Against the Wall*, NBC 2011); Abby Kowalski (Rachel Carpani, *Against the Wall*, NBC 2011); Shawn Spencer (James Roday, *Psych*, NBC/Universal 2006–14). This trope continues in other supernatural crime shows, with characters like Raimy Sullivan (Peyton List, *Frequency*, The CW 2016–7) and Kate Lockley (Elisabeth Röhm, *Angel*, The WB, 1999–2004).

2. For a remarkable breakdown of all instances in which Lucifer calls Decker "The Detective" vs. the number of times that he calls her "Chloe," please see youtube user mariadeckerstar's compilation/count at https://www.youtube.com/watch?v=p2O1WMy8T1c

Works Cited

Brunsdon, Charlotte. "Television Crime Series, Women Police, and Fuddy-duddy Feminism," *Feminist Media Studies*, vol. 13, no. 3, 2013, pp. 375–94.
Creeber, Glen. *The Television Genre Book*, 3d ed. BFI, 2015.
Daly, Carroll John. *The Snarl of the Beast*. Resurrected Press, 2013.
Ferguson, LaToya. "Lucifer Throws a Little *Law & Order* Into Its Devilish Mix," *A.V. Club*, 28 November 2016, https://tv.avclub.com/lucifer-throws-a-little-law-order-into-its-devilish-m-1798189660

Garland, Tammy S., et al. "Prime-Time Representations of Female Federal Agents in Television Dramas." *Feminist Criminology*, vol. 13, no. 5, Dec. 2018, pp. 609–631.
Jenner, Mareike. *American TV Detective Dramas: Serial Investigations*. Palgrave, 2016.
Kompare, Derek. *CSI*, Wiley-Blackwell, 2010.
Mittell, Jason. *Complex TV: The Poetics of Contemporary Television Storytelling*. New York UP, 2015.
_____. "Narrative Complexity in Contemporary American Television," *The Velvet Light Trap* no. 58, 2006, pp. 29–40.
Nichols-Pethick, Jonathan. *TV Cops: The Contemporary American Television Police Drama*. Routledge, 2012.
Örnebring, Henrik. "The Show Must Go on ... and On: Narrative and Seriality in Alias." *Investigating Alias: Secrets and Spies,* edited by Stacey Abbott and Simon Brown, I.B. Tauris, 2007, pp. 11–26.
Piper, Helen. *The TV Detective: Voices of Dissent in Contemporary Television*. I.B. Tauris, 2015.
Sparks, Richard. *Television and the Drama of Crime*. Open UP, 1992.
Turnbull, Sue. *The TV Crime Drama*. Edinburgh UP, 2014.
Winston, Robert Paul, and Nancy Mellerski, *The Public Eye: Ideology and the Police Procedural*. Palgrave, 1992.
Worthington, Heather. *Key Concepts in Crime Fiction*. Palgrave, 2011.

About the Contributors

Simon **Bacon** is an independent scholar based in Poznan, Poland. He is the author or editor of several books, including *Growing Up with Vampires* (2018) with Katarzyna Bronk, *Gothic: A Reader* (2018), *Dracula as Absolute Other* (2019), *Horror: A Companion* (2019), *Eco-Vampires* (2020), and *Monsters: A Companion* (forthcoming).

Teresa **Cutler-Broyles** has an MA in cultural studies and a master's certification in architectural historic preservation. She teaches film and cultural analysis at the University of New Mexico, and creative writing at the Umbra Institute in Perugia, Italy. Her research interests include architecture, historical preservation, science fiction, Italy and Italian history, cultural studies, and, gender and sexuality studies.

Shawn **Edrei** teaches at Tel-Aviv University and is a researcher of digital narratology. He has published numerous articles and has coedited *Crossing Channels, Crossing Realms* (Inter-Disciplinary Press), and has edited two collections on science fiction studies (Cambridge Scholars Publishing). His own manuscript, exploring the latest developments in interactive fiction, is forthcoming from McFarland.

Phil **Fitzsimmons** is an educational consultant, independent researcher, and adjunct at Avondale University College, Australia. His research interests include adolescent spirituality as well as supernatural and horror representations in film and literature.

Mary **Going** is a Ph.D. candidate at the University of Sheffield, exploring depictions of Jewish characters, myths and legends in late 18th- and early 19th-century literature. She contributed a chapter on Jewish vampires to *Horror and Religion* (July 2019) and has also published on witches, Jewish persecution, and sexual violence in *Ivanhoe*.

Lynn **Kozak** is an associate professor at McGill University whose work primarily focuses on the ancient Greek epic and contemporary North American serial media, with forthcoming chapters and articles on *The Exorcist*, *Stranger Things*, and *iZombie*.

Cynthia J. **Miller** is a cultural anthropologist specializing in popular culture and visual media. Her writing has appeared in numerous journals and collections, and she has edited more than a dozen essay collections. The editor for Rowman & Littlefield's *Film and History* book series, she serves on the editorial advisory boards for the *Journal of Popular Television* and *Bloomsbury's Guide to Contemporary Directors* series.

Michelle D. **Miranda** is an associate professor within the State University of New York system. She has a Ph.D. in criminal justice from the Graduate Center of the City University of New York. She worked as a criminalist and as both a medical photographer and a death investigator. She is the author of *Forensic Analysis of Tattoos and Tattoo Inks*.

Scott **Rogers** is a professor of English at Weber State University in Ogden, Utah. He teaches courses on 18th- and 19th-century British literature and popular culture.

Adam James **Smith** is a lecturer in English literature at York St. John University. His work explores the relationships between politics, news, and literature. His doctoral research examined 18th-century periodicals covertly sponsored by political parties. He coedited *Poetry, Radicalism and Conspiracy in Sheffield* (2016), a volume of late 18th-century protest poetry.

Ashley **Szanter** is an independent scholar and professional writer based in Northern Utah. She earned an MA in English and has published in a variety of scholarly journals and publications. She coedited *Romancing the Zombie* with Jessica K. Richards (2017) and has several other collections forthcoming. Her primary research interest concerns the evolving role of zombies in popular culture with an emphasis on generational concerns.

A. Bowdoin **Van Riper** is a historian who specializes in depictions of science and technology in popular culture. He is the author or editor of a wide range of volumes, from science to science fiction to horror. He is the editor of the *Martha's Vineyard Museum Quarterly* and coeditor, with Cynthia J. Miller, of a variety of collections, including *Elder Horror* (2019) and *Horror Comes Home* (2019).

Mark **Yates** received a joint Ph.D. in English literature at the University of Salford and Ghent University. He is the author of a variety of articles on William Blake, and is an associate lecturer of English literature at the University of Salford and a trustee for the UK–based charity, Book-Cycle.

Index

abduction/abductive reasoning 57–60, 63n29
"The Abominable Bride" (*Sherlock* episode) 50, 63n24
Abrams, Jarold J. 103–4
AC/DC 76
"The Adventure of the Abbey Grange" (1904) 50
"The Adventure of the Creeping Man" (1923) 54
"The Adventure of the Crooked Man" (1893) 49
"The Adventure of the Norwood Builder" (1903) 50
Against the Wall (1987) 187n1
AIDS 5, 80–98
Alighieri, Dante 167
Allen, Robert C. 32, 36–7
Amélie (2001) 136
An American Werewolf in London (1981) 66, 72
Angel (1999–2004) 5, 101, 104, 106, 187n1

Barnum, P.T. 52
Barnum effect 52
Barry, Peter 18–9
Bennett, Andrew 30
The Big Sleep (1946) 110n10
Black Sabbath 76
Blair, Linda 77
The Blair Witch Project (1999) 78n1
"The Blind Banker" (*Sherlock* episode) 55–6, *Blood Ties* (2007)
The Blue Dahlia (1946) 110n10
Blue Öyster Cult 72, 76
Bones (2005–2017) 159, 176
Booker, Keith 13
Boomtown (2002–2003) 187n1
Boyer, M. Christine 105
Brimstone (1998–1999) 158, 160, 163, 165–6, 168–9
Brooklyn Nine-Nine (2013–) 5, 101
Brown, Mary Ellen 34
Brown, Simon 13–5
Buckman, Peter 34, 36, 43n15
Buckner, Brad 75

Buffy the Vampire Slayer (1997–2003) 5, 101
Burton, Tim 136

Cagney and Lacey (1981–1988) 42n7, 134
camp 80–3, 85, 88, 90, 98n4, 99n16
Campbell, Joseph 116, 112
Carlin, Shannon 136
"A Case of Identity" (1891) 54
Castle (2009–2016) 68, 159, 161, 176
The Castle of Otranto (1764) 67
Cawelti, John 164
characterology 52, 62n14
Chernaik, Warren 16
Christianity 7, 96, 99, 117, 120, 126, 143, 154, 163
City of Demons (2018) 148, 153–5
cold reading 52–53
Collins, Wilkie: *The Woman in White* (1859) 3
Conan Doyle, Sir Arthur 5, 46–65, 101; "The Adventure of the Abbey Grange" (1904) 50 "The Adventure of the Creeping Man" (1923) 54 "The Adventure of the Crooked Man" (1893) 49 "The Adventure of the Norwood Builder" (1903) 50; "A Case of Identity" (1891) 54; "The Final Problem" (1893) 46; *A Study in Scarlet* (1887) 46
Confessions of a Justified Sinner (1984) 78n1
Constantine (2014–2015) 5–7, 142, 147–57
Constantine, John (character) 6–7, 142, 147–57
Cooke, Elizabeth 103
Cracker (1993–2006) 173
Criminal Minds (2005–) 1, 169
Criss, Jami 169
Crowley, Aleister 47–8, 61n7
CSI (2000–2015) 1, 10, 68, 75, 78, 103, 134, 144n5, 159, 173
CSI: Miami (2002–2012) 68
CSI: New York (2004–2013) 68

Dacre, Charlotte 16; *Zafloya* (1806) 17
Dallas (1978–1991) 34
Daltrey, Roger 76
Dante *see* Alighieri, Dante
Dark Passage (1947) 110n10

191

Index

Dark Shadows (1966–1971) 3, 4
Daughters or Darkness (1971) 110*n*3
Daybreakers (2009) 110*n*3
de Brabant, Nicholas/Nick Knight (character) 80, 83–98, 99*n*31
deduction/deductive reasoning 4, 48–51, 53, 55, 57–60, 63*n*29, 64*n*33, 148, 151–2, 155
Delano, Jamie 151–2
Derrida, Jacques 18–9, 22
Desmet, Christy 42*n*1
the Devil 3, 7, 17, 69, 124, 149, 158–171, 173–4, 180, 185–7
Divia (character) 94, 95, 99*n*30
divination 48, 53, 56
Dolan, Marc 32, 42*n*11
doubling 24, 29–45, 87
Dracula (1897) 66, 86, 101, 109
Dracula's Daughter (1936) 102
Dragnet (1951–1959) 68, 134, 159
DuCharme, Janette (character) 82, 84, 88–90, 95, 99*n*28
Duchovny, David 14

Edlund, Carver 78*n*4
Elementary (2012–) 4, 173
Eliade, Mircea 117–7, 163
"The Empty Hearst" (*Sherlock* episode) 58, 62*n*17, 63*n*27, 64*n*27
The Exorcist (1973) 77

Fables (2002–2015) 144*n*7
Fabrikant, Geraldine 33
fandom/fans 4, 14, 33, 46, 60, 74–75, 141, 169
Feinberg, Joel 168
femme fatale 81–2, 107
Féval, Paul: *Vampire City* (1867) 78*n*1
film noir 5–6, 35, 81–3, 88, 101–11, 138, 160, 163
"The Final Problem" (1893) 46
Fiske, John 31, 33, 39, 42*n*5, 42*n*7
forensic science 6, 10, 46–7, 62, 68, 73, 75–6, 114, 116, 134–45, 173, 190
Forever Knight (1992–1996) 5, 80–100, 101, 134, 141
Frankenstein (1818) 66
Frequency (2016–2017) 187*n*1
Freud, Sigmund 4, 29–31, 43, 87
Fringe (2008–2013) 135, 147
Frost, Mark 29, 33–6, 38, 42*n*10, 43*n*12
Fukunaga, Cary 112
Fuller, Bryan 135–6, 143

Gaiman, Neil: *The Sandman* (1989–1996) 141
Gall, Franz Joseph 62*n*14
genre hybridity 66–9, 74–5, 77, 148, 150, 172–3
Gentlemen Prefer Blondes (1953) 32
Girard, Rene 87
The Glass Key (1942) 110*n*10

Golden Boy (2013) 187
Gomez-Gallisteo, M. Carmen 13
Gothic 17–8, 46–7, 49, 61*n*2, 63*n*24, 66–79, 83, 113, 148–50
Gothic play 66–8, 74–5, 77–8
"The Great Game" (*Sherlock* episode) 55, 63, 64
Grimm (2011–2017) 135
Gross, Hans 53–4
The Gun for Hire (1942) 110*n*10

Haggerty, George 87
Hall, Stuart 85
Halskov, Andreas 35, 42*n*4, 43*n*12
Hannibal (2013–2015) 143–4*n*4
hard-boiled detective fiction 5–6, 101–11, 151, 174
Harrelson, Woody 112
Harrison, Thomas: *Red Dragon* (1981) 110*n*6
Harriss, Chandler 10, 69–74
Harrowitz, Nancy 57–8
Haven (2010–2015) 135, 148
Hill Street Blues (1981–1987) 34, 45, 42, 134, 159
"His Last Vow" (*Sherlock* episode) 58
Hislop, Rev. David 120
Hogg, James: *Confessions of a Justified Sinner* (1984) 78*n*1
Homicide: Life on the Streets (1993–2003) 10, 141, 162
homosexuality/homoeroticism 89–93, 95
Houdini, Harry 47
House of Dracula (1945) 102
The Howling (1981) 74

I Am Legend (1954) 110*n*3
incest 41–2, 84, 90, 92–5
induction/inductive reasoning 57–60, 63*n*29
intertextuality 31–9, 41, 147, 151
Interview with the Vampire (1976) 86–7, 105

Jack the Ripper 3
John Constantine Hellblazer 142, 150–7
Johnson, Earvin "Magic" 86
Justice League Dark (2017) 156–7

Kansas 76
Kaveney, Roz 148
Kerr, Paul 33
Key Largo (1948) 110*n*10
Knight, Peter 14–5
Knight Rider (1982–1986) 75
Knowles, Christopher 151
Knowlton, Steven 149
Kolchak: The Night Stalker (1974–1975) 3, 4, 43*n*13
Kompare, Derek 114, 172–3
Koshi, Genevieve 135–6
Krantz, Tony 42*n*8

Kripke, Eric 66-7, 69
Kristeva, Julia 31, 119

LaCroix, Lucien (character) 84, 88-9 91-7, 99n23, 99n30, 99n31
Lambert, Natalie (character) 82, 88
The Late Show (1990) 34
Law & Order (1990-2010) 1, 10, 134, 159
Law & Order: Criminal Intent (2011) 143, 144n5
Law & Order: Special Victims Unit (1999-) 1, 144n5
Led Zeppelin 76
Ledwon, Lenora 32, 39, 42n2
Legend of Tomorrow (2016-) 156
Lévi, Éliphas 47, 61n7
Levine, Gary 33
Lie to Me (2009-2011) 173
London After Midnight (1927) 102
Lost (2004-2010) 136
Lost Girl (2010-2015) 135, 148 156
Lovecraft, H.P. 66
Lucifer *see* the Devil
Lucifer (2016-) 7, 142, 158, 161, 164-70, 171-88
Lynch, David 4, 27, 39-30, 32-3, 35, 38, 41, 42n8, 42n9, 42n10, 43n12

MacLeod, Tracey 34
Madonna 31-2
Malach, Michele 10-11, 19
Man Against Crime (1949-1954) 1, 4
Manhunter (1986) 110n6
Manson, Marilyn 76
Mark of the Vampire (1935) 102
Matheson, Richard: *I Am Legend* (1954) 110n3
McConaughey, Matthew 112
McTaggart, John 167
Méliès, Georges 162
melodrama 81-4, 85, 89-90, 99n16
The Mentalist 161
Mercury, Freddie 86
Miami Vice (1984-1990) 75, 134
The Middleman (2008) 161
Mill, John S. 57
Millman, Joyce 13, 14
Mission: Impossible (1966-1973) 161
Monroe, Marilyn 32
Moonlight (2007-2008) 5-6, 101-11, 135
Moore, Alan: *Saga of the Swamp Thing* 148, 151, 152
Mulder, Fox (character) 3, 9-27, 143n4, 144n5
Murder, She Wrote (1984-1996) 173
"Murders in the Rue Morgue" (1841) 3, 26n1
Murnau, F.W. 106, 162

Nadja (1994) 110n3
NCIS (2003-) 1, 68, 134, 159
necromancy 48, 54, 60, 62n15
Nestorowich, Max 154, 156

Neumann, Hans-Joachim 162
Nietzsche, Friedrich 21-2, 119
Nochimson, Martha 11
Nosferatu (1922) 107
noosphere 6, 114-29
NYC 22 (2012) 187n1
Nyland, Jopi 103

Once Upon a Time (2011-2018) 135, 141-3, 144
Osbourne, Ozzy 76

Paranormal Activity (2005) 78n1
Peirce, Charles S. 57
Pepper's Ghost 63n24
Picarelli, Enrica 13
Pizzolatto, Nic 112
Poe, Edgar Allan 16, 63n26; "Murders in the Rue Morgue" (1841) 3, 26n1
police procedural 1-8, 9-12, 15-7, 21-5, 29, 31-6, 41, 43n13, 46, 56, 66-79, 80-1, 83 85, 135-46, 147-59, 160-88
Poltergeist (1982) 66
Profiler (1996-2000) 143n143-4
Psych (2006-2014) 187n1
Pulp Fiction (1994) 110n8
Pushing Daisies (2007-2009) 6, 134-46, 161

Radcliffe, Ann 16-7, 78n1
Rammstein 76
The Raven (nightclub) 88, 93, 95
Reaper (2007-2009) 7, 158, 160-1, 163-4, 165-6, 169
Red Dragon (1981) 110n6
"The Reichenbach Fall" (*Sherlock* episode) 48
Rice, Anne: *Interview with the Vampire* (1976) 86-7, 105
Robert-Houdin, Jean-Eugène 50
The Rockford Files 161
Rodley, Chris 30, 38
Rookie Blue (2010-2015) 1
Route 66 (1960-1964) 63
Royle, Nicholas 30
Russell, Jeffrey Burton 162
Rymer, Malcolm: *Varney the Vampire* (1845) 102

Saga of the Swamp Thing 148, 151, 152
Salazar, James B. 40, 43n43
Sanctuary (2008-2011) 135
The Sandman (1989-1996) 141
Satan *see* the Devil
"A Scandal in Bohemia" (1891) 50, 62n19, 62n20
Schreck, Nikolas 162
Scully, Dana 9-13, 14, 17-20, 22-5 144n5
Sheldrake, Rupert 117
Shelley, Mary: *Frankenstein* (1818) 66
Sherlock (2010-) 4-5, 46-65
The Shining (1980) 66

Simon, David 141
The Sixth Sense (1999) 78*n*1
Sleepy Hollow (2013–2017) 135, 141–2
Sontag, Susan 82–3
spiritualism 47, 54, 112
Spivey, Michael 149
Stevenson, Diane 41
Stoker, Bram: *Dracula* (1897) 66, 86, 101, 109
"A Study in Pink" (*Sherlock* episode) 58, 62*n*17, 63*n*27, 64*n*64
Sturgis, Amy 147–8
Supernatural (2005–) 3, 5, 8*n*1, 66–79, 135
Swales, Martin 16

Taylor, Charles 14
Taylor, Ken 120
Taylor, Laurie N. 27–8
Thelema 61*n*7
Theseus 119, 129
T.J. Hooker (1982–1986) 187*n*1
Todorov, Tsevtan 150
Torchwood (2006–2011) 135
Training Day (2017) 187*n*1
True Detective (2014) 6, 112–33
21 Jump Street (1987–1991) 187*n*1
Twilight Saga 110*n*9
Twin Peaks (1990–1991, 2017) 4, 10, 29–45
Tyndall, John 58

Ultraviolet (1998) 110*n*1
uncanny 29–45, 77, 84
Underworld (series) 106

Vampire City (1867) 78*n*1
vampires 3, 6, 7, 48, 76–8, 80–100, 101–11, 141, 149–50; noir 101–11
Varney the Vampire (1845) 102
Vidocq, Eugene 53–4
Vilain, Robert 16

Walpole, Horace: *The Castle of Otranto* (1764) 67
Warehouse 13 (2009–2014) 135
White Collar (2009–2014) 161
The Who 76
Willingham, Bill: *Fables* (2002–15) 144*n*7
Wise, Ray 38, 43*n*14
The Woman in White (1859) 3
Woodward, Richard B. 33

The X-Files (1993–2002, 2016, 2018) 3, 4, 9–28, 63, 66, 103, 134–5, 143*n*4, 144*n*5, 176
X-Files: I Want to Believe (2008) 9, 16, 22–3, 24

Zafloya (1806) 17
Žižek, Slavoj 110*n*7

www.ingramcontent.com/pod-product-compliance
Ingram Content Group UK Ltd.
Pitfield, Milton Keynes, MK11 3LW, UK
UKHW042010140426
5217IPUK00015B/1084